THE CHURCHES MILITANT

THE

CHURCHES

MILITANT

THE WAR OF 1812 AND AMERICAN RELIGION

BY WILLIAM GRIBBIN

NEW HAVEN AND LONDON, YALE UNIVERSITY PRESS, 1973

Library of Congress catalog card number: 72-91313
International standard book number: 0-300-01583-6

Designed by Sally Sullivan
and set in Linotype Janson type.
Printed in the United States of America by
Vail-Ballou Press, Inc., Binghamton, N.Y.

Published in Great Britain, Europe, and Africa by
Yale University Press, Ltd., London.
Distributed in Canada by McGill-Queen's University
Press, Montreal; in Latin America by Kaiman & Polon,
Inc., New York City; in Australasia and Southeast
Asia by John Wiley & Sons Australasia Pty. Ltd.,
Sydney; in India by UBS Publishers' Distributors Pvt.,
Ltd., Delhi; in Japan by John Weatherhill, Inc., Tokyo.

TO MY MOTHER AND FATHER

PREFACE

The last half decade has not been an auspicious time for dispassionate examination of old wars. This investigation, nevertheless, was not undertaken with a view to relating its findings to any situation other than that of the United States under James Madison. It may be that some ideas expressed in these pages are applicable to other times, other crises. It may be that other periods of foreign conflict and domestic upheaval have laid bare and accelerated developmental processes in the body politic. It may be that the resulting group pressures and countervailing forces have acted like scattered magnets to rearrange the pieces of the social order into new, enduring patterns of attraction and repulsion. Just as the troubles of 1812 foreshadowed much about the next several decades, perhaps in other troubled times we can see drawn long-lasting lines of commitment and vectors of opposition to them. Some readers, adept at discovering circumstantial parallels, may choose to find in this volume a commentary on matters not germane to the second war with Britain. "It well may be," concluded Edna St. Vincent Millay, "I do not think I would."

This study was begun as a dissertation at the Catholic University of America under the direction of Harold D. Langley, whose lively encouragement deserves an expression of appreciation here beyond the customary prefatory thanks. The influence of Thomas West's stylistic criticism in these pages should be obvious to him, although I suspect they could have profited from yet another of his readings. I hope Sister Marie Carolyn Klinkhamer and other friends whose advice and willingness to listen have been helpful in this effort are not disappointed at the result. The help of my brother Wally in preparing the manuscript was invaluable. By their receptivity and thoughtfulness, my students at Virginia Union University have at times made easier the formulation of the material herein, parts of which first appeared in *Church History* and *The Historical Magazine of the Protestant Episcopal Church* and are incorporated here with the kind permission of the editors. Finally, credit must be given to those who have long fostered respect for learning and reverence for both words in print and people in thought. For all of which, the dedication of this volume is insufficient acknowledgment.

CONTENTS

INTRODUCTION

*As a considerable part of my travels was near the
Frontier it will probably be expected that I should give
some account of the war among the rest of my Notes
& observations, But as people are generally much divided in their political sentiments, & apt to give credit
to that only which is agreeable to their own wishes or
Ideas I thought it most prudent to say but little about
it, leaving everyone to his own Political belief & avoiding censure from any.*

Aaron Hampton's diary, July 1813

American religion in the early nineteenth century can be likened
to the proverbial patchwork quilt, with the proviso that the pieces
of the whole pattern were ever growing larger or smaller, amal-
gamating, dividing, sometimes appearing out of nothing. If change
is the first law of life, then America's churches were exuber-
antly alive. They were at once the products of ancient traditions and the ideas carried in each morning's papers. Rooted in
the Old World, many were distinctively products of the New.
Represented in them was every theological tradition familiar
to Europe's divines, as well as a few that might have been entirely new to them. The multiplicity of American religion was
sure to provoke the wonder, if not the amusement, of foreign
visitors, who could find in any one of several American cities
more distinctive groups of Christians than existed in most European nations.

In the more than half century preceding the War of 1812,

American Christianity had experienced great upheavals. In the fifth decade of the eighteenth century, the series of revivals known as the Great Awakening had hit Britain's seaboard colonies with repeated waves of conversion and mass participation in outpourings of the spirit. For generations thereafter, the community revival or "season of grace" remained the joyous hope of believers; and equally long, in fallow years as well as good times, the vivified spirituality of the Great Awakening characterized the religion of Americans.

A second awakening, the Great Revival, occurred at the turn of the eighteenth century and so captured the soul of the frontier that it set the pattern of western religion for the next half century. Thousands gathered in camp meetings to hear the Gospel preached, and the pious part of the nation turned with confidence to the task of combating international infidelity and domestic godlessness. Even the churches which stood aloof from revivalism, such as the Episcopalians, were drawn into the current of evangelical fervor and moral reform.

That current was in full tide at the time of the second war with Britain. From the years of the Great Awakening, a self-assertive Christianity, a crusading spirit of righteousness had permeated the nation's life. It was a bond of union. For although Americans may have been motivated by economic drives, social conflicts, racial fears, national prejudices, altruism and selfishness, territorial greed and humanitarianism, almost all of them could take at least nominally a united stand upon the ground of Protestant Christianity. It provided the symbolism of their oratory, the values of their ideology, even the cosmology of their science. All their various motives were apt to be expressed and justified with reference to moral values and religious goals.

This ground of agreement was, to say the least, ample in its bounds. Within the limits of American Protestantism there existed enough conflict and discord to perplex contemporaries and bewilder later scholars. In a very real sense, the Christian public was engaged in ecclesiastical guerrilla warfare in which, at any one time, an indeterminate number of forces opposed one another for the sake of true religion. The early Republic witnessed a substantial increase in the number of churches. In the years immediately before and after the War of 1812, schisms and secessions were epidemic. In the aftermath of the War of Independence, many churches suffered the rancorous and intricate ordeal of establishing national structures independent of Old World ties, only to be confronted by further disagreements and divisions. The Methodists had early lost some adherents who preferred their own egalitarian brand of "Republican Methodism" to the church's episcopacy. Presbyterians suffered the loss of the "Cumberland presbytery," a separation which proved to be most enduring, as well as various minor schisms along the frontier, where the highly organized and educated ruling structure of their church seemed somewhat out of place. Most believers watched with horror the spread of the Shakers, whose communism and rejection of marriage placed them beyond the pale of respectable Christianity. This did not, however, prevent their winning converts, the only source of new members inasmuch as the Shakers outlawed procreation. Equally as bad was the Universalist heresy, the devil's own rebuttal of the Mosaic Decalogue, assuring sinners that eternal punishment was but a myth devised by corrupt priesthoods to subdue mankind. In America's lusty theological life, even the tiny New Jerusalem church could find the means to publish its own periodical, explaining the visionary cosmology of Emanuel Swedenborg. Rejecting all sectarian labels, the unflinching iconoclasm of the Christian Connection was yet another body blow to the security of Reformation Protestantism. Even the Society of Friends suffered a rupture of its membership in the Hicksite schism not long after the war. Whether all these events are interpreted as the result of poor church structure or as the inevitable reaction of social units to their democratic environment, participants in the process were often quite explicit in avowing that it was a second Reformation, perhaps more meaningful than the first.

These divisions and disputes were limited to no region of the country and concentrated in no single branch of Protestantism. They occurred, moreover, in a religious community already extremely pluralistic. Denominational identity among the older churches, however small, was strong. Sabbatarian Baptists remained quite distinct from their brethren who observed Sunday as the Lord's Day, and the Arminian "Freewill Baptists" were in essential disagreement with all Calvinist Baptists. Intricacies of organizational purity as well as doctrinal distinctions maintained the separation of the Associate, Associate Reformed, and Reformed Presbyterian churches. Traditions and national pride explained in part the separate identities of the German Reformed and Dutch Reformed churches, which, in spite of their doctrinal kinship with Presbyterianism, reserved their own ecclesiastical organizations.

America had become a theological testing ground. If older religious systems could not meet a practical need—bringing the Gospel to the frontier, for example—the need itself would produce its own remedy, in this case democratic churches short on book learning and long on comfort and hope. Survival of the theologically fittest was the central fact of ecclesiastical life. Those churches which adapted to the country's steady development of egalitarian and libertarian values would thrive, eventually becoming masters of their new environment by virtue of their superior harmony with it. Conversely, denominations unready to hurry into the uncertain future would weaken, sicken, perhaps perish as surely as a species caught up in a fundamental change of living conditions.

Because competition under these circumstances encouraged denominational enmities, church disputes were seldom marked by mutual forbearance. Each church possessed its own collective consciousness, the accumulated memories of past injustices wrought upon their fellow believers by other Christians. Congregationalists remembered Anglican persecutions, while Baptists recalled their treatment at the hands of both Anglicans and Congregationalists. Methodists chaffed at the scorn heaped upon their irregular ministry by older churches, while Quakers had worse complaints against the intolerance of their fellow Christians. Various small offshoots of Presbyterianism kept alive the memory of religious outrages in Scotland and Ireland, while Irish Catholics in America knew firsthand that similar outrages were still common. Newer churches condemned all of the older, while traditional believers condemned equally Universalists, Freewillers, Smithites, Swedenborgians, Shakers, and Campbellites as sons of Satan. All the disputants did agree that the Roman Catholic church remained earth's chief evil, and so they handed down to successive generations the record of Babylon's heinous crimes. This agreement, however, was hardly sufficient to overcome centuries of denominational dispute reinforced by controversies immediately at hand.

In the years preceding 1812, America was as discordant politically as it was fragmented religiously. The young and still uncertain party system trembled with the rancor engendered by disagreements over financial policies, territorial acquisition, issues of sectional pride, and personal acrimony. Most of all, the country's political life was kept simmering by the enduring conflict between Britain and France and their corresponding admirers and detractors in the United States. Just how that simmer eventually boiled over into war was none too clear at the time and ever since has been a subject for debate. One interpretation would lay the responsibility upon congressional "war hawks," whose western and southern constituencies hungered for land in Canada and Florida. Another analysis stresses the widespread outrage at Indian attacks, especially when British influence was suspected in them. The economic depression in the Mississippi Valley prior to war has been cited as a contributing factor in the development of a martial spirit there. It has also been suggested that the war was meant to vindicate republican government in a world of rampant monarchism and that the vote on the declaration was determined by party affiliation rather than sectionalism. Those who actually decided for war offered their own reasons. Defending national honor, they would uphold America's maritime rights and end the impressment of seamen into the British navy. This explanation was derided by their critics, who were sure most of the sailors in question were Irish deserters and who wondered why slaveholding landlubbers were so concerned with impressed tars from New England. This original debate has long continued, and little has been settled in the process.[1]

It is not likely that more can be settled here. By the tag end of the twentieth century we have surely realized the folly of hunting a war's causes, in the sense of isolated factors upon which a safely impersonal or satisfyingly individual blame can be placed. And as psychology and sociology more and more reinterpret the human past in terms comfortingly irresponsible and guiltless, it seems less and less important to pin down the reasons for one politician's vote and still less meaningful to explain mass behavior in terms of lofty issues and diplomatic rodomontade.

Why, then, dissect anew the War of 1812, attempting again to impose patterns on emotions and logically categorize the willfulness of men? The answer to that would have to be as pretentious as the question, but it would probably have something to do with man's refusal to accept any limitations, past or present, to his control over events, if not over himself. Be that as it may, there is additional reason to look one more time at popular attitudes—the word is correctly vague—during the second war with Britain. Without disparaging any interpretations of the War of 1812, without denying the economic and sectional and partisan factors involved, we can yet profit from studying still another facet of human behavior by attending to the religion of Americans as they fought their war. For after commercial statistics have been compiled, election results tallied, and individual minds analyzed, this other part of the national experience, central to what the country was in 1812, may put us in still closer touch with the mind of warring America.

Even the most skeptical observer would not explain American involvement in the world wars of this century as the result only of economic forces, personal piques of leaders, or the playing out of an international scenario just fated to end in tragedy. He would necessarily consider too the epidemic belief that Pershing's Expeditionary Force would preserve the civil religion of democracy or that the second war's goals, rightly or wrongly, transcended the predictable interests that have formed the usual stuff of world affairs. And in both cases he would attend to the way in which Americans formulated moral images of their enemies and friends to the extent that the world seemed divided into sheep and goats, awaiting final judgment. All this would be important because it is from just such elusive beliefs, attitudes, conceptualizations, that the quicksilver current of public opinion flows.

If we are unable to grasp what modern wars have meant for the

American people without considering what we might call, for want of better words, the popular ideology of warring citizens, then perhaps we do the past an injustice and ourselves a disservice by neglecting that component in the War of 1812. For ideology there was aplenty, albeit in a premodern form. And it was being nurtured, if so deliberate a term can describe its mushrooming spontaneity, from the very roots of American culture: its Christian religions. As Ralph Henry Gabriel has expressed it,

> the secular faith of democracy and the religious faith of a changing Protestantism were not only closely interrelated but were mutually interdependent. They complemented one another. There was no suggestion of rivalry between them. Together they provided the American with a theory of the cosmos which gave significance and direction to human life, and with a theory of society which gave a meaning not only to the relation of the individual to the group, but of the United States to the congregation of nations.[2]

It is a loose concept, an impression more than a definition, but an incisive summary, nonetheless, of the Republic's creed in a period that yields its meaning more readily to theologians than to secular sages. And if the American mind of that era is to be fathomed, one might begin by observing America's churches in the laboratory setting that the war provided.

It is likely that most men of 1812, like those of the atomic age, could not make the total commitment that is war without the psychic support of a system of values and hopes, whether it be called religion or philosophy or ideology. And we dare not ignore this aspect of their behavior lest we turn wonderfully complex creatures, each of them a marvel of contradiction and impossibilities, into artificial mimics of themselves. We can justifiably look askance as the rulers of Mississippi Territory pledge their "sacred honor" to end Britain's violating of "her most sacred pledges."[3] But we do well to consider, as Charles Carroll doubtless did when he became the first signer of Anne Arundel County's antiwar petition to Congress, that "the United States are, in the aggregate, a moral and religious people."[4] Otherwise we can not grapple with honest emotions like those of a martial convention in Sara-

toga County, New York, which affirmed that "trusting in the
support of an all wise God in a just cause, we shall yet preserve
our liberties, and independence." [5] Otherwise we smilingly miss
the relevance of fervent journalism that could hail Thomas Mac-
donough's victory on Lake Champlain by declaiming, "But it was
not he! It was the Lord of Hosts!" a sentiment with which the
hero, noted for his piety, probably agreed.[6]

Those statements from the war years boldly imply a whole set
of axioms: that the justice of causes can be measured, that the
citizens of 1812 enjoyed liberties worth preserving, that a benef-
icent deity cares for men, hears their prayers, and grants them
assistance in bad times. If some now dissent from those doctrines,
that does not discredit them or lessen their usefulness as a framework upon which wartime public opinion can be displayed. For
even if their dogmas be rejected, the vigorous believers of Saratoga County had considerably more experiential evidence to
support their faith than would later pietists who thought that
through communication and sincere striving the human family,
organized in council, could swear off its long habit of fratricide.

When the United States went to war in June 1812, its ecclesiastical life was still further complicated. It goes without saying
that a state of war, like any great crisis, intensifies all the forces at
work within the national machine; and like a complex instrument
being tested under great stress, the body politic reveals what
strengths and weaknesses may be inherent in its structure. The
fight with Britain is a case in point. In its course, America showed
what positive virtues it possessed and realized what internal frac-
tures enervated the country. Religious divisions of course were
exacerbated by the state of war as surely as a machine's points of
friction grate more harshly under increased pressure. For the
crisis was both a challenge and an opportunity to the American
churches, a change in operating conditions requiring individual
responses, adjustments, adaptations on the part of each. Some approved the war, others condemned it. To some it came as an
advantage in the aforementioned ecclesiastical competition, while
to others it was a decided handicap; and in still other cases, it
seemed to have little effect at all. The record of American religion

during the war, composed of these many varied reactions, provides an unmatched opportunity for studying the young Republic's most important social institutions, its churches, during a time of maximum strife. This may well be the closest one may approach a study of public opinion in America's formative years.

Extrapolating public opinion from denominational opinion is not as audacious as it might at first appear. If the churches represented only a minority of the populace, the voting rolls often held a much smaller minority. Aside from the churches, there were few groups to which Americans could voluntarily adhere as an expression of their deepest beliefs and aspirations. There was probably no organization as representative of a community's stated values as the religious congregation. For if it included only the respectable part of the populace, it thereby contained a high proportion of the opinion makers, the spokesmen, the leaders, the property owners, the voters. Admittedly, America's churches were but a few cells in a much larger social organism. But sometimes isolated cellular behavior and development reveal the progress or pathology of a whole body. So too the response of American Christians to their country's plight may be informative of conflicts and events beyond the limits of purely theological concern.

If we assume that human reactions to war and civil disruption change little from one decade or century to another, then denominational responses to the troubles of 1812 take on added meaning. If it be granted that modern wars have wrought great internal changes in the country, breaking up old patterns of life and anticipating future ones, then it is worth considering that public affairs during the second war with Britain may also have prefigured subsequent events. Just as we can now read accounts of domestic developments during World War II and find in them pointed hints, ignored at the time, of the problems and conflicts of the postwar era, so too a careful attention to apparently trivial opinions and behavior during the War of 1812 may discover early indications of what lay in store for the country after the fighting stopped. The possibility that such is the case should make us especially careful to avoid prejudging antiwar zeal or prowar fervor. For if they did not terminate at war's end but only underwent transformation, then assessing their full import demands from us an appreciation of their more enduring impact upon the country's religious commitment.

But any study of public opinion, historical or contemporary, faces one major procedural difficulty. What material can be used? What reflects the popular mind without distorting it? Which leaders truly speak for their followers? One is tempted to an unrestrained impressionism, throwing together prominent characters in the hope they really did personify their constituencies. But even that does not suffice. For although we document the words of politicians, they are made less useful by the very fact that they do come from the lips and pens of public figures, who, if not dissimulating, must nonetheless calculate, whose very honesty is a matter for display and hence suspect. Moreover, great men may represent the folks back home but are rarely representative of them. And even if we could find some hypothetical member of the Congress who embodied the will of his people, we are yet challenged to determine his motives, dissect his values, give names to ideas that may have been nameless even to him. He would be a poor guide to the public opinion of 1812, a changeling thing with unnumbered components: illiterates trudging behind oxen, city workers longing to be prosperous, gentlemen itching to be powerful, dandies and patriarchs, citizens who married, multiplied, and feared old age with seldom a thought of what transpired in the nation's capital.

We have looked at their economic motives, studied their regionalism, weighed their partisanship and class antagonisms. We should now give similar care to their religion, the nearest thing to a universal in their wildly varying experience. This is not to say that their churches had a hand in declaring or ending the war, although churchmen played leading roles in defending and damning it. It is not to suggest that public officials were motivated by religious factors in their decisions, although some were. It is only to insist that the Americans of 1812, concerned about a great many things, will not reveal themselves to us unless we too are concerned with the full range of their interests. If the resulting wisdom will not substitute for conventional views of the war, it perhaps will fill in the vacant background of traditional portrayals.

Or to switch metaphors in the middle of an apologia, the religious aspects of the war set the stage for all else that happened, provided the props and special effects for the drama's military and political actors. Thus there is good reason to add to the many vectors that directed the course of events still another: the religious dimension of foreign conflict and domestic rancor.

But American religion encompassed church members and the unaffiliated, learned theologians and backwoods mystics, antique dogmatists and thinkers born before their time. We can scarcely hope to comprehend all parts of that mélange. Some groups were so weak that, if their members did have a uniform political stand, it had no significance for the larger community, while in some cases small churches could, by their social standing or dedication or effective leadership, have influence beyond the confines of their own fellowship. Even so, for many of the smaller churches, meaningful material is either unavailable or sufficient to reveal only the isolated facts that interest ecclesiastical antiquarians. But if it is true that American religion comprised more than the adherents and beliefs of the country's major denominations, it is also true that those churches, the great body of Christian America, represented most variations and nuances of wartime opinion. And it was the membership of the numerically large or prestigious churches that could exercise political power. So even if one looks at only the biggest and brightest pieces of the aforementioned patchwork quilt, it should be possible to sketch with fair accuracy the contours of public sentiment during the war.

Examining the country's major churches as they responded to the circumstances of war need not presume any denominational unanimity. Although there was not political uniformity among all Irish-Americans in 1916, all German-Americans in 1920, or all Afro-Americans in 1964, in each case certain shared attitudes toward a common situation were evident. So too there are obvious practical reasons for dealing with the beleaguered Christians of Madison's America on a denominational basis. It is of course the easiest order to impose on very disorderly events. But the ultimate justification for this approach is that it is precisely the way the faithful of 1812 would have dealt with the matter, because their compartmentalization into rival groups was for them a vital fact, unfortunate perhaps, but awfully important. We do well, then, to let them impose their own pattern of social divisions, antagonisms, and alliances on the historical record.

Because it is sometimes impossible to reach the great masses of believers, we must hearken to their natural spokesmen, hoping thereby to hear not only the clergy's views but also the opinions of those who paid their salaries. Congregations had simple and direct means to express approval of their pastor's conduct, just as they usually could effectively make it known that their minister did not speak for them by withdrawing support or instigating local controversies. For this and other reasons, there was between the ordained leader and his followers less of a gap in learning, purpose, and sophistication than we might now expect. Bluntly said, we come to the study of a past war with our receptivity distorted, our attitudes sensitized by our own vivid experience. And part of that experience may be skepticism as to the ability of those who have traditionally been a community's leaders, like clergymen, to speak the minds of the mute multitude behind them. If we do thus distrust public opinion when it is focused through the eyes of any elite, it should be reassuring to remember that there were times when leadership, especially in the churches, grew more directly out of the people and could speak to their needs with more forceful precision, albeit less polished urbanity, than its modern counterpart.

As churchmen and their followers chose sides politically and selected heroes and villains from among the nations, they were themselves acting as negative reference groups. Thus a godly man might have hated Britain because his godly neighbors, whom he despised, loved her. The process is still with us. An ethnic or religious, regional or economic group can still grow hostile to a foreign interest because the group's domestic antagonists are friendly to that interest, or vice versa. Contemporary examples are easy to find, especially if we examine our own opinions as well as those of the general public. We might thereby discover some kinship with those Americans who found the War of 1812 an opportune occasion for affirming their own religious identities by contradicting the loyalties of other believers. Observing the way public reaction to world crisis was shaped by this push-and-pull interaction of mutually hostile factions, we may be better able to follow subsequent attitudes toward foreign affairs. For if a citizen's view of international events was in part dependent upon feuds and alliances among the many interest groups within his own small community, then any attempt to study his country's foreign relations must attend to the way America's internal divisions were projected out upon external conflicts. In that light, clerical bickering was more important than it might otherwise seem.

The amalgamation of foreign conflicts and internal politics is always an unstable compound. Factional strife within exaggerates and in turn is magnified by enemies without. Rather than stopping at the water's edge, partisanship can be heightened when divisions at home seem to parallel firing lines abroad. To explicate circumstances so complicated, it might be useful to employ the analytical methods of sociology and psychology. There was, indeed, much about wartime religion and politics that lends itself to those methods. For example, the patterns of fear and suspicion among both antiwar and martial Christians may resemble the "paranoid style" which some scholars have found in other parts of the American past. One might speak of an antiwar "persuasion" or a Republican "mind-set." Those who are so disposed may apply those concepts to the record of public opinion during the war and may thereby illumine what sermons and broadsides did not bring to light. The tools of the social sciences may reveal more about Madisonian America than a metaphysical historiography could hope to find there. They may also, in the process, fundamentally misconceptualize the human condition. It is a risk well left for more ambitious investigations to undertake.

A further caution is necessary. Christians of the warring Republic were faced with choices and judgments that have been a recurring part of moral man's attempt to reconcile world and faith, ethics and exigencies. So there may well be some value in their experience for a later generation, no less perplexed by the same matter. But if the moral issues of 1812—the nature of a just war, the limits of civil obedience and disobedience, the dilemma of a moral minority, the meaning of national calamity and international holocaust—take on a special interest to modern Americans, they might lose in the process their most authentic meaning. For human responses, delicate things as they are, cannot without damage be uprooted from their native soils to form a psychic landscape in another time, unless one intends an artificial garden of plastic precedents. We must forbear imposing upon the Americans of 1812 the concerns of a later era, lest by aligning their fate with ours we facilely prove what is already believed in. We must, then, be content to let the consciences of the past, agonized, confident, tremulous, dishonest, define their own issues in their own terms. If in our enlightenment we see what they could not and understand better than they what drove them or led them or enticed them, they deserve the courtesy of a hearing, even if their words reflect a world view antique, unscientific, and worst of all, no longer useful. This much at least we owe them.

We owe it to ourselves also. For in their understandable need to justify themselves and convict their opposers, the Christians of 1812 had a penchant for using the lessons of history as remedies for their own ills. Scripture, the church fathers, centuries of European upheaval and decades of North American progress all proved the war was necessary and righteous. They all also proved, incidentally, the exact converse. That amazing dexterity of the past in sanctifying the political faith of almost anybody is the only true relevance of an analysis of American religion during the war. That does not minimize the significance of such an endeavor. More than ever, it makes it witness to what is most in need of saying.

1 ✠ GOD'S CONTROVERSY WITH AMERICA

Our hope is not in our armies, it is not in our generals, it is not in our counsellors, it is not in our constitution: it is in this, that the Lord is long-suffering, and slow to wrath, and repenteth him of evil.

Arthur Stansbury, September 9, 1813

As Great Britain and France continued throughout the first decade of the ninteenth century their bloody contest for the hegemony of Europe, one nation after another became involved in their struggle. Repeatedly the complications of transatlantic wars had drawn the United States into the international arena; repeatedly diplomacy and the turn of fate had combined to prevent American participation in the carnage. Whether diplomacy or luck failed, accumulated grievances provoked the Twelfth Congress to approve military action against Britain on June 18, 1812. The long threat of war was turned into the reality of bloodshed, and plans were put into operation for the conquest of Canada.

Several months thereafter, a "public debate" was held in Baltimore, admission twelve and a half cents for benefit of the poor. The topic was, "Can a Christian go to war and be justified by the Bible and his conscience?" [1] This was a question which was being discussed in one form or another from the pulpit by scores of ministers. It was not, however, a mere debating point for clergymen. It was also of great concern to their congregations, who were ready to pay their twelve and a half cents to hear or participate in arguments on both sides of the question. Thousands of assemblies of all religious persuasions formed an important segment of the electorate; and while clergymen declaimed on the morality of warfare, political factions sought to win support from this morally aware populace.

In the weeks before June 18, citizens of all political sentiments had addressed their government concerning the course of foreign relations, sending petitions to Congress from all over the country. It is impossible to determine what effect these displays of public opinion had upon the congressmen who finally determined the nation's policy. The people's representatives were already close to their communities, and so it was unlikely that memorials from a part of their constituency could substantially change their minds. The petitions did serve another purpose, perhaps their intended purpose, as partisan propaganda, for which they were well designed. As such, they directly appealed to religious voters.

A good example was the most defiant Federalist petition, issued by a citizens' convention in Rockingham, New Hampshire, during the crisis of early summer, 1812. This partisan manifesto foreshadowed the worst excesses of future discord and, vowing military resistance to any tie with France, won great notoriety. The resolves were soon reprinted in antiwar papers and even quoted from the pulpit. George Sullivan, member of Congress from Exeter, was the featured speaker at the gathering and freely indulged in the apocalyptic rhetoric that soon became a hallmark of such performances. A French alliance, he told the audience, "is the wormwood, it is the gall, which the wrath of heaven has mingled for the nations." [2] In the context of his hearers' intellectual presuppositions, Sullivan's scriptural warning cannot be dismissed as emotional verbiage. It was a consistent theme in antiwar petitions.

In Massachusetts, for example, the Essex County Convention condemned America's leaders for violating the biblical precept that "they who rule over men, must be just, ruling in the fear of God," and warned that a French connection "is of itself sufficient to draw down upon our country the judgments of Heaven." [3] The assembled citizens of Worcester County deemed the federal government beyond reform and decided not even to bother sending their resolutions to Washington.[4] Toward the Canadian border, in areas likely to suffer directly from military action,

Vermonters addressed Congress concerning the moral dangers of war. Indeed, this subject was given primary place in their petitions, which gathered several thousand signatures. They deplored "loans, taxes, and a thousand other concomitant evils"; but before all these, they anticipated the first evil of war "as inevitable, a general corruption of morals." [5] Even in Boston, where questions of commercial advantage were naturally uppermost in men's minds, the town meeting held three days before the final vote on the declaration of hostilities called America's willing involvement in Europe's strife "a wanton and impious rejection of the advantages with which the Almighty has blessed our country." [6]

In Philadelphia too men were interested in the fate of Atlantic commerce; and there opponents of war circulated two petitions, the more popular of which concerned itself with the economic hardship sure to come with a resort to arms. The other, less widely circulated, condemned belligerence for far different reasons. Some of the memorialists, "of several various denominations of Christians," opposed war of every description as wicked. Others deprecated only their country's involvement in the present European carnage. But "however differing in other respects," all the subscribers expressed the wish that Congress and the president would try "to DESERVE and OBTAIN the blessing pronounced by the FOUNDER of Christianity, on the makers of Peace." [7] Their scruples were shared by many citizens in Cumberland County, who ascribed America's long years of peace to the kindness of that being "who overruleth the ruler" and who as yet refrained from punishing their country with "the most awful dispensations— desolating judgments, and terrific convulsions in the physical and political world, which ever could afflict suffering humanity." [8] Similar considerations inspired Marylanders in Anne Arundel County, who declared that if carnage, aggressive invasion of Canada, and national sin were requisite to defending national honor, "we protest against it; the United States are, in the aggregate, a moral and religious people; they have not made honour an object of their foederal compact." [9] These recurrent moral arguments prepared the ground for the most authoritative anti-war statement, the address of dissenting members of Congress to their constituents.

The congressmen concluded their address with three pages of trade statistics, demonstrating the economic folly of war with Britain to preserve a worthless commerce with France. Here was their primary concern. Yet the manifesto was directed not only to a citizenry worried about making a living but also to a society deeply wedded to Christian moral concepts. So the dissenters did not equivocate their appeal to the religious public. "Moral duty requires," they declared, "that a nation, before it appeals to arms, should have been, not only true to itself, but that it should have failed in no duty to others." "Moral obligation" demanded that the protection of the American flag not be extended to Irish deserters. "Every consideration of moral duty" coincided with practical wisdom to argue that the United States should avoid Europe's quarrel. How could a heaven-blessed people dare to pray, they argued, or dare to look to heaven for future blessings when they prepared to wreak needless suffering upon their northern neighbors? The concluding paragraph summed up their entire argument: "At a crisis of the world such as the present, and under impressions such as these, the undersigned could not consider the war . . . as necessary, or required by any moral duty or political expediency." [10]

Federalist opposition to the war on religious grounds could be met in kind by advocates of military action. In the capital of Virginia, for example, they expressed horror at British attempts to foment discord by sending a spy "stealing to our fire-sides and altars." [11] Another rebuke came from the First Congressional District of Pennsylvania, where Republican citizens, in obvious rebuttal of a Federalist cliché, affirmed their trust "in that Being, who sometimes in his inscrutable providence afflicts the just, but oftener requites their constancy." [12]

It goes without saying that the motives of those who signed petitions advocating or opposing war may have had little to do with morality. Economic interest, regional bias, local party affiliations, or the artificial fervor of partisan alcohol may have accounted for their righteous indignation. This does not necessarily indicate insincerity, nor does it lessen the validity of their religious rhetoric as a meaningful expression of public opinion. This was true of every petition blustering with moral outrage, every editorial invoking Christian values, and every oration based on scriptural themes. For political employment of religious sentiment was not really an exploitation of it. The relationship between religion and politics was not competitive but, on the contrary, can best be described as a social symbiosis. In a culture self-consciously proud of its role in the historical progress of Christianity, any separation of religious and political values would have rendered them both inoperable. Religious issues were bound to be political controversies as well, and every political crisis was at the same time a moral one. Decisions of state were also moral decisions, and antagonists in partisan disputes were likely to be also participants in theological arguments.

This was best exampled in the use of fast days, occasions of public prayer in times of national crisis, when citizens could jointly seek guidance for their beleaguered country. Public fasts proliferated during the War of 1812. Some were local, others national. Although New England observed more than its share, they were held in other regions as well. Fasts were often extremely controversial occasions and showed that the religion and politics of Americans were too closely related to be studied separately.

There were three such occasions during the summer of 1812 alone. Even before the decision of June 18, the General Assembly of the Presbyterian church and the General Synod of the Dutch Reformed church agreed with the synod of the Associate Reformed church to observe July 30 as a fast day. The Presbyterian body warned that the low state of vital religion, the prevalence of vice, and "the variegated visitations of heaven's justice" were "national judgments, which there is too much reason to apprehend may be 'the beginning of sorrows.' " [13] While Congress debated the war resolution, the Dutch synod spoke stern words to a worried people:

Under the dominion and dispensation of Jehovah, the peace and prosperity of our common country are threatened. The rod of his indignation is shaken over us, and it becomes us to hear its voice. . . . Brethren, we are a guilty people; a sinful nation—and iniquity abounds in our land. As individual crimes go to fill up the measure of national guilt, we are each one personally implicated in that mass of crimes, which rises up as a cloud to the heavens, crying out for the vengeance of the Almighty upon us.[14]

Because it was a venerable custom to petition civil rulers that "by their authority and command" local governments might lend their support to fast observances,[15] the governors of New York and Pennsylvania, where the cooperating denominations were numerically large and socially influential, set aside July 30 as a day of public prayer. Needless to say, the warnings of the petitioning churches became still more pertinent when Congress at length decided for war.

Several New England states observed still another fast. Governor Caleb Strong of Massachusetts, whose recent electoral defeat of Elbridge Gerry created hopes for a national Federalist resurgence, set aside July 23 as a fast day for his state and was soon followed by Governors Roger Griswold of Connecticut and William Jones of Rhode Island. Strong's proclamation of the observance was pious, humble, and forcefully political. It pleaded for protection from an alliance with infidel France, asked justice for the persecuted Indians, and begged pardon for the country's many sins. The combining of official rhetoric, religious sentiment, and partisan argument rendered the proclamation a curious mélange, a travesty of both personal prayer and state paper. Its reference to Britain as "the bulwark" of religion against impious France gave mocking Republicans a vulnerable target for years to come. But to God-fearing Federalists, the governor had spoken accurately and devoutly. His words were soon quoted in sermons and religious magazines, as well as in antiwar papers, where readers knew the necessity of praying "that [God] would break in pieces the power of the oppressor, and scatter the people that delight in war." [16]

President Madison too set aside a day, August 20, as a national fast. His announcement to that effect came too late and was too imprecise for those citizens who believed the war was divine judgment for the country's sins. The president was more con-

cerned with asking a blessing on American arms than with con-
fessing America's guilt. He attributed the conflict to "the injustice
of a foreign power" and was careful to avoid specifically Christian phraseology, apparently because of his scruples concerning
governmental sponsorship of any creed.[17] Moreover, he only
recommended religious observances; he would not "direct and
require" them. These scruples were themselves offensive to the
president's adversaries, one of whom published a pair of fast
sermons, the rambling title of which made clear the difference
between the presidential and other fasts. The former was only
"*recommended* by the President of the United States for a
NATIONAL FAST," while local observances were "*appointed* by the
governor and Council for a STATE FAST." [18] The Reverend John
Fiske of New Braintree, Massachusetts, made the same point more
bluntly. The very words he used in attacking hypocritical rulers
were taken in part from Madison's proclamation. Scoffing at
wicked leaders who "are reduced to the necessity of appointing a
season, when all, who are disposed, may united look to God for
direction and aid, by their religious teachers, in whom the people
have confidence as men of God," Fiske would not condemn his
country's foe and asked, for himself and his colleagues, "Must
they curse because the king commands it?" [19]

Fiske was only one of a multitude who would not curse on
command. Madison's proposal that the fast observances beseech
help for the army was met by widespread contempt. A Bostonian
critic was horrified because, while Christians prayed for mercy in
a time of public calamity, Madison "is not content with forcing
upon the nation a war that must destroy it, but he asks you to
supplicate your God for its success . . . for success in a battle
against your liberties and your God." [20]

From the pulpit came more rebukes to the president. Nathaniel
Thayer quoted Madison's fast message and announced, "I add,
with my persuasion of the unrighteousness and tendency of the
war, I cannot make the prayer which is recommended." [21] Samuel
Austin urged his hearers to "pray for the success of our arms so
far as, and no farther than, they are employed in support of a
cause which [God] himself can approve." [22] After a sermon in
which he gave no quarter to the president, John Lathrop declared,

"I must be excused, if I do not pray, that God would bless our armies on an expedition, to which I could not give my services with a good conscience." [23] Although Noah Worcester had earlier delivered moderate sermons which drew praise from administration spokesmen in New Hampshire, on August 20 his plea for mutual benevolence was joined to an outright rejection of Madison's suggested prayers. Years later he explained, "Though I could not pray for the success of our arms, I could pray that the lives of the soldiers on both sides might be preserved, and such were my prayers during the war." [24] Perhaps the wittiest disrespect for the fast day was that shown by a Federalist editor in Virginia, who faithfully printed Madison's proclamation, as did antiwar papers generally. Five weeks later, on August 21, the day after the fast, the editor discovered a typographical mistake. "In copying the fast day proclaimed by the President, we inadvertently committed an error," he explained, "in stating Tuesday to be the day instead of Thursday the 20th inst. This error escaped our observation until too late to correct it." [25]

A year later, when the war seemed decidedly less glorious, Madison again set aside a day of prayer in a message that seemed a direct answer to his critics of the previous year. "If the public homage of a people can ever be worthy the favorable regard of the Holy and Omniscient Being to whom it is addressed," he contended, it must be freely performed, not commanded by civil authority. This would prove the power of religion,

> freed from all coercive edicts, from that unhallowed connection with the powers of this world which corrupts religion into an instrument or an usurper of the policy of the state. . . . Upon these principles and with these views the good people of the United States are invited, in conformity with the resolution aforesaid, to dedicate the day above named to the religious solemnities therein recommended.[26]

"These principles" pleased Madison's admirers; but as a Baltimorean enthusiast noted, they were received with scorn by opponents of the war.[27] Another Republican charged that Federalist obstruction of fast observances out of spite for the man who recommended them was unworthy of even the Essex Junto.[28]

This was probably his ultimate deprecation, and it was not inappropriate.

The influential *Federal Republican*, for example, did not appreciate the president's didactic essay on the principles of liberal religion and urged its readers to refuse participation in religious services on the fast day because "the hypocritical cant of the production" was "perfectly in character with the professions and conduct of the dominant party." [29] Madison might have believed that casually "recommended" worship was alone worthy of the Supreme Being, but "A Bible christian would say—this has been worthy the indignation of Jehovah in every age and nation—this has been the horrid spectacle christians have viewed with sorrow in every age of the church, and I hope they will continue to do so." [30] Many Federalists must have agreed with the suggestion of one antiwar wit who announced his intent to pray for peace every Thursday of the war, excepting only the Thursday recommended by Madison. To discover the reason, he added, one need only read the impious fast day message.[31]

Antiwar righteousness also fell upon William Plumer of New Hampshire, who, unlike other governors in New England, failed to appoint a state fast in the summer of 1812. Some men, an editor in Portsmouth observed, "consider themselves so firmly grounded, that their seats cannot be shaken and even to *deity* refuse to acknowledge their offences." Plumer's impiety came as no surprise because his chief, Madison himself, had waited for Congress to solicit his announcement "before he proclaimed the gathering of the people, to adore the Sovereign of Heaven and Earth." The concluding warning was repeated over and over during the war: "When the wicked rule, the people mourn." [32]

The following spring, Plumer did declare a state fast; and his message to that effect was a martial and partisan document, praying that dissident ministers would be made to teach obedience to civil powers. Republicans thought this would please all sincere Christians and contrasted Plumer's message with "the hypocritical and factious inuendoes" of the governor of Massachusetts upon similar occasions.[33] Plumer's prayers were decidedly practical. One of them asked the ruler of all armies to "teach our hands to war and our fingers to fight." This use of scriptural diction amused a Federalist in neighboring Vermont, who mocked, "This looks like a *slap* at the Virginia practice of *gouging*. Or does his Excellency seriously mean to recommend to the people of New-England, a game of *fisticuffs*." [34]

Fast day controversies were not all one-sided, of course. The governor of Massachusetts was especially unfortunate in this regard, as one of his supporters lamented: "Nothing has called forth such vile taunts, nay, such bitter execration, against the pious Gov. STRONG, as that clause of his *Fast Proclamation*, where he speaks of Great Britain, as 'the Bulwark of the religion we profess.' " [35] When Strong appointed another fast in the spring of 1813 according to the custom of his state, a Republican editor took issue with his partisan message and reprinted for patriotic Bostonians the fast order of 1776, recommending that it be substituted for the governor's own seditious call to prayer. [36]

A similar furor was provoked in Rhode Island when Governor William Jones in a Thanksgiving Day message urged public repentance for America's sins to avert future punishment. Outraged Republicans scorned the proclamation, cataloged Britain's crimes, and demanded to know if "there was no national sin in the murderous affair of Copenhagen; in the avaricious capture of the Spanish frigates with dollars; in the horrid murders and barbarities committed in India and Ireland, and in our own country." [37] If the peppery Republicans of Rhode Island settled no moral issues in their fast controversy, they may have won a few votes in their efforts to gain an electoral majority, the final arbiter in America's theological democracy.

However controversial the role of politicians in wartime fasts, it was the clergy who held center stage on those occasions. It was theirs to outrage or delight their hearers, win notice in the local papers, perhaps even publish their sermons if public favor so warranted, all the while applying as best they could their own moral insights to a very complicated situation. The Congregationalist clergy of the northeastern states were especially adept in this procedure, perhaps because their region had so long cultivated the tradition. Two of their number, Jedidiah Morse and Elijah Parish, spoke of the matter in their popular textbook history of New England:

This pious custom originated with their venerable ancestors, the first settlers of New England; and has been handed down as sacred, through the successive generations of their posterity. A custom so rational, and so happily calculated to cherish in the minds of the people, a sense of their dependence on the Great Benefactor of the world for all their blessings, it is hoped will ever be sacredly preserved.[38]

The Congregational church was the heart of religious opposition to the war, and both Morse and Parish observed the various fasts in the manner of their ancestors with appropriate sermons. Parish's orations were so appropriate to the mood of his Federalist hearers that his name soon came to be used in the farthest reaches of the land to portray malicious treason. His counsel was forceful:

Rise in the majesty of your unconquerable strength, break those chains under which you have sullenly murmured, during the long, long reign of democracy; batter down those iron walls, which have incarcerated your souls and bodies so long, and once more breathe that free, commercial air of New England, which your fathers always enjoyed.[39]

The reaction was also forceful. A more patriotic discourse by a Dutch minister was soon published with a prefixed fold-out sheet containing excerpts from Parish's diatribe and headed "INFERNALISM." [40] "Let the reverend madman peaceably pursue his career of folly, treason, political and religious phrensy," advised an editor, who thought honest Federalists would repudiate the culprit.[41] But the "young Judas" continued his orations and became the embodiment of antiwar religion.[42] His dissent was not made more reputable when one of his sermons was published in Halifax with a British editor's comment that "this sermon claims *the suffrage of every soul that loves the best of constitutions—* namely that of OLD ENGLAND!" [43] The compliment was duly noted by Republicans; and when Mathew Carey published his popular tract, *The Olive Branch*, it included a chapter on the priestly treason of men like Elijah Parish. "Of all the abominations that disgrace and dishonor this country in these portentous times," he wrote, "I know nothing more deserving of reprobation than the prostitution of the pulpit for party or political purposes." [44]

This was by no means an unusual sentiment, and the fiery and quotable speeches of Parish and a few cohorts have long provided historians with a concise picture of the antiwar clergy.

But the picture drawn from Parish's hyperbole was a caricature, useful for illustrating by way of exaggeration but inappropriate for accurately portraying ministerial dissent. Like any determined combatants, Republican propagandists aimed at vulnerable limbs, attacking the weakest points of their clerical opponents to secure maximum political advantage from the excesses of a few ordained extremists. While Parish raised the specter of secession from his pulpit in Byfield, scores of his colleagues in Massachusetts and neighboring states were delivering more moderate sermons. Jedidiah Morse, for example, his colleague in both the ministry and literary efforts, counseled his congregation concerning their duty in the present crisis. He discussed the character of a good ruler, the limits to Paul's admonition to obey authorities, and the duty of Israel's watchmen to sound the warning trumpet, lest they themselves be held accountable for failing their priestly calling.[45] This was much more than a simple denunciation of the month-old war and represented the generality of antiwar preaching more accurately than the few openly seditious sermons so angrily attacked by Republicans.

A unique significance must be granted to that preaching. Granted, each sermon was the handiwork of but one individual, whose words may have represented nothing beyond his own political preferences. Moreover, because most of the protesting sermons were delivered by Congregationalists, they bore none of the authoritative cast of an episcopal address or synodal decree. This limits their usefulness as expressions of denominational policy. On the other hand, those sermons were delivered by community leaders who were second to no civil officials in the molding of public opinion. Intending to point out a danger, a Republican leader testified to this fact. "There is perhaps no order of men that possess equal means of influence with you," he warned the clergy. "The very duties of your profession, and your relative situations in life, have a natural tendency to acquire and preserve a great influence over your fellow men. The nature of your office necessarily connects you with the people, in the most important concerns of human life." [46] The pulpit, then, could be something like a community's pulse point. The many fast days during the war provided repeated opportunities for a close reading of that pulse.

In their overall context, the fast sermons of 1812 form an introductory schematic for charting the emotions, fears, and hopes which the vehemence of Elijah Parish could never fully express. This hostile response to the war, taken as one uneven unit, falls into three divisions. The first, denunciation of Madison's policies on religious grounds, formed a fairly standardized argument to which the ministers devoted most of their dramatic oratory. Equally important was the clergy's defense of their right to dissent from public policy not only as citizens but also, in the phrase of Jedidiah Morse, as the ordained watchmen of Israel. Finally, the most important part of the sermons, the concluding application of the discourses, outlined plans of political action to oppose the unrighteous conflict. It is necessary to remember that the antiwar sermons were indeed sermons. There is always danger of emphasizing the accident, the political dissent, to the neglect of the substance, the sermon itself. In the America of the early national period, the preacher was rare who generalized, theorized, and emoted without some application of his theme to the lives of his audience. Printed sermons were often ended with an "application," "reflection," or "improvement," clearly headed as such. Discourses on moral conduct, condemnations of theological opponents, even internment sermons were incomplete without the application of beliefs, however abstract, to the immediacies of worldly existence. Similarly, by the very nature of its literary form, an antiwar sermon was likely to contain clear applications of the preacher's opinions to quite practical circumstances. More attention is due to these applications than to the preliminary generalizations. For like most sermons of the period, those delivered on the summer fasts of 1812 had definite purposes for their eloquence.

The arguments advanced in those sermons were not to be easily dismissed. Napoleonic France was an infidel nation, controlled by the antichrist foretold in the Book of Revelation or by the false prophet of the papal antichrist. Only Britain prevented this Beast of Babylon from conquering the world. Britain, moreover, had recently taken the lead in spreading Protestant Christianity over the globe through evangelical societies. No good could come from warring against the enemies of God's enemies, especially in an offensive invasion of Canada, in which no honest Christian should take a willing part. Aggressive war was always contrary to the commands of the Gospel; and this particular war was the instrument of deists, slaveholders, Francophiles, and the great antichristian league. Americans were to be allied with all of papal Europe against the land of their Protestant fathers. Elijah Parish could very reasonably remind his congregation that it was in Maryland, "that State in this country, where the papal religion *has* predominated," that the administration's mobs had begun a reign of terror.[47] He was referring to a murderous encounter between supporters and opponents of the war at the office of the *Federal Republican* in Baltimore, the see city of Archbishop John Carroll. It was little consolation that Napoleon himself had abolished the Spanish Inquisition, that the pope was his prisoner, and that antiwar forces in Maryland enjoyed the prestigious support of Charles Carroll, the bishop's illustrious kinsman. The extremity of the situation overruled these considerations. On the other hand, considerable justification was required for such strenuous clerical participation in the public crisis.

The United States that fought the War of 1812 had as yet come to no grounds of agreement concerning the role of religious teachers in a multidenominational republic. Apparently this disagreement lay heavy in the thoughts of the antiwar clergy. Their frequent comments on this point indicated their awareness of the reaction they would provoke. Nathan Strong of Hartford reassured his congregation, "I do not address you in the character of a politician," and then set about strongly praising Connecticut's Federalist leadership, who could be trusted because "the oath of the Lord is upon them." [48] No stranger to the rough-and-tumble of American religious controversy, Samuel Austin began his sermon of July 23 bluntly: "It is denied that this sermon is political. . . . Facts of a political nature are adverted to. But they are produced in evidence to a point of religious instruction." [49] This disavowal did not, however, prevent him from denouncing the "phrenzy and madness of governmental office-holders." On the next fast day, Austin made not even the pretense of an apolitical discourse but began with an extended justification of his own "grand heresy": "As prejudices are known to exist against me, founded partly in religious, partly, perhaps most, in political consideration; and some have carried their most unfounded resentments so far as, for a time at least, to leave my congregation, a short personal apology will not be deemed improper." [50] Austin asserted his right as a minister to exercise the privilege of any citizen to speak out for good government; the intimate relationship between religious truth and civil prosperity made that right even more important. Certainly, few members of his congregation would have objected to those ideas. In all probability it was his next axiom which provoked the defections of which he spoke. Concerning his own position as a clergyman, he asserted, "There is no situation in life, more exempt from those sinister influences which blind the understanding, and pervert the judgment." [51]

The theological politics of Nathan Beman were so far unperverted that he could tell his hearers unequivocally, "Here let it be understood, that I shall not meddle with the political contests of the day. I preach only the politics of heaven;—I inculcate the spirit of the bible." [52] It was heavenly politics, he thought, to remove from office impious men who would interfere with the activities of British evangelical organizations by a needless war. John Lathrop assured his congregation that he would not need to apologize for discussing political matters. Apologies were not called for because the Bible, Vattell, and Puffendorf showed that "sound political morality, and the morality of the New Testament, come so near together, that the christian minister who inculcates the moral duties which were inculcated by Jesus and the Apostles, must and will inculcate the best political morals." [53] Jedidiah Morse spoke for all his ministerial brethren, to whom Scripture threatened punishment if they failed to warn Israel of approaching calamity.[54] This consideration above all else united antiwar clergymen. It was cited by David Osgood to justify his various fast sermons, which were among the most extreme antiwar pronouncements:

> As a teacher of righteousness, as a minister of Christ, I feel myself under obligations infinitely superior to all human laws,

most solemnly to testify, both in public and in private, every where, in the hearing of all persons, rulers and subjects, against this atrocious wickedness, and to lay down my life, rather than cease this testimony.[55]

Still avoiding rancor, Noah Worcester closed his discourse on August 20 with a similar justification, picturing a dying soldier who suddenly sees the present war's immorality and accuses the preacher of failing his holy calling by not warning of this sin.[56]

Other clergymen directed their apologia directly against the barbs of their opponents. Micah Stone noted that some objected to political preaching on the grounds of impropriety; but "All I shall reply to such is, I did not receive, neither shall I hold, my office, on such a condition." [57] Failure to guard the liberties of his country, he contended, would make him both a perjured traitor and an unworthy minister. Stephen Rowan of the Reformed Dutch church in New York published his fast sermons specifically because of the attacks made upon them for their political content. Any partisans offended by his preaching, he insisted, would thereby save him the trouble of making a concluding application by exhibiting themselves as the targets of scriptural rebuke.[58] Brown Emerson exhibited the same facetious righteousness in his sermon on Governor Strong's fast day. After a series of pointed rhetorical questions, he avowed, "I only ask, and leave the questions to be resolved by facts. I have always discarded the idea of making the pulpit a place for mere political discussion." [59] It remained for Timothy Dwight, one of the most actively partisan clergymen in America, to abide by such a disavowal of political preaching. On both the state and national fasts of 1812, he preached in the chapel of Yale College. On both days his subject was the approaching millennium, for which the present carnage was the preparation. On both occasions his hatred for Napoleonic France and his disapproval of America's war were obvious.[60] Compared with his colleagues' sermons of the same days, however, those of the "Protestant Pope of Connecticut" were remarkable for their restraint.

Having either sidestepped or summarily rejected objections to their partisanship, the antiwar clergy were confident of the propriety, indeed, the moral necessity, of their dissent. Nor were they without a program for accomplishing righteous goals. Elijah Parish offered concise advice: "Protest, did I say, protest? Forbid this war to proceed in New-England." [61] The great body of fast sermons were a little more moderate, much more sophisticated politically, and committed to the processes of constitutional government. It was, after all, an election year. The state-by-state choosing of presidential electors was to begin but two months after the August fast. More than any other factor, this consideration moderated the tenor of antiwar preaching. The mere possibility of a change in leadership in the autumn must have meliorated the despair that came so naturally to many churchmen.

There was sufficient cause for alarm. Soon after the declaration of war, the office of an antiwar newspaper in Baltimore was sacked by a Republican mob. Late in July shots were exchanged between another mob and a band of armed Federalists, who, having been taken into protective custody, were besieged in the jail. The nation was soon shocked by stories of murder, torture, and mutilation, reports which the Federalist press naturally stressed and detailed. In the partisan tumult, exact information was as hard to obtain as it was unwanted. But protesting clergymen thought a Jacobin reign of terror was at hand and feared mass martyrdom. One of them drew a parallel between the horrors at Baltimore and the awful fate of Jerusalem which had caused the Redeemer to weep over his beloved city; for the Maryland carnage "reminds us of that furious mob, who wreaked their vengeance on Stephen, the first martyr." [62] Samuel Worcester delivered a special sermon, "The Martyrdom of Stephen," on the same theme and warned his listeners that the violence was not yet ended. "The blood still cries to heaven; and God is the avenger," he declared.[63] In private he expressed the same terrible foreboding. He confided to his brother in early August, "You will have heard of the horrible scenes at Baltimore! The same spirit is here, but as yet is kept under restraint. The friends of peace, however, think it prudent, to have their arms in readiness for any want. May God preserve us, and our beloved country." [64]

Another preacher fearfully drew a personal parallel with Jeremiah, who, "because he was faithful, and testified against the rulers of Israel, and against a sinful people, was persecuted, cast into prison, and confined in a dungeon." [65] His pessimism was matched by Reuben Holcomb, who foresaw moral defeat in American victory, in which case "the minister of the meek and lowly Saviour, must be driven into exile, or fall a sacrifice to Gallic insolence and madness." [66] Allowing for the hyperbole characteristic of the times, one must nevertheless be impressed with the clergy's heartfelt fears.

Almost always, however, the approach of the presidential election acted as a safety valve. Amid the apprehension of July and August, amid the mob violence and the uncertainty that exaggerated it, there was some ground for hope if constructive political action could take advantage of electoral possibilities. Almost unanimously, the summer fast sermons proposed political moderation, as opposed to the extremist rhetoric which so infuriated the administration's supporters.

A stalwart of the Federalist social apparatus in New Hampshire, John Hubbard Church, summed up his entire sermon of August 20 in its title, *Advantages of Moderation*. Calm, deliberate, prudent measures alone could reverse the fearful state of the country, he warned.[67] He was joined in this opinion by the great majority of his colleagues. Reuben Holcomb, who foresaw a general slaughter of Christian ministers, nonetheless cautioned his congregation, "In the present state of political discord, be very careful that you do nothing seditiously." [68] Freeman Parker was just as definite: "We have no right, with force and arms, to oppose any constitutional measure of the government." [69] After condemning both the mobs of Baltimore and the tyranny of Congress, Micah Stone denounced all illegal measures to rectify the situation: "While we remain firm, we must keep ourselves cool, and take no step but in conformity to the Constitution and Laws." [70] Similarly, Nathaniel Thayer's pathetic catalog of American suffering at the hands of the national government was followed by surprisingly mild advice: "The only safe and sure remedy for present evils is a vigilant and Christian use of your elective rights." [71] Though a layman, Jeremiah Evarts was secretary to the American Board of Commissioners for Foreign Missions and so was as much a part of the ecclesiastical establishment of New England as any minister.

In his Independence Day oration in Charlestown, Massachusetts, soon after the resort to arms was decided, he too advised restraint. Although the liberties of the people were in danger, "We must do nothing inconsistent with our constitutional obligations. If laws constitutionally enacted are oppressive in their operation, we must seek a constitutional remedy." [72] Like his clerical friends, Evarts urged moderation because relief was readily available in the autumn elections.

It was not only the threat of civil disorder which terrified protesting clergymen. A moral malaise had been for some time evident in the workings of the American government and was additional cause for alarm during such a crisis. It would have been difficult to find many American church members in disagreement with the maxim of the antiwar preacher who declared, "God is either obeyed or disobeyed, honoured or the opposite, by a ruler, in every part of his official conduct; and that conduct is, of course, right or wrong, in a religious point of view." [73] At a time when separation of church and state was by no means an unchallenged tenet of the American creed, the separation of government and moral righteousness was completely unthinkable. To assume that demands for a government respectful of religion were unique to Federalism is to accept a rather poor piece of that party's propaganda. The religious character of candidates was campaign material for both parties. In local elections during the war, Republicans often accused their opponents of fielding impious candidates and did so with a moral hauteur usually associated with Federalist impeccability. So when antiwar preachers advised the election of candidates conforming to scriptural requirements for office, their frame of reference was not peculiar to one political faction. No matter how narrowly partisan the intention or the final result of their advice, it was directed to a general ground of agreement among American Christians.

Jeremiah Evarts represented his fellow laymen as well as his ordained associates in urging support for men "shewn to be worthy of public confidence, by lives of private virtue; such men as are actuated by a regard to conscience, and the fear of God." The preservation of American institutions was at stake, for "there never was a republic worthy of the name, unless among a people who were in a considerable degree under the influence of Christianity." [74] This was axiomatic to all the antiwar clergy. Even the erudition of William Ellery Channing could not elaborate upon such simple truth. "Let us remember that there is no foundation of publick liberty but public virtue," he said, "that there is no method of obtaining God's protection but adherence to his laws." [75] Along with many others, Jedidiah Morse thought the Constitution itself imperiled the United States by its failure to set religious tests for national officeholders. Without pious rulers, ruin was inevitable: "Under rulers of no other character, has any christian nation ever flourished, for any length of time. Under rulers of a different stamp, nations have always degenerated, and been finally brought to desolation and ruin." [76]

Other preachers illustrated this same point by presenting histories of the rise and fall of nations from the chastisement of Israel to the punishment of America. Scripture confirmed them in their diagnosis of the country's malady, for "when the wicked bear rule, the people mourn." Recent events also afforded harsh proof that annihilation awaited any republic which compromised its religious purity. The Dutch Calvinists had tolerated infidels; the Swiss cantons had grown lax in their ancient creed; the German Protestants had turned from the paths of their fathers to dally with modern philosophy. Now they were all fallen beauties, Timothy Dwight warned, chained to the plaguy corpse of antichrist.[77] The European vortex yawed its way westward to the last republic; and religion alone, not war, could preserve its republican institutions from the peril. Lyman Beecher had good reason to plead with his New Haven congregation a few days before the presidential election that they would consider moral character the sole criterion in their voting. The stakes were immense, for "neither we nor our children shall ever see another New England, if this be destroyed." [78]

Even though the clergy's view of international affairs was as somber as their forebodings of a domestic reign of terror, in both cases pessimism stopped short of despair. Even in the face of the divine retribution that had overtaken the entire western world except Britain, the antiwar clergy's program was still an orderly resort to electoral process. In general, they advocated nothing more seditious than the elevation of DeWitt Clinton to the presidency.

Their exhortations to that effect, although couched in generalities, often seemed quite explicit. Sometimes their phraseology was identical with that of Federalist editors. Any ruler governing in the fear of God, declared Micah Stone, "will administer the government in the spirit of the constitution, and will not attempt to exalt one part of the Union on the ruins of another." All party spirit must be renounced to act "in concert with the Friends of Peace, Commerce, and Independence." [79] James Abercrombie asked his flock if they had, as individuals, acted to secure divine mercy for their country by disregarding partisan feeling to "place in the important station of Rulers, men of wisdom, integrity, firmness, magnanimity, and disinterested attachment to the public welfare; the dignity, the honour and property of the nation?" [80] His meaning was clear to Republican editors in Philadelphia, who excoriated his political preaching.[81]

Ministers had been reprobating partisan rancor as an unchristian display of enmity long before the war. But their concern in the summer of 1812 was not to rebuke political hostility but to urge an electoral fusion of Federalism and Clintonian Republicanism. "The humble professors of the christian religion" should use all their influence "to bring the parties in our country to think more candidly of each other, and unite in some measure for the safety and happiness of the whole." [82] No campaign committee expressed the Clintonian platform more succinctly than did Nathaniel Thayer, who desired, "without distinction of name or party, to invest with office the friends and lovers of peace, who will have a sacred regard to the agricultural and commercial interests of the community." [83] And no other clergyman more completely identified Christian morality with one electoral ticket than did Stephen Rowan when he deprecated party loyalties and recommended, "whether you eat, or drink, or vote, do it for the glory of God, and the good of your country." [84] Samuel Worcester demanded the same nonpartisan cooperation—"a coalition, a union"—to insure that "internal tranquility and order will be established on solid foundations." [85] The clergy's reliance on the electoral process was justified by the possibility that Madison might be de-

feated in the fall election by the major of New York. Renegade
Jeffersonian that he was, DeWitt Clinton's candidacy nonetheless
presented the fortuitous coincidence of Federalist policy and
scriptural qualifications.

The issues of the presidential campaign, such as it was, cannot
be neatly analyzed. Without candidates' orations and policy statements, electioneering was intensely local, developing regional
issues and personal antipathies. Clinton did, however, deliver one
address which was used nationwide as a campaign speech, the
candidate's own pronouncement on vital issues. It was explicit and
committal but concerned domestic disorder rather than the incipient war.

One of Clinton's duties as mayor of New York was delivering
the "charge" to that city's grand jury. In early July 1812, his
charge concerned recent incidents in which ruffians had attempted
to chastise opponents of the war by destroying their property in
the manner of the Baltimore vigilantes. With the clergy's fears of
organized repression serving as emphasis, Clinton's denunciation
of mob violence was soon reprinted in Federalist papers all over
the country. It was editorially praised as the candidate's own
statement of principles and was the closest approximation to a
campaign pledge in the contest of that year. Clinton's own jour-
nalistic organ, the *New York Columbian*, reprinted accolades bestowed on the jury speech by another Republican editor. But the
added commentary was more important: "The handsome, unqual-
ified eulogiums on the mayor's charge, in differing federalist
papers, we have foreborne to copy." [86] The *Columbian* did not,
however, forbear to publish a "Solemn Appeal to the people of
New-England" from a "Republican Clergyman," who strongly
recommended Clinton's candidacy. Voters need only examine his
"impartial animadversions upon every class of public offenses." [87]
A Federalist clergyman was more explicit. In his fast sermon of
August 20, Jonathan French discoursed on the rights of free
Americans and quoted the patriots of the Revolution as authori-
ties. "To these noble sentiments," he wished to subjoin "the late
patriotic and truly republican observations of his Hon. De Witt
Clinton of New-York." [88] The "observations" were extracts from
Clinton's jury speech.

It merited this attention. To silence criticism in time of war, he contended, would degrade republicanism:

> We have therefore prepared ourselves for the crisis; and, with the blessing of Heaven, we shall not only suppress tumultuous and riotous assemblies, but we shall bring the authors and abettors to condign punishment. And as long as we occupy these seats, be assured, that we shall put down and punish, in the most exemplary manner, all attempts to invade the public peace, to destroy the lives and property of individuals, and to impair the freedom of opinion and enquiry.[89]

It is true that the antiwar clergy expected Clinton, if elected, to restore peace with Britain. But it was also true, as Republican spokesmen pointed out, that the mayor's agents in some states were promising a more effective prosecution of the war and not its cessation. This ambivalence was possible at a time when campaign platforms had not yet come into vogue. The only issue for which Clinton's own words could readily be cited as a definite policy was the crisis of domestic disorder.

In addition to his one specific pledge, Clinton secured ministerial support on more intangible grounds: his character, his piety, his public witness to the Christian religion. Of course, this might be poor material for political argumentation; and his electioneering literature did not exploit it.[90] The reason is a matter for conjecture. In light of the bitter denominational hostilities of the period, it was only prudent to avoid antagonizing more voters than might be won over by displays of Clinton's Presbyterian piety. Then too, Clinton had long functioned in the multidenominational politics of New York, while the experience of his ministerial supporters was largely confined to congregations homogeneous in both religion and politics. They could apply religious criteria to the candidates with much greater security than could professional politicians seeking to please all and alienate none. However that might be, a Republican editor in North Carolina was correct in noting the Clintonians' failure to exploit their candidate's piety to the detriment of that of Madison: "Further, Mr. Madison possesses the most unblemished moral character; nor have his vile calumniators dared to hazard the attempt of attacking him on this point, which with the *supporters* of the '*bulwark of our most holy religion*,' is generally a consideration of the first importance." [91]

It was indeed a "consideration of the first importance" that DeWitt Clinton was one of the most publicly religious politicians in the country. As another Republican noted, Federalists claimed Clinton was "a peace-loving, Quaker-thinking, meek-eyed Moses; a religious, pious pattern of benevolence; shuddering at the name of war." [92] While Clinton administered the government of New York City, his regular attendance with his family at services of the Presbyterian church testified to his religious beliefs and was well noted in the community.[93] He was later to become the vice-president of the American Bible Society and of the Presbyterian Education Society and was the patron of numerous humane organizations. In addition, in 1812 and for many other years, his running mate Jared Ingersoll was a distinguished trustee of the General Assembly of the Presbyterian church.[94] Two more godly candidates would have been difficult to find.

When Clinton died in 1828, a New York paper summed up his character: "he bowed in homage to the name of JESUS; and to the virtues of a truly great mind, added the faith of a CHRISTIAN." [95] Clinton's friend, the Reverend Alexander Proudfit, eulogized this rare politician who had never felt superior to religion and who had confided his wish that his children might become advocates of Christianity.[96] On this same occasion, Clinton was recalled by the Reverend James Milnor, who sixteen years earlier had been one of Pennsylvania's two congressmen voting against the war. The angry reaction of his constituents had caused his withdrawal from public life and eventual entrance into the ministry. His sermon on Clinton's death did not mention the bitterness of the war years but testified to the personal esteem Milnor felt for the deceased statesman. In a way, it was a reaffirmation of the principles of the antiwar clergy of 1812, who had so admired Clinton for publicly supporting the Christian religion:

And, hence, he was ever ready to give the weight of his personal, and when it was proper his official sanction, to its institutions. Yes, amidst the clamours of infidelity Clinton shrunk not from the avowal of his attachment to Christianity; and though immersed in the varied cares of public life, he found a pleasure in affording his countenance and aid to the diffusion of its influence.[97]

To determine the sincerity of Clinton's renowned piety is not within the competence of historians. Nor does it matter if his own estimable religious character served his supporters as a pretense for the furthering of economic, sectional, or partisan ambitions. It is difficult to conceive of the antiwar clergy as a body condemning any Federalist candidate for high office on the grounds of immorality; and Republicans made much of this contradiction whenever the opportunity presented itself, as in the Rhode Island elections in the spring of 1812.[98] But political inconsistency need not be a sign of insincerity. It does not matter if the antiwar preachers of 1812 would have endorsed less pious men than Clinton. It matters greatly that the clergy faced no such dilemma, that Clinton was simultaneously a leader acceptable to the Federalist party and a man qualified by scriptural standards to govern a Christian people. This happy circumstance justified ministerial intervention in the election and made it all the easier to employ ecclesiastical influence as a political instrument.

But whatever significance is attached to the fast sermons of 1812, it will be of dubious validity as long as the clerical value-system that structured those sermons is suspected of hypocrisy. The clergy's fulminations would have had value only as curiosities if their beliefs had not had currency among the congregations too. If awareness of the nexus between a nation's virtues and its prosperity, if millennial expectations and fear of antichristian anarchy were not within the milieu of a great many citizens, then pulpit endorsements of Clinton would have been no different from other pieces of electioneering material. The vital import of the sermons, however, is that they did indeed reflect the pattern of emotional responses interwoven in the fabric of American religion. In the final analysis, it was the congregation's world view that was the catalyst in the reaction between religious values and political programs. For the explication of that world view, the antiwar sermons of 1812 are only a necessary introduction.

2 ✠ FEDERALIST ARMAGEDDON

> *To conclude—a new era seems opening on Europe and the world.*
>
> William Ellery Channing, June 15, 1814

When William Channing preached on Governor Strong's fast day, he revealed the heart of antiwar sentiment. "To see [the war] in its true character," he believed, "we must consider *against what nation it is waged,* and *with what nation it is connecting us.*" [1] Though his statement was formulated with political intent, his congregation's criteria for deciding what nation deserved America's friendship or hostility were largely religious. World diplomacy was to them a grand morality play, in which various states represented good or evil. International affairs were not so much the interaction of governments as the continuing clash between Christian peoples and agents of Satan. Officials charged with deciding American foreign policy may have acted on the basis of national interest or party policy or personal ambition, but a large part of the electorate had very different concerns. They expected their country to champion the interests of Christianity against its worldwide foes, and they knew very well who were its enemies and allies. They had ample information on the subject, provided by scores of humanitarian societies, whose reports, bulletins, appeals were reprinted in newspapers, church periodicals, and mass-produced tracts. Literate American Christians and the many citizens they influenced could thus develop their opinions about international events by judging the moral character of the various participants.

Pious Federalists had long since decided the French government, whether Jacobin or Napoleonic, was morally depraved.
Its revolutionary excesses were thought to be the inevitable result
of deism and radical democracy. By 1812 this was an old story.
For a generation New England's religious leaders had rehearsed
it so that French wickedness was an unquestioned dogma of the
antiwar creed. As already mentioned, their fears of Gallic infidelity were expressed in antiwar sermons. And the way in which
those fears were turned against the Republican party is too well
known to require explanation.[2] There were, however, other actors
on the international stage, other nations whose moral character
concerned American Christians as they debated their country's
foreign policy. Russia was of central importance in European
events, as was the papacy under Pius VII. More important than
either, of course, was the nation against which James Madison was
making war.

To American Christians, British support for international evangelical enterprises was both a great hope and a constant incitement
to emulation. The American Board of Commissioners for Foreign
Missions could not have been more blunt in their appeal for financial assistance in the autumn of 1811: "Shall the four American
missionaries then be cast upon the London funds? Is not the
American public as well able to supply £600 annually, the sum
estimated to be sufficient for the support of four missionaries, as
the British public is to supply £10,000?" [3] The possibility of war
was very real two months later when the board published their
annual address to the Christian public, which demonstrated no
increase in subtlety. Although "fighting an unexampled conflict,"
Britain was still supporting missionaries in foreign lands, and
Americans should do likewise.[4] A year later, after the declaration
of war and the many sermons protesting that decision, the board's
prudential committee boldly declared that Britain, while "sustain-
ing a conflict unexampled in the history of the world, is displaying
a liberality, a zeal, and a spirit of enterprise for imparting the
word of life and the blessings of salvation to all people, to enemies
as well as to friends, not less strikingly unexampled. . . . By her
admirable example, America should be provoked to emulation." [5]
The board's address to the Christian public, the handiwork of

Jedidiah Morse, Samuel Worcester, and Jeremiah Evarts, again praised the missionary accomplishments of "the country to which we now stand in the relation of a public enemy." [6] The antiwar trio's effusive praise for Britain's religious character was a consensus of, rather than an affront to, the sentiments of their readers.

Toward the end of the eighteenth century, British Christians had united in evangelical activities that culminated in the formation of the British and Foreign Bible Society.[7] This became the parent organization to scores of local societies throughout Britain, and similar ones were soon flourishing in many American states. Although the first decade of the nineteenth century witnessed unprecedented human slaughter in Europe, it also felt a missionary impulse throbbing out from the British Isles, sending waves of Christian enlightenment all over the earth. In spite of the darkness that covered much of the western world, Christians could find cause for hope. From the moral gloom of Lexington, Kentucky, the editor of a Presbyterian journal addressed his readers on this subject. Missionaries preaching where no Christian had ever prayed, evangelical societies at home supporting their efforts, and the rapid dissemination of the Bible were sure indications, he thought, of great events to come. "The Gods of the nations are famishing," he rejoiced, "and the kingdoms of the world rapidly becoming the kingdoms of our Lord and of his Christ." [8] Two years later another frontier Presbyterian expressed the same opinion. It was indeed true, as he asserted, that combined British and American expenditure of "one million and a half of money" in 1813 for missionary work would have been deemed a fantasy only a decade earlier.[9] But by 1813 anyone at all concerned with the progress of Christianity could read accounts of the United Brethren's missionary outposts, the adventures of British evangelists in Burma, and the latest translations of the Bible into strange tongues. But most of all, the American religious public applauded and gloried in the labors and writings of the Reverend Claudius Buchanan.

A Scotsman and fervent Episcopalian, Buchanan spent twelve years in India as an advance agent of Christian civilization. His writings about the moral condition of the Orient electrified British public opinion and provoked a veritable crusade of missionary zeal. His epitaph understated the accomplishment:

BY HIS "CHRISTIAN RESEARCHES" AND OTHER
VALUABLE PUBLICATIONS
HE PLEADED THE CAUSE OF NEGLECTED INDIA, NOR PLEADED IN VAIN.
BRITAIN WAS STIRRED TO A SENSE OF HER DUTY,
AND SENT FORTH LABOURERS TO THE HARVEST.[10]

Buchanan's graphic account of his travels, *Christian Researches in Asia,* was a best seller in the United States during the war. Several American editions were published, and most of the church periodicals of all denominations printed excerpts of unusual length. It was part of the advertised stock of most bookstores, whether or not they were generally oriented toward works of piety. It was advertised in the public press of both political affiliations in all areas of the country. Its author was the subject of admiring versification, and his death provoked heartfelt eulogies. It was a milestone in the awakening of Americans to the call of a worldwide mission. More important than this, it provided material that figured mightily in the rhetoric of both antiwar dissent and prowar reaction. As a mass-circulation testimony to British religious fervor, it made clear to those Americans who opposed the War of 1812 "against what nation it is waged."

The portions of Buchanan's book usually reprinted by American editors concerned Indian idolatries and the author's visit to the headquarters of the Inquisition at Goa, an institution still functioning in the Portuguese overseas province in spite of its recent demise in Europe. Compared with conventional religious reading material of the time, the book was strong stuff with its descriptions of Hindu sacrifices, wife burnings, infanticides, and all the gross horrors of paganism. Particularly shocking was Buchanan's account of the Juggernaut festival, which entered into both the religious mentality and political oratory of Americans. Continually referring to the idol as "Moloch," he described the mass carnage attendant on the god's worship, which turned the area into another Valley of Hinnom, the biblical prototype of hell: "He laid himself down in the road before the tower as it was moving along, lying on his face with his arms stretched forwards. The multitude passed round him, leaving the space clear, and he was crushed to death by the wheels of the tower. A shout of joy was raised to the God." [11] Buchanan's account was sadly inaccurate concerning the extent of human self-sacrifice in the Juggernaut ceremony. But inaccuracy aside, it gave expression to the honest pity felt by Anglo-Saxon Christians for the heathens of the Orient.

Even more shocking was Buchanan's report that the British East India Company, the agent of imperial government in much of India, collected a "Juggernaut tax" from pilgrims wishing to participate in the festival and its supposed sacrifices. Part of this tax, indeed, was used to subsidize temple courtesans. Moreover, for understandable practical reasons, the company preferred heathen natives to Christian converts for positions of local responsibility. For equally practical reasons, the company also limited the activities of British missionaries, fearing that Christianization, as one American editor surmised, might "prove fatal to the British government in India." [12] In addition, to discover that the Inquisition operated in territory so close and so vulnerable to British power was an affront to the sensitivities of people who had consigned that institution to history in the progressive dissolution of the antichristian world. Religious publications reminded their readers that the East India Company's charter was about to be renewed and "that no man can stand acquitted by God, or by his own conscience, who shuts his eyes to the magnitude of the questions which Dr. Buchanan has brought before him." [13] They warned that if Parliament did not yield to the joint supplications of pious people in both Britain and America "the result would be long and deeply lamented." [14]

Although opposition to missionary activity in India came from the East India Company and not from the British government, the sponsorship of paganism by the de facto instrument of British control was a challenge to British religious pretensions, which American war hawks did not fail to exploit. In November 1812, a Republican paper in Rhode Island ran a small item to inform its readers of an upcoming feature: "An Enemy to Juggernaut and Juggernaut's Bulwark is received, and shall be served up in our

next, for the edification of federal religionists." [15] Printed three
weeks later, the promised article was accompanied by an editorial
stressing the importance of the subject, especially since so many
homes were already supplied with Buchanan's book. "Those religionists," it added, "who regard the assertion of Gov. Strong as
orthodox, will do well to read and ponder." The article itself
questioned whether the phrase "Church of England" should not
be changed to the more accurate "Church of Juggernaut," because that too was under the sponsorship of the British government, which would encourage the worship of Beelzebub if it
could be made a source of revenue.[16] This article was soon reprinted in other papers together with a small item announcing the
safe arrival in India of a team of American missionaries, the joy of
which occasion was shattered by their expulsion by local authorities. The editorial columns of the *New Hampshire Patriot* demonstrated the eagerness with which advocates of the war seized
upon this opportunity to register their position with religious
Americans. Great Britain, the paper noted, was supposed to be a
holy nation, "But with all their religion and goodness, they can
take a premium from the poor ignorant Asiatic idolater to indulge
him in falling down and worshipping the moulten image, Juggernaut.—By this piece of religious fraud, they raise a handsome
revenue to the British government."

This propaganda must have been well received by Republicans,
for the *Patriot* returned to the Juggernaut scandal many times
before the end of the war.[17] And other papers similarly used religious indignation to stir enthusiasm for their country's military
efforts. "A Christian politician" writing in a Vermont paper
linked British support for the "Moloch of the East" to British
cooperation with the Roman church of Canada, which many
Vermonters probably feared as much as British invasion.[18] The
writer of a series of articles in the *Newark Centinel of Freedom*
emulated Buchanan's spirit of hyperbole by mocking British missionaries who had supposedly watched thirty-six million Indians
starve to death.[19] *Niles' Weekly Register* best demonstrated the
partisan use of the missionary controversy in an article which
served as an example for successive attacks on "Juggernaut's bulwark" throughout the war. The British, charged the *Register*,

were less scrupulous than the Jews of old, who at least had refused to put Judas's blood money into the temple treasury. The
blood money from Juggernaut supported both pagan prostitutes
and parliamentary stockholders. The *Register* touched a matter
dear to the hearts of all American Christians, who at that time
were beginning what would become a great missionary crusade:

> The piety of certain people in the Eastern states fitted out a
> religious mission to *India*. Two excellent men, Messrs. *Judson*
> and *Newell*, with their wives, sailed from *Salem* on this laudable
> business. . . . They arrived safe in *India*—but the government
> immediately ordered them back, and they have returned home.
> The revenue of *Juggernaut* must not be unhinged! [20]

A year after its first printing of the Juggernaut article, the
Columbian Phenix invited its patrons to visit the newspaper office
to see for themselves a copy of the London *Times*, in which the
prime minister himself declared support for Christianizing India,
but only to the extent that it would not interfere with British
interests there. The *Phenix* was triumphant; it had discovered still
another reason to war against impious Britain. For "we find the
official organ of the government publicly announcing, that the
Religion of the Most High God must not be suffered to interfere
with the arrangements of the British government." [21] Such a consideration must have had substantial weight for the congregations
which had been repeatedly told by their ministers of the dangers
involved in fighting emissaries of the Gospel.

When public pressure caused Parliament to alter the charter of
the East India Company, guaranteeing greater efforts to evangelize
the East, those who shared Governor Strong's esteem for "the
bulwark" of religion were jubilant. This was news that must "very
much interest the feelings of the Christian world." [22] The in-
domitable Board of Commissioners for Foreign Missions showed
how much the news interested them. Was it nothing, they asked
in their annual address in 1813, that reports just received told of
the parliamentary triumph? Was it nothing that nine hundred
petitions loaded the tables of Parliament, signed by nearly a half
million people, "a greater number than ever before offered petitions in their own handwriting, for one common purpose, to any

government on earth?" [23] But this was by no means the end of the controversy. The moral character of the British nation continued to be a matter for vituperative debate in the American press. The frequency with which this subject was exploited and the intensity of the arguments used on both sides can only begin to suggest the depth to which public opinion was permeated by religious sentiment.

The exploits of Dr. Buchanan were but one part of Britain's missionary accomplishments. The nerve center of Christian expansion was the British and Foreign Bible Society. A year before the war, the Bible Society of Philadelphia expressed its joy in being united with the British parent organization to extend the heavenly kingdom, "an empire infinitely more glorious and durable than any which is acquired by arms and cemented with blood." [24] This transatlantic unity was strained but hardly broken by the advent of hostilities. Its American participants remained determined to surmount international enmity for the sake of the Gospel. One of them expressed the belief of many of his fellows. "Even while the ambition of rulers may contrive to embroil the nations in hostilities," he observed, "the spirit of union among Christians, who are connected in Bible Societies, will soften the rigors of war." [25]

A symbol of this international fellowship was the meeting of John Quincy Adams and Lord Gambier at the peace negotiations in Ghent. The latter was a famous patron of Bible societies, an interest shared by his American opponent across the bargaining table.[26] Adams was undoubtedly more polite in discussing their common activities than was one British journalist, who described Gambier as a man "who sung psalms, said prayers, and assisted in the burning of Copenhagen, for which he was made a lord." [27]

Instances of sarcasm were far outnumbered by kindlier expressions of transoceanic amity. In its annual report for 1814, the Bible society of Massachusetts expressed gratification "that we have been able in any measure to assist the operations of the British and foreign Bible Society, that noblest institution of modern times, and the parent of all similar institutions through the world." The spread of the Scriptures was a cause "which is destined to survive the schemes of statesmen and the trophies of conquerors." Antiwar Americans could find comfort in providing British prisoners of war with Bibles to make their captivity less burdensome, just as British Christians distributed Scriptures to American inmates of Dartmoor Prison. In the same report, the Massachusetts society gave even more substantial evidence of its gratitude for British benevolence. A cargo of Bibles dispatched for the Cape of Good Hope through the generosity of the British and Foreign Bible Society had been acquired by an American privateer in its capture of the British ship *Falcon*. The owner of the privateer assisted the society in repurchasing the Bibles and speeding them on their way to the intended destination. For this magnanimity Benjamin Crowninshield earned the gratitude of antiwar citizens, which he was not likely to win as Madison's future secretary of the navy. "This transaction," the society declared, "affords a laudable example in all cases, which may occur, wherein property of a destination and nature so peculiarly sacred and interesting, is by events of war placed at the disposal of American cruisers, or their owners." [28] This was a particularly pleasant occurrence, especially when compared with a previous incident of privateering in which a cargo of Bibles was sold for maximum profit and a monetary restitution made to the British parent society by outraged American Christians.

Equally magnanimous were the members of the New York Bible Society, who sent French Bibles to the benighted Catholics of Canada, thereby demonstrating "that generous and truly Christian spirit, which, in the midst of war, knows no war." [29] The same spirit was time and again shown by the British organization. Its gift of one hundred pounds to the Norfolk Bible Society was especially gracious because made during wartime, presenting "a delightful contrast to the gloomy spirit of war." [30] Its two donations to the Philadelphia Bible Society of one hundred pounds each were doubly gracious, and the directors of the British society hoped that the gifts "will be accepted as a pledge of the union they desire to maintain with their American brethren in promoting the interests of Christ's kingdom." [31] "Their American brethren" responded to their generosity by deprecating the military conflict that threatened to rend apart the transatlantic Christian community.

In the context of the very real emotional ties between Christians in the two countries, some suspiciously political aspects of antiwar sermons take on a new cast of sincerity. When Nathan Beman condemned the war for disrupting missionary activities, his congregation must have understood his references. His choice of words revealed his reading of Buchanan's *Christian Researches:* "The temple of *Moloch,* that *cruel* and *sanguinary* deity of the heathen, already begins to be deserted." [32] The Reverend Jesse Appleton, president of Bowdoin College, used similar references to emphasize his opposition to the carnage by which two Christian peoples worshiped, as it were, an idol more hideous "than the Moloch of the Hindoos." [33] The General Assembly of the Presbyterian church in 1814 also invoked Buchanan's metaphor in its annual report: "The altars of the East *will* be overturned; the images of Moloch *will* be broken down; and the only question is, whether the work shall be performed, and the reward enjoyed by others, or by you? O brethren, our hearts beat high with hope." [34] Reuben Holcomb's hearers no doubt sympathized with his denunciation of the war, which was directed against the home of missionaries and translators of the Scriptures. That, he insisted, was the reason Britain was hated "and her destruction sought for, by the antichristian powers of Europe." [35] Benjamin Bell concurred, although his words intimated the opposition the subject could provoke from Republican congregations. He admitted he had said "that to oppose Great Britain in attempting to spread the Gospel throughout the world, as she was doing, was to fight against God; and I say it still." [36] When Thomas Andros delivered a series of sermons concerning the battle of Armageddon, it gave him confidence in a Christian victory in that encounter to reflect upon the missionary exploits of America's enemy. For "the bloody persecuting sword" was torn from the hand of "Popish malice and cruelty," and British Christians were pouring Bibles into "these Catholic nations to whom the reading of Scriptures has been for ages prohibited." [37] Little wonder, then, that all these men longed for peace to restore evangelical cooperation and hasten Christ's reign on earth. Little wonder that they condemned a war against "a nation which embosoms a great multitude of devout men and women, precious pledges of her safety, and formidable for her defence against all assailants; whose prayers, like a cloud of incense, daily ascend up before the throne of God for protection." [38]

Even Britain's armed forces, the plunderers of many American towns, received their share of praise. When a Baltimorean mockingly regretted "that no efforts have as yet been made to spread the benign doctrines of the gospel among the army and navy of Great-Britain," he was corrected by a journalist in Albany, New York. Far from the burned ports of Chesapeake Bay, the editor of the *Christian Visitant* had statistical evidence of the enemy's religious character: "The army and navy of Great-Britain are supplied with chaplains, who perform Divine Service regularly: And, if we mistake not, it will be found recorded in several numbers of the *Christian Observer*, that the Bible has been distributed among them, in great numbers, by the British Bible and Auxiliary Bible Societies." [39] He was not mistaken. Evangelical societies were exerting great efforts to bring the Gospel to military men, whose employment and living conditions seldom inclined them to piety. Nor was he mistaken in his source. The *Christian Observer*, the main periodical of the Anglican church, was reprinted in the United States and conveyed the good news of souls won and hearts converted.

Items from that journal were favorite material for American church magazines. Within days of the war declaration, an editor in New York reprinted a report of evangelism among the enemy's sailors and soldiers not only in Europe but even in India, where the imperial regiments were witnessing to Christianity among the heathen. [40] A month later another editor reprinted evidence for reports of such saintly soldiers. This was a lengthy letter to the Edinburgh Bible Society from the Rosshire regiment of militia, contributing twenty-nine pounds in gratitude for Bibles received from the society. [41] While most of the American coastline was blockaded by enemy vessels, the Massachusetts Bible Society reported that the British government had supplied Scriptures to warships in its service. It was satisfying that the supply could not meet the demand from seamen seeking consolation in their perils. "In England," the report continued, "great efforts are made to furnish soldiers and seamen with the word of God; and officers of distinction have born testimony to the happy influence of these pious efforts." [42] It consoled another antiwar editor to report, some months after the beginning of hostilities, that regimental schools were being formed throughout England for the education of soldiers' children, particular attention being given to moral and religious instruction.[43] The American military position was critical in early summer 1814, when many religious journals published the report of still another British Bible society for soldiers. If the story were intended to portray a typical enemy fighter, it was indeed bad news for the American militia. A British soldier, the recipient of a free Bible distributed by pious citizens, proclaimed himself doubly armed to fight for both king and church with the comfort of Holy Writ.[44]

Enemy evangelism even reached American military forces but in a roundabout manner. Shortly after the end of hostilities, many periodicals reprinted the annual report of the London Missionary Society, which had sent preachers to French and American prisoners of war interned in Dartmoor Prison. Great hopes were entertained for the fruition of this labor, especially among the American inmates.[45] About a month thereafter, the same prison was the scene of serious bloodshed. A suspected escape attempt, overzealous guards, and a great deal of confusion left seven prisoners dead and many injured. Republican papers were once again filled with accounts of British butchery. One of them, for instance, pictured wounded prisoners pleading for mercy, "to which they received the *British-religious* reply of 'no—you d——d yankee rascals, you shall have no quarters!' " [46] Another summed up the whole bloody affair as "a customary specimen of their religion." [47] There is no evidence, however, that the massacre at all impaired Britain's reputation among opponents of the war. The religious character of Great Britain was yet another controversy for which the Peace of Ghent provided no definite settlement.

When Americans read the reports of pious societies, whether British or their own, they were informed not only about the triumphs of Governor Strong's "bulwark" but also about Czar Alexander of Russia, the greatest Christian of the era, whose holiness was surpassed only by his glory in fighting the Napoleonic scourge. He was, of course, politically important to antiwar Americans. He was anxious for an early end to the North American squabble so that his British allies could devote their military and financial resources single-mindedly to Europe, and the possibility of Russian mediation between the Anglo-Saxon combatants was a recurrent source of controversy. Alexander made his first proposal as early as September 1812; and for years thereafter, Federalists accused Madison of rejecting the chance for peace, while Republicans blamed Britain for refusing to parley. All the while, underlying the diplomacy and its partisan repercussions was a significant lode of public opinion concerning Russia and its famous ruler.

It was military prowess rather than godliness that occasioned most accolades for the Russian autocrat. When the *Panoplist* compiled its yearly chronology for the Christian public in 1813, it termed the ruin of Napoleon's army in eastern Europe "one of the most overwhelming events which ever took place in the whole history of the wars of ambition. . . . The history of the world affords no parallel." [48] A speech by arch-Federalist Robert Goodlow Harper revealed the narrowly partisan use to which Alexander's victories could be put. To the emperor Americans owed the liberty they still enjoyed, he contended. To him they owed even their ability to rejoice in the little American navy, whose victories would have been but steps to ruin had not Russian power thwarted French ambitions. Harper therefore saluted the man they had gathered to honor, toasting him with "the most glorious title that mortal man has ever received, the most glorious title that man has ever deserved—Let us drink the health of—ALEXANDER THE DELIVERER." [49] In like manner, Russia's military advance across Europe gave the gadfly editor of the *Federal Republican* a satisfaction which had nothing to do with the czar's religious character. "The uneasiness of Mr. Madison, at the celebration of the Russian victories is amusing," the paper mocked, "though it is cruel sport, it must be confessed." [50] This sport needed no other justification than partisan opportunism. As long as Alexander was successfully fighting France he would have been a hero to Federalists, whatever his morals. But Federalists were fortunate in that they did not find it necessary to exalt an irreligious ruler.

As the religious part of the electorate well knew, Alexander was the most pious sovereign in Christendom, the foremost spokesman of the international evangelical community. The apotheosis he enjoyed during the war years defies analysis in purely political terms. His admirers themselves contributed passionate testimony to the religious sentiment underlying the facts of international relations. A Carolinian poet praised him not only for his conquests but also for his devout magnanimity, his restoring crucifix worship to the Catholic world, for example. Entitled simply "Ode to Alexander," the verses began,

> High on the peak of glory stands
> The Russian! Saviour of a hundred lands! [51]

The same idea was expressed in a thanksgiving sermon by Samuel Jarvis in April 1815. The glory of Christian Russia was the primary reason he gave thanks, for he certainly could not imply any approval of his country's recent military adventure. While the United States had plunged willfully into carnage, "the world beheld the sublime spectacle of a christian people, rising with the sword in hand, and the cross in the other, to repel an insolent invading foe." [52] The contrast between the two nations was obvious.

Given the lack of accurate information in America about the Russian Empire, it is probable that Jarvis and those who agreed with him based their esteem for Alexander and his people on the widely disseminated reports of the British and Foreign Bible Society. Alexander possessed a remarkable ability for issuing proclamations in defeat, in victory, on anniversaries and celebrations. Because of their pious phrasing and because of the czar's liberality toward religious societies, many of his state papers found their way into the literature of foreign organizations. By this indirect procedure, readers of church periodicals in the United States were informed that at least one nation had the good fortune to be governed by a professed Christian.

The Ninth Annual Report of the British and Foreign Bible Society, for example, reprinted the czar's order that the traditional corn tithes should revert to their original purpose, the printing of Bibles for the peasantry. Christians rejoiced in this report that the imperial government would repay popular tribute "with the rich treasure of the Word of Life." [53] Alexander's witness to the sacred Scriptures, a Baptist editor wrote, "must be peculiarly interesting to the American public at the present time, as it serves to develop one trait in a character which the world so justly admires." [54] Later the same year, another report of the British society reprinted Alexander's ukase on the first anniversary of national deliverance from France, along with several miscellaneous letters from imperial officials promising their support for local evangelical efforts.[55] Yet another royal proclamation in 1814 offered thanks to heaven for the success of Russia's armies and reminded subjects that the victory was God's.[56] This too was deemed a religious document and found a place in the report of the British and Foreign Bible Society. It was consequently reprinted in dozens of American journals and antiwar papers.

The Second Annual Report of the fledgling New Hampshire Bible Society presented still greater evidence of Alexander's faith. The board could not refrain "from mentioning a most interesting event, which has recently transpired." [57] The czar had given ten thousand dollars to the Saint Petersburg Bible Society. Indeed, in order to sign the constitution of that body he had delayed his departure from the city to confront the French at Wilna. The coincidence of this display of piety with the Russian victory in the subsequent battle was seen as cause and effect by one Federalist clergyman, who jubilantly declared, "He lost nothing by the delay." The Russian success was pregnant with warning for the American war effort, so noticeably wanting in official piety. For "the event proves, that GOD honors those who honor HIM." This was in pointed contrast with "the war people," who hated Alexander because he combated "their idol of atheism." [58] True to form, after the battle of Wilna, Alexander issued yet another proclamation, quoting the thirty-seventh psalm and urging his subjects to "acknowledge then, Divine Providence in this wonderful event." [59] His advice was duly followed by the Federalist press.

Alexander's righteousness was good propaganda. His proclamations made a telling contrast with those issued by rulers in other lands, "the inhabitants of which, notwithstanding, profess to be

Christian." [60] His attributing victory to divine help was far different from the shameful boasting of Americans every time their
navy captured a ship.[61] Against the background of Bible society
reports and periodical sketches, Federalist oratory must have been
well received. At an Independence Day rally of "the friends of
peace of the state of New-Jersey," Lucius Horatio Stockton
exulted that heaven had answered the "fervent supplications of
the Russian church and people," inspiring Alexander to stand
"unmoved in the strength of his God." The resurgence of Christian Russia was "worthy a martyr's crown." [62] And with that
example before them, New Jersey's Federalists refused to take
part in the war; for "duty to God and their conscience" forbade
it.[63] On the same day, the Federalists of Charlestown, Massachusetts, heard Joseph Tufts recount the virtues of Alexander the
Deliverer in an address that seemed less commemorative of the
founding fathers than of the Cossack cavalry. The cause for joy
was that "this Christian conqueror entered Paris on the 31st of
March in triumph." [64] If the political ambitions of Federalists
were not yet realized, at least their prayers were answered.

When an enthusiastic preacher suggested that Alexander might
have already fought the battle of Armageddon at Moscow,[65] his
hearers probably thought the idea not at all eccentric. Much of
America lived, as it were, on the brink of apocalypse, awaiting the
fulfillment of Saint John's visions and the overthrow of the Roman
Catholic church. Like other players in the international drama,
the papacy held a religious significance for American Protestants
that figured mightily in the contest for public opinion.

When a Baptist editor surveyed the worldwide state of the
Church in 1811, he reported "an event, as wonderful in all its
concomitant circumstances, as propitious in itself." This was

The overthrow of Antichrist, and the destruction of the seat of
the beast . . . plainly foretold in New Testament prophecy.
Our forefathers have made the fulfilment of these prophecies
the subject of their prayers in public and private for many
centuries. God is fulfilling these prophecies, and answering
these prayers, in a surprising manner.[66]

The refusal of Pope Pius VII to countenance French encroachments upon his authority had led to his imprisonment by Napoleon in 1809. The emperor later ordered the Spanish Inquisition abolished, thereby answering generations of prayers from Protestant Christendom. Typical of the American reaction was the response of a journalist who could hardly restrain his emotion. "Let all the world rejoice," he proclaimed, "and let the third day of February be annually, for ever, celebrated by all nations, because, on that day in the year 1813, the SPANISH INQUISITION WAS ABOLISHED." [67] Napoleon was indeed the scourge of Catholic Europe, more effectively combating the papacy than had any ruler of recent centuries. His bloody repressions in the Iberian peninsula seemed to be a fitting retribution for centuries of Spanish butchery in the eyes of American Protestants, who had long been tutored in the stories of the "black legend." They noted with righteous amazement that the worst slaughter seemed to be falling on "popish countries." [68]

Therein was a dilemma for opponents of the war. If they hated Napoleon, how could they delight in his progress? If they loved the "bulwark" of their religion, how could they explain that Britain was also the champion of Pius VII and was the last hope of absolutism in Latin Europe? Britain's armies fought for monarchy in Spain and sheltered the Portuguese royal family in their flight to Brazil. It was an embarrassing predicament, especially when exploited by Republicans.[69]

The explanation formulated by Federalist Christians of this peculiar alignment was in the best tradition of theological adaptation to social necessities. Fortunately the Book of Revelation was sufficiently vague to allow political considerations to alter traditional views. Theories were proposed to explain how great good, such as the end of the Inquisition, could come from such an evil man as Napoleon. One scholar suggested that the pope was not really the antichrist foretold in New Testament prophecies. Rather, the papacy was the whore or beast, which would propagate and nourish an offspring, the infidel king, who would turn upon her and persecute her as she had once persecuted the saints.[70] Britain's alliance with Catholic nations was justified by the need to crush France and was no indication of approval for their corrupt religion. To one extent or another, most antiwar Christians accepted some version of this interpretation. It allowed them to maintain their abhorrence of Napoleon without compromising their ancestral hatred for Rome. Church periodicals frequently printed commentaries on the contemporary application of the Apocalypse. One very popular article proved that the Wahhabite schism in Islam had occurred "exactly about the same time" as Voltaire had begun his infidelity and that the Muslim world would be destroyed along with the papacy at Armageddon.[71] The parallel between the branches of Babylon was almost too wonderful to believe.

Assuming, then, that Napoleon's contest with the pope confirmed rather than confused the visions of Saint John, Federalists could participate unequivocally in the joy occasioned by European events. The only alteration in New England's hereditary world view was that the pope would no longer be called antichrist. That name was transferred to Napoleon, but all the other pejorative titles of the pontiff remained valid. The change was demonstrated by Freeman Parker's fast sermon in July 1812. He sincerely believed "that every seventeenth year of a century, great things happen in religion," and so he looked with foreboding to the year 1817, which might be marked "by the overthrow of the only independent state in Europe, and a fatal alliance of the United States with Daniel's infidel king, the tyrannical antichrist[.] Great God forbid it!" [72] Whatever one may think of Parker's numerology, his application of the term "antichrist" to Napoleon indicated an important change in scriptural interpretation, a change so widely accepted by opponents of the war that the reputable Elias Boudinot, writing anonymously at the end of the war, expected no one to disagree. No observing mind would deny, he thought, "that the antichrist foretold, as coming on the earth after the Man of Sin, had literally appeared in the new government of France, having Napoleon Buonaparte for her head." [73]

The apocalyptic drama being enacted in Europe held fast the attentions of antiwar Christians. The opening months of 1814 were not propitious for Republican patriots, but the optimism of Federalist believers was unaffected by national perils. It was their comforting conviction that, "whatever evils await a sinful world,

the darkest times of the church are undoubtedly, past." The as-
surances of Scripture, in the Book of Revelation no doubt, pointed
to "the general prospect which now pervades the nations, believers and unbelievers, of the approach of a period of universal
peace and prosperity to the world." [74] This millennial vision may
have been hidden, however, from anyone operating within the
more mundane framework of lagging military operations and a
threadbare treasury. From the theological wilds of Maine, another
Congregationalist editor also anticipated the future with minimal
concern for America's immediate situation. Parts of Maine were
actually occupied by invading armies, but there were other factors
to consider. "It is indeed a time of distress in the world," he
admitted,

> of devastation, carnage and misery. But amidst all this gloom
> the friends of religion have "light and gladness and joy." For
> God is marvellously building the walls of his spiritual Jeru-
> salem in these "troublous times." The world is rapidly prepar-
> ing to submit with one accord to the sceptre of the Prince of
> Peace.[75]

This stoic acceptance of national calamity was not an eccen-
tricity of religious journalists. It was a recurrent theme in the
reports of pious societies, official pronouncements of churches,
and the statements of private individuals. Optimism like that expressed by editors at the beginning of 1814 was echoed throughout the year. It was the worst year of the war for the United
States but the grandest year of progress for international Christianity.

In May, the Congregationalist General Association of Massachusetts decided that, all in all, the cause of religion was progress-
ing. Although the future was to see the fall of the American
capital and fearful days of domestic division, the optimism of the
association was unrelated to narrow political considerations. In
view of the prospects before them, they anticipated the time "not
far distant, when it shall be said to Zion, 'Arise, shine; for thy
light is come, and the glory of the Lord is risen upon thee.' " [76]
The General Association of Connecticut seemed to agree. Meeting soon after their Massachusetts brethren, they too saw "animat-

ing prospects" and felt "called to rejoice in the prosperity of Zion" because daily evidence showed Jehovah's remembrance of his people.[77]

Several months later, when the military situation was even more critical, a member of the General Association of Connecticut described the happy situation of Christianity still more emphatically. Henry Rowland assured the Auxiliary Foreign Mission Society that, however depressed the Church might be, "the time for her deliverance is at hand. She will soon exchange her habiliments of mourning for garments of joy and rejoicing.—The days of her mourning are almost ended. She may, even now, lift up her head with joy and behold her redemption drawing nigh." At the time, the British invasion fleet for New Orleans was also drawing nigh, as were Canadian-based armies. So Rowland took cognizance of the dangers awaiting guilty nations but added, "We hope that the Church of Christ will not be greatly affected by them." His sermon must have been well received. It was deemed sufficiently meritorious for the format of the *Connecticut Evangelical Magazine* to be altered for its publication. That journal had long been running a series of articles on the credibility and inspiration of the Bible, which, befitting their importance, had always been allocated the opening pages of the magazine. In the November issue, however, the opening article was Rowland's sermon, which temporarily displaced the authenticity of Scripture as the most pressing concern of the Connecticut faithful. The following month, the series on the Bible was restored to its rightfully prominent position.[78]

The devout members of the New Hampshire Bible Society also expressed their happiness during the worst year of the war. Their annual report did refer to tremendous international events, but the reference was not to America's plight. "When was there a more signal period," they asked, "than the last twenty years, of war and carnage, of calamity and distress to nations? Is not Babylon falling? Is not the papal power almost annihilated?" [79] The Missionary Society of Vermont declared, "We live in an age of wonders. The predictions of the Bible, respecting the latter-day glory of the church, are rapidly fulfilling." [80] Even the Bible Society of Kentucky agreed that great things were in store for the Church. For the allied victory in Europe had had one all-important result: France was now opened to the dissemination of the Scriptures through the efforts of Bible societies. Obviously "this is a subject that calls alike for astonishment and gratitude." [81]

Like all great expectations, these millennial visions died hard. When the allied powers restored the ancien régime in the Catholic countries of Europe, when Babylon resurged from its ashes, Federalist Christians were confronted with harsh realities. To heighten the horror, even the legions of Babylon were resurrected: a papal decree of 1814 re-created the Jesuit order on an international basis. On the frontier a pious editor could be forgiven if he was still insisting in March 1815 that the papacy, the fourth kingdom prophesied by Daniel, was "rapidly wasting away, or already come to its end." [82] In the eastern states, Christians were apt to be better informed of the course of European events and could no longer entertain such notions. Looking back on the momentous changes of the past year, a prominent Presbyterian minister in Richmond, Virginia, saw "events truly of evil omen." It was impossible "without unutterable feelings of indignation and sorrow to contemplate the re-establishment of the Inquisition, the massacres of Protestants," and the restoration of the pope to temporal power.[83] The many erudite treatises on Revelation were rendered useless. The *Connecticut Evangelical Magazine* manfully admitted that contemporary application of scriptural prophecies was probably a violation of their intended purpose.[84] Clearly, for Protestant Christendom, the agony was not yet over.

There were many who were not surprised by this turn of events, many who all along had interpreted the European cataclysm differently. There were devout Americans who did not admire British religion, did not think Napoleonic France was antichrist, and did not believe Alexander's legions were the armies of Light. Republican Christians developed their own interpretation of Revelation, in which the power of Babylon was as present in Boston as in Rome. To many pious Americans, the War of 1812 was not a partisan crime but a Christian crusade.

3 ✠ REPUBLICAN CRUSADE

Such a war God considers as his own cause, and to help in such a cause is to come to the help of the Lord.

John Stevens, April 8, 1813

It was Federalist dogma that Christian America disapproved of "Mr. Madison's war," but then it was also their belief that virtually all of the country's faithful were numbered in their ranks. During the angry summer of 1812, John Fiske and his congregation were comforted to know that immoral military adventures would soon grind to a halt as the public refused to participate without the approval of their "religious teachers." "The religious part of a people will have this privilege," he insisted, "and this sanction from those who speak to God for them, if the cause deserves it, and if not they will have no part of it." [1] Nathan Beman consoled his congregation by declaring that "most of the religion in this country and Great Britain is *strongly* and *vitally* opposed to this war." [2] Jonathan French too forecast a united opposition to the unholy conflict. "With few exceptions," the country's ministers would support "rational liberty, true republicanism, and good government; and if they believed the present war to be just and necessary, no class of citizens would more zealously advocate it." [3] The Federalist wits who satirically reprinted the sermons of John Giles to reveal his Republican infidelity similarly were sure that, "with a few wretched exceptions," the pulpits had not been tainted with the corruption of democracy. [4]

If historians have not agreed with them, they have at least not offered much of an argument. Most accounts of the war understandably make some mention of antiwar religion.[5] After all, dissension was at the time provocatively controversial and can provide dramatic highlights for any study of the war. But protesting preaching was localized, both geographically and denominationally, representing, in fact, little more than the Congregationalist churches of New England, a few allied Presbyterians, a handful of Episcopalians, and a scattering of disparate others. Benjamin Bell was more realistic than most of his antiwar colleagues when he lamented that most ministers were neglecting to teach the scriptural condemnation of warfare. Whether or not he was justified in charging that "it appears to be no great matter with them whether their nation be guilty of murder or not," [6] it was true that his resistance to public policy was a minority position. A diarist in Massachusetts lamented that "so many who name the name of Christ engage in [militia drill] and in Military duty so cheerfully," [7] and there is every reason to believe most pious Americans were on the side of the militia.

But clerical dissenters had certain advantages in circulating their views: a literate audience, their own superior education, a habit of printing their handiwork. Most of the religious journals of wartime America were Congregationalist or Presbyterian; and for every sermon published by a Baptist or Methodist, dozens were produced by their theological foes. It may seem oversimplified, but the antiwar churches dominated the religious media of the day.

Although prowar Christians were not as literate as their opponents, they were equally fervent in their beliefs, partisan as well as creedal. Their opinions not only represented many more voters than did antiwar sermons but also were more authentic evidence of the nexus between religion and politics. For among the very churches that supported the war effort were those which soon grew into the country's largest denominations, and the melding of their faith and patriotism was essential to the forging of American nationalism. They included some of the freshest religious energies in the nation: the new sects, the older left wing of Protestantism —Baptists, Methodists, splinters and dissidents among splinters.

They had little theological agreement and oftentimes were themselves mutually hostile, but certain political interests did bind them together.

Most of them were loyal not only to the Republican party but also to the person of James Madison, the champion of religious freedom in Virginia. When David Benedict published his famed history of the Baptists in 1813, its appendix contained significant documents in the church's past, the very first of which was Madison's "Memorial and Remonstrance" of 1785 in behalf of religious liberty in the Old Dominion. "The style is elegant and perspicuous," Benedict noted, "and for strength of reasoning and purity of principle, it has seldom been equalled, certainly never surpassed, by any thing on the subject in the English language." [8] A Baptist journalist was even more effusive, asserting that Locke himself had never stated the cause of equal Christian liberty with such clarity and force. Moreover, in light of efforts then being made in Massachusetts to remove the special tax for support of the clergy, the document had a special significance. As the editor put it, "We therefore recommend it to the candid perusal of all our readers, especially those in this Commonwealth, as being peculiarly seasonable at this present time." [9]

During this same controversy in Massachusetts, the Baptist firebrand John Leland taunted fellow members of the state legislature for their backwardness, reminding them that Virginia had long ago established full religious liberty and had "given birth and education to a Henry, a Washington, a Jefferson and a Madison, each of which contributed their aid to effect the grand event." [10] Another legislator assured his colleagues that Madison's words, "like apples of gold in pictures of silver, will stand an eternal monument to crown him with everlasting honors when generations yet to come shall rise up and call him blessed." [11] Elias Smith, the apostle of democratic religion, greeted Madison's reelection in 1812 by predicting "greater and more successful exertions made in favour of civil and religious liberty than ever has been made in any four years since the Declaration of Independence." [12] Because these men and the sectarians they represented so admired the president, the term "Madison's war" was to them an endorsement rather than a criticism of American foreign policy.

Even without the president's special popularity, many Christians would have been all too delighted to fight Britain; for like their Federalist neighbors, Republicans were adept at formulating theological interpretations of world affairs. They matched antiwar Christians prophecy for prophecy, apocalypse for apocalypse, as both parties awaited the imminent Armageddon in Europe. Martial Americans adhered to the traditional reading of the Book of Revelation. Whatever they might think of French infidelity and Napoleon himself, they knew antichrist was the pope of Rome and all other opponents of religious liberty, including the Congregationalist leaders of New England. Moreover, many denominations cultivated ancient grudges against the church and crown of Britain; and 1812 seemed a felicitous year to even up old scores.

The papal beast of religious tyranny seemed mortally wounded. The Freewillers of the northern frontier were jubilant because "the mother of harlots and abominations of the earth, is trembling; and it is hoped that the time is not very far distant, when the waiting posts shall be furnished with the long expected news. 'Babylon is fallen! Babylon is fallen!' " [13] But the Freewillers knew that Babylon encompassed all persecuting power, including the official religious structures of their own states, from which those radical democrats received only derision and contempt. They therefore rejoiced in the plight of both Rome and their domestic foes, "the merchants of Babylon," who "hang down their heads and mourn." [14] A Virginian Baptist made the same point in a poetic effort cataloging Babylon's fallen minions—"scribes, and priests, and lawyers, and mitred bishops too; Popes, Cardinals, and friars"—and bringing the point home to American dissenters:

> See troops of mourning merchants,
> And tradesmen stand aloof;
> They wring their hands for sorrow,
> And cry that awful truth:
> Alas! Alas! she's fallen,
> And all our wealth is gone;
> There's none to buy our purple,
> We're utterly undone.[15]

In like manner a Sabbatarian observed that although the entrenched Protestant churches called the papacy "Babylon" and "mother of harlots" appearances could be deceiving. "Let us remember that God does not always call things by the same name that man does," he warned, and that Congregationalists and Presbyterians shared Rome's hunger for civil power.[16] Methodists too nipped at the heels of New England's "false prophets" who would use their ministry to betray republican government.[17] These and other angry Christians formed quite a phalanx in political contests, and their evangelical fervor turned the War of 1812 into a veritable jihad.

Republican editors were eager to assist in the metamorphosis, and in the process they more than compensated for the limited publishing capability of the prowar churches. Their propaganda took advantage of both historical and contemporary enmities. It was militantly, aggressively Christian; and its first hapless victim was the governor of Massachusetts.

When Caleb Strong's fast day proclamation called Britain "the bulwark of our religion," Republicans were outraged. They sarcastically toasted the enemy's sanctity: "its text bible and missionary societies; the comment intrigue and corruption; the application, the temple of Juggernaut, and the scenes at Hampton, Havre-de-grace, and St. Innegoes."[18] All over the country editors recommended a recently printed map of America's northern frontiers, which would register "the practical correspondence between the *bible societies* and the *tomahawk*—between *vital religion* and the *scalping knife*—between *professions of faith* and the *practice of piety*."[19] Almost all Republican accounts of Indian attacks, British atrocities, or Federalist perfidy made some reference to Strong's "bulwark"; and his words were often used as headlines for grisly reports of scalpings, rapes, and the Juggernaut festival. His detractors agreed that he had "prostituted the most sacred subject to the worst of purposes. He deserves not the tolerance of silence."[20]

Strong's statement faced factual contradiction on many points, not the least of which concerned the moral character of Britain's rulers. However great the piety of those Britons who supported missionaries and Bible societies, their monarchs made exceptionally poor bulwarks for any system of religion. Readers of Repub-

lican papers were regularly informed of the latest scandals in
the royal family, the rumored illegitimacy of the princess royal,
the marital troubles of the prince regent, and the notorious
escapades of his brothers; and this propaganda was especially
effective when counterpointed with references to Britain's evangelical fame. "These societies for so pretendedly pious purposes,"
one editor scoffed,

> are mere political engines, and my Lord CASTLEREAGH would
> laugh most heartily at the suggestion, that piety had a share
> in the patronage they receive from the government. With
> England religion is merely a political engine. Of what profession
> it is, is scarcely thought of, so it pays a tribute in cash or in ser-
> vice or pretences.[21]

It was a good talking point; and if voters wanted more details,
they were often furnished with accounts of the depraved British
nobility, all intended to reflect upon American anglophiles. One
example should be sufficient to suggest their vehemence:

> If a man were, *immediately* after his marriage, to desert his
> wife, and appear with "common-sewer"-women in the streets,
> . . . to have FAME and REPUTE in every brothel and gambling
> house of his vicinity, and be carried home drunk from three
> to six times a week, *we* should not choose him for the *"patron
> of a* BIBLE *society*." [22]

The priestly admirers of Britain, the press noted, would have to
decline invitations from the saintly duke of Clarence because
his mistress presided at his table. The people of Massachusetts,
who feared that their bulwark would be destroyed by Napoleon
after he abolished the Spanish Inquisition, were urged to read Lady
Hamilton's recently published memoirs, which portrayed adulter-
ous Lord Nelson and his equally depraved country.[23]

It was not simply that the British government was corrupt. Its
pretensions to piety, so strongly applauded by Federalists, were
insufferable. One report of enemy atrocities in the towns of the
Chesapeake Bay informed the public that the commander of
the ravagers was Admiral Cockburn, president of the Halifax
Bible Society, and that Sir John Sherbroke, whose men occupied

American soil at Castine in Maine, was prominent in another of those devout organizations.[24] "A Bible Society has been organized at Halifax," Republicans mocked, as they suggested Americans should reconsider their esteem for "this new prop of 'the bulwark' in our hemisphere." [25] They had not forgotten the revelations of Claudius Buchanan. If a Bible society could exist at Halifax, it could exist in India, where "the creature who receives the revenue from the *prostitutions* and *murders* in honor of *Juggernaut*, may be a member of one of them." [26] Thus Republican advocates vied with one another in following the advice of William Channing, judging the war by examining "against what nation it is waged." And if any reader was not yet convinced of the enemy's depravity, if the reports of the British and Foreign Bible Society still seemed too admirable, Republicans could furnish added reminders of Britain's crimes against religion.

There were yet in America deep reservoirs of hatred for Britain's established Anglicanism. The *Boston Yankee* warned that the majority of New England's population would see to it that twenty-five eccentrics at Hartford did not league them with "this modern Babylon, this plunderer of nations, this scourge of the earth. We detest her venal government," continued the editor, "abhor the deep and abominable depravity of her *state* religion, which is no better than popery." [27] Many Americans agreed with him. "What has *Britain* done for the *Protestant* cause," one of them asked: "Why, she has persecuted a large majority of *her own* Protestant subjects, dissenting from the dogmas of her *national church*, with inquisitorial cruelty, and yet persecutes them—and she makes war as cheerfully against *Protestants* as *Catholics*." [28] The evidence to that effect was overwhelming. Britain not only tolerated but even established Romanism in Canada. Thus "the pious cabinet of St. James" consorted with the mother of harlots to nurse its political funds.[29]

When the legislature of Massachusetts refused to express delight in an American naval victory because such rejoicing was not "becoming a moral and religious people," Republicans called this a "blind and subservient attachment to 'the old whore of Babylon,' England." [30] The cliché was meaningful to those

Christians who remembered the lash of Anglican intolerance and were warned that a British victory would "not only take from you your political, but your religious privileges." No man held office in England without satisfying the sacramental test, participating in Anglican communion services in return for public position. Republicans could ask, "Is this religious intolerance, this system to make hypocrites and false swearers, to prevail in New England?" [31] Christians in Maryland and Pennsylvania were urged to remember the sufferings of the early Quakers, who knew the real meaning of British piety. "How then is *England* the *'bulwark'* of OUR *religion*," they demanded. "Was it the conformity of the views of WILLIAM PENN or of CECELIUS CALVERT to the holy 'bulwark' which first planted Pennsylvania or Maryland?" [32] Britain was plainly the archenemy of "our holy religion, which she forbids your missionaries to preach to the victims of Juggernaut, and for professing which she burnt your very ancestors at the stake." [33]

As the war grew longer and less successful than had been expected, events in Europe unhappily confirmed the worst charges of Republican propaganda. No one could deny that "the most important and immediate consequences of the success of the allies have been the reestablished tyranny of the *Holy Office*" and the reopening of the slave trade.[34] If Britain rewarded her friends with the Inquisition, her enemies could expect much worse. The thought was frightening even in frontier communities, where local papers reprinted the full text of King Ferdinand's decree reviving that institution.[35] That "poor, miserable, infatuated bigot" was also persecuting Freemasons, whose fellows in America could consider this effect of British victory.[36] The Bourbons and bigotry were returning together, it seemed, and perhaps another Saint Bartholomew's Day was imminent.[37] The fault was Britain's, spreading slaughter over the world "to revenge the cause of the church of Rome on the French nation." [38] The eminent Alexander McLeod warned that future generations would scarcely believe how some Christians were so terrified of French infidelity as "to hail like the millennium, an event which tended to consolidate European despotism; which restored to power the man of sin, with all the gloomy terrors of the Roman Inquisition." [39] With good reason, then, John Hargrove of the

New Jerusalem Church could lead his congregation in thanksgiving for their country, "where no Inquisition, or religious
proscription can possibly exist, together with our sacred charter
or Bill of Rights. Turn your eyes, my favoured hearers, towards
the eastern continent, or Old World, and what do you see?" [40]
What any Republican Protestant could see was the triumphant
coalition of Great Britain, righteous Alexander, and papal Rome.

Prowar Christians were quick to add another villain to that
nefarious alliance, for the antiwar clergy were too closely associated with Britain and religious tyranny to escape inclusion in
the forces of antichrist. Consequently, religious propaganda justi-
fying the war had a domestic as well as foreign application. It
sought not only to denigrate British morality but also to discredit American Federalism by invoking sectarian antagonism
against the Congregational church and its anglophile ministry.
Of course, there had long been an affinity between New England's
sectarians and Republican leaders, who had long worked to dis-
establish Congregationalism. But the fact of war and the greater
fact of Congregational opposition to it placed an entirely new
significance upon traditional hostilities. The preexisting symbiosis
of Republican politics and dissenting religion was intensified, as
both became predatory, cooperating to attack their long-stalked
prey, the "puritanical saints of the east," who had made themselves vulnerable by opposing the national crusade. [41]

The Congregationalist clergy were at the heart of a controversy
that was the most important single prelude to war in a large part
of New England. Many of them served as chaplains to local
branches of the Washington Benevolent Society, which in spite
of its title was primarily devoted to Hamiltonian politics; and for
their services they won both Federalist praise and Republican
abuse. The Benevolents, as their detractors called them, coun-
tered criticism of the clergy by their appreciative toasts:

The Rev. Clergy—Venerable for piety, respectable for talents,
useful as men, and a blessing to the world.

The Clergy—Like their divine Redeemer, they preach *peace*
and good will to men.

> The Clergy of our Country—May their zeal, sound principles, and exemplary piety, prove a phalanx against the itinerant minions of corruption.[42]

The matter soon went beyond drinking bouts when Wait Chatterton, deacon of the Congregationalist church in Rutland, Vermont, and Sylvester Pond, member of the church in Castleton and a former member of the Washington Benevolent Society there, informed the public that the society admitted to membership immoral men, scoffers at religion to whom their own churches would deny fellowship. Although Pond hoped his revelations "may not interrupt the harmony of the people of God, nor injure the pure religion of our divine Redeemer," less concerned Republicans were faced with imminent state elections and could overlook his scruples.[43]

While Federalists published sworn depositions declaring the accusations false and malicious, the shocking exposé of the Benevolents was spread throughout New England as Republicans chided, "this society, this federal caucus, has become your God, and Great-Britain your Saviour." [44] An anonymous Congregationalist warned that any society rejecting pious men on partisan grounds while admitting politically orthodox sinners was no Christian fellowship; and several members of the church in Lancaster, New Hampshire, showed their agreement by publicly denouncing their minister for lending the force of religion to the service of sedition by participating in the society.[45] When Republicans lamented that churches were separating, pastors being dismissed, and congregations dissolving amid partisan dissension,[46] the situation may not have been as serious as they imagined. But even so, the worst of it was that the controversy did not keep Federalists from winning heavily in the spring and summer elections.

This is not to say that the antiwar clergy were vindicated. As the fighting continued, Congregationalist ministers sometimes found their flocks politically recalcitrant. Some churchmen in Dalton, Massachusetts, issued a manifesto refusing further support for their pastor, whose antiwar invective had demeaned his pulpit.[47] That extremity was averted in Walpole, New Hampshire, only when the Reverend Mr. Fessenden agreed to a written retraction and apology for his objectionable fast sermon.[48] Timothy Flint resigned his pulpit in Lunenberg, Massachusetts, because "my people were democratic, and the mania of democracy always ran high here. It rendered the last years of my residence here very uncomfortable. Starvation and insult exhausted my health." [49] The same mania led Moses Dow to request dismissal from the Second Church in Beverly, Massachusetts, because of "insufficient support. The true reason [*sic*] he was a Federalist of the genuine Washington School!!" [50] In Edward Payson, the Republicans of Portland encountered a more formidable opponent. When the town's Committee of Public Safety ordered all church services suspended so that all men could work on the fortifications on the Sabbath, he refused compliance, held services, and had a large attendance.[51]

Clergymen like Dow and Payson bore the brunt of Republican outrage in the first months of the war. When partisans gathered to resolve approval of Madison's policies, they usually turned their attention to recent sermons and issued statements like that of the Hancock County convention in Maine. There Republicans viewed with disgust "those men cloathed with the sacred character of religion, who descend from their high station to become the heralds of discord, the low instruments of sedition." [52] "We would regard with tenderness and candor the aberrations of our most useful class of citizens," avowed the Republicans of York County. But when ministers defiled their pulpits by antiwar preaching, they became "public incendiaries, the decided adversaries of their country, the open auxiliaries of the common enemy, and men who have forfeited all claim to public respect and public support." [53] Like many another gathering, the convention in Providence, Rhode Island, condemned those who had been bribed to "prostitute the priestly dignity, for bandying into party, and profaning the sacred altar by blowing thereon the coals of faction with unhallowed breath.[54]

Thus it was that Republican rallies, especially in New England, usually included in their partisan drinking toasts some pointed references to antiwar ministers, with innumerable variations on the same theme:

The tory-clergy; may they fight more against the devil, and less against their country.

New-England—may she renounce the old bulwark of Essex Junto Religion, and return to her first love.

Religion—the corner stone of our republic, unconnected with priestcraft.[55]

And so on. An especially popular salute, with many different wordings, probably was heartily cheered by sectarians longing for disestablishment of the Congregational church:

Our Clergy—May all those who preach sedition or treason from the pulpit, be branded with eternal infamy and left to earn their bread by the sweat of the brow.[56]

The jubilant Philadelphians who celebrated the victory at New Orleans by hailing "David Jones, the patriotic chaplain," added another toast to which that Baptist war-horse could have answered a fervent "Amen." "A good text for a Yankee sermon," they joked, "those who neglect all their duties, forfeit all their rights." [57]

All through the fighting and well after it, Republicans flailed away at Federalist religion and British piety with virtually any weapon that came to hand. They cited the authority of two Baptist greats, Isaac Backus and David Benedict, to document the sufferings of their coreligionists in Britain and to accuse Congregationalists of contemplating similar persecutions.[58] They reported British harassment of Methodists, who were all of England's "most serious, zealous, and lively professors of religion." [59] They warned that Canadian children were legally illegitimate and unable to inherit property unless their parents had been married under Episcopal or Catholic auspices.[60] They predicted that an unsuccessful war would result in a "NATIONAL RELIGION; all must be Episcopalians; the clergy must be paid out of the national chest." [61] At election time voters were bluntly told what was involved in the contest. "It is a fact," they declared, "Sectarians, as the standing order call them, are almost universally in favor of the Government, and the standing order are nearly as universally against it." [62] The former should therefore elect men like Madison, "who have been denounced as infidels and atheists, because they have advocated and established universal *freedom of opinion in religion.*" [63] No less a figure than Governor William Plumer of New Hampshire wrote a treatise against the antiwar clergy; and when one of their number caustically responded, Republicans charged that his answer "has the mark of the beast upon its forehead." [64] When the Republican minority in Rhode Island's House of Representatives protested the decision to send delegates to the Hartford Convention, they too aimed a blow at Congregationalism by warning that the planned nation of New England would bode no good for the land of Roger Williams, which would be overwhelmed by its powerful neighbors. "The new confederacy would not establish a religion to suit this state," they predicted. "Let what is past premonish us of the future." [65] When Republican editors warned the Federalist rulers of New England that attempted secession would bring on civil war, they must have had in mind those martial Christians who would not tamely submit to another Babylonian captivity.

John Fiske may have been correct in believing that Christians would not participate in the war without the sanction of their "religious teachers." What Fiske and Federalists generally failed to realize was that the antiwar clergy were but a small part of America's ministry. The first Independence Day of the war presaged what was to come, as martial preachers all over the land observed the anniversary in a way that should have made Fiske see his error. When John Gemmil told the patriots of West Chester, Pennsylvania, that his participation was a duty second only to preaching the Gospel, he spoke for a legion of his fellows, ministers like William Harrenten and Nathaniel Kendrick in Vermont, Ariel Kendrick in New Hampshire, and a host of nameless others.[66] In the northern extremity of Massachusetts, where faith in British magnanimity was considerably less than in the Bay State proper, the Republicans of Saco gathered at the Reverend Mr. Cogsell's meetinghouse and after services expressed themselves in a more festive manner by toasting, "The Clergy of every denomination—May we ever distinguish between the mes-

sengers of Heaven and the movers of sedition." Both the Reverend Mr. Morrill and the Reverend Mr. Jenks supervised the services
at Bath, while Martin Ruter won the audience's admiration with
his fervent invocation in the Reverend Mr. Dean's meetinghouse in
Portland, after which the Reverend Mr. Blood read the Declaration of Independence "after some solemn prefatory remarks,
referring to the days of the Revolution (in which he participated)." [67] Another veteran, Deacon Parker, presided at Georgetown, while Samuel Baker did the same at Thomaston and, like
all the others, "entered with lively feeling and warmth, into the
present unpleasant situation of our public affairs, and urged the
instant and imperious duty of arming and making patriotic and
vigorous exertions in the cause of our country." [68]

Throughout New Jersey too, ministers demonstrated that
united clerical opposition to the war was a Federalist delusion.
In a patriotic homily in Bloomfield, Cyrus Gildersleeve traced
divine superintendence in American history; and Stephen
Saunders's oration in the First Presbyterian Church there envisioned American expansion to the western ocean, a continental
Republic inspiring all who struggle against imperial powers.
While the Reverend Mr. Duryee delivered the invocation at the
Republican rally in Paterson, the Reverend Mr. Picton in West-
field was urging his fellow Scottish Christians to flee that "infatuated, distracted, devoted island" before Britain suffered the
fate of Sodom.[69] Abel Jackson presided at yet another celebration in Bloomfield, where a toast was raised to "the Federal
Clergy—Alas! Alas!" John Dow of the Dutch church in Belleville
recounted heaven's guidance of the Republic from the battle
of Trenton to more recent events which so thrilled his hearers.
His colleague, Dr. Solomon Froeligh, on the same day delivered
a rousing sermon, which the Republican press soon serialized. Recalling the fall of Holland, his hearers and readers well knew
that theirs was the last Republic and probably shared his confidence that "The Lord will plead our cause, and execute judgment
for us; he will plead our cause, in the cabinet of Britain, and in the
palace of St. Cloud; he will plead our cause in the highway of nations, on the banks of the Wabash, and even before the walls of
Quebec." [70]

In Kentucky there was similar optimism as Jesse Head's sermon recalled the Revolutionary struggle, "which eventuated in the achievement of our *civil* and *religious liberties*," and urged his hearers to defend those freedoms.[71] The Republicans of Richmond County, New York, cheered Peter Vanpelt's plea for divine help in coming battles and must have understood that he hoped to avert from his adopted country the ruin which had recently befallen his Dutch homeland.[72] Other exiles shared his feelings and soon would be voicing them before their congregations.[73] Hundreds of other clergymen would appear at local celebrations to offer Republican prayers, to preach patriotism and damn sedition. They would often lead their congregations to work on fortifications and would remind the laborers their bulwarks were built against "that government, the throne of which is stained with the blood of the saints, which can forbid the progress of missionary labors, which supports Moloch in the East, lifts up Antichrist in the West, and keeps down or only tolerates what is good at home." [74] No wonder they often summoned the people to arms with Scripture's alarm, "To your tents, O Israel!"

Some of them evinced their support for the war by ministering to the soldiers who fought the battles of Israel. These informal chaplains were of many creeds, but in their heterogeneity they showed a broad base of religious approval of the war. The role of chaplains in the American armed forces was as yet undeveloped. Ordained personnel willing to take upon themselves such responsibilities were rare, but local ministers often held services for troops stationed in the neighborhood. Sometimes a commission as militia chaplain was awarded to a prominent clergyman because of his popularity with the soldiers, as was the case of Peter Vanpelt, whose Independence Day sermon in 1812 led to his appointment as chaplain to a local regiment.[75] It was a surprisingly casual way to provide for the spiritual needs of military forces. Of course, kind remarks about the state of military piety were seldom heard, especially among the antiwar clergy, who considered the army a school of vice. Nor did the appointment of someone like Chaplain Booge, a suspended Presbyterian minister, create greater respect for the moral side of camp life.[76]

Those who ministered to the fighters, however, did not share

the pessimistic view of military service. The Baptist Elisha Cushman told "a Company of the United States' Troops, about to
March upon the Frontiers," that when a soldier deserved re-
proach "it is due to his character and not to his calling." [77] When
the Lutheran George Lochman assured the departing militia of
Lebanon County, Pennsylvania, that they resembled King
David's army marching from Jerusalem to stop the invaders
of Israel, he too mentioned the supposedly immoral character of
the army but urged them to emulate the Christian legion of
Marcus Aurelius, Gustavus Adolphus of Sweden, or General
Washington, whose piety was by now legendary.[78] Another
Lutheran, David Schaeffer of Frederick, Maryland, recruited men
in the city's streets to form a volunteer company but limited his
services to a three-mile march with his flock, a sermon, and
prayers for the kneeling warriors.[79] Perhaps this should qualify
him as a chaplain. Certainly he matched the performance of that
office by John Brodhead of the Dutch church in New York,
whom Governor Tompkins appointed chaplain to a regiment
of artillery and who often visited the soldiers at their stations.[80]
Apparently such visits constituted sufficient presence to fulfill the
duties required by a formal commission.

Similar service was performed by Matthew Henderson of
the Associate Reformed church, who preached to volunteers
gathering in the neighborhood of Pittsburgh. His colleague,
John Dunlap, who had participated in the Revolution as a boyish
exile from Britain, was naturally pleased to address sailors of the
navy docked at Whitehall, New York, those *"five hundred conquering heroes."* [81]

Usually the navy received much less exposure to the Gospel.
There were probably only two clergymen among the navy's wartime chaplains, most of whom were only officers with a degree of
education.[82] This did not mean that Israel's maritime forces were
necessarily irreligious. Even when incarcerated in Dartmoor,
American seamen often attended church services, although when
the minister provided for them by their captors prayed for his
royal sovereign, he was left without a congregation. "He went
off and we have not seen him since," one inmate recorded. His
place was in part filled by Black Simon, a local preacher who

held services for Negro prisoners in their part of Dartmoor and whose preaching was frequently attended by white inmates. When several prisoners were slain in the Dartmoor massacre, it was Black Simon who provided consolation to their comrades by preaching about the tragedy.[83]

No matter how much or how little religious activity was carried on among American soldiers and sailors, the antiwar clergy knew that all the wickedness in the country was involved in the unholy fight. After all, the very men who preached the military Gospel, Baptists like David Jones and Horatio Jones, were themselves considered notorious sinners by Federalist standards.[84] Nor was a host of Methodist itinerants thought likely to improve the state of military piety. Be that as it may, they were well suited to dealing with Republican crusaders. Andrew Jackson himself selected Learner Blackman, presiding elder of the Nashville district, as chaplain to the three thousand volunteers under his command, whom Blackman visited from boat to boat as they descended the Ohio and Mississippi rivers.[85] Generals Winfield Scott and Jacob Brown encouraged Gideon Lanning to preach to their troops in western New York, and both officers were among his regular hearers.[86] Both Joseph Merrill and the bellicose Billy Hibbard for some time ministered to troops at Boston, while other Methodist circuit riders did likewise in the Chesapeake area and in the West. One of their number in Indiana rode the Whitewater circuit carrying a gun in case of Indian attack and singing a favorite hymn to the delight of frontiersmen: "And are we yet alive!" [87]

It goes without saying that few clergymen were actually involved in the war effort even to the extent of serving as makeshift chaplains. The ones who were so involved, however, were parts of a larger pattern of religious support for the war. They represented unnumbered thousands of Americans marching in the armies or praying for their success, Christians awaiting a Republican millennium after the defeat of Pius VII and his British friends, persecuted sectarians planning vengeance on old foes. Their response to the national crisis transcended partisan interests, for once again North America was the scene of conflict between a foreign power and the armies of the Lord.

4 ✠ ARMIES OF THE LORD

I now call upon the priests of every christian denomi-nation, to show yourselves and call out "who is on the Lord's side?"

Isaac Hilliard, 1814

The prowar churches were theologically disparate, often suspicious of one another, factious and competitive; but like the partisans of James Madison, they were united in their hatred for Britain and her American admirers. If Republican Christians did not have many outlets for publicizing their opinions, if the ministers did not often publish their wartime sermons and the congregations patronized few journals, they nonetheless left ample testimony to their political beliefs; and that record reveals an enthusiasm for the war far more extensive than the religious opposition to it.

Foremost among the prowar churches were the Baptists, whose martial patriotism transcended regional and economic interests, class conflicts and party loyalties. Generations of accumulated grievances against both Anglicanism and Congregationalism made them fervent patriots, for the war had been declared contrary to the wishes of the Baptists' domestic theological opponents and against a government historically hostile to their communion.

Because of their extremely decentralized system of government, the political temper of the Baptist churches during the war can be determined only by a composite of fragmentary evidences. But several semiofficial Baptist statements concerning the national crisis greatly appealed to the Republican press and were extensively reprinted. These expressions of denominational support for the war made up by their wide circulation what they lacked in ecclesiastical authority. In its yearly meeting of October 1813, the Philadelphia Baptist Association, one of the most influential, considered moral issues raised by the war. One of the two members chosen to draft a circular letter on the topic of nonresistance was Horatio Gates Jones, chaplain to the Roxborough regiment of Pennsylvanian militia.[1] Little wonder, then, that the letter lamented that many Christians preferred to see their families slaughtered rather than fight to defend them. According to the association's reading of Scripture, pacifism was contrary to Christ's own command to the Roman soldiery that they be content with their wages; for surely he would not have advised them to enjoy the wages of sin. The circular closed with the Pauline command to obey authorities, "not only for wrath, but for conscience' sake." [2]

Baptist associations all over the country issued letters concordant in spirit, if not in complete substance, with the Philadelphian circular. The North Carolina General Meeting of Correspondence, for example, early in the war urged its members to observe the fast day recommended by the president, "taking into consideration the calamitous state of the country in being involved in a war by the injustice of a foreign power." [3] While the Philadelphia Association was convened, the Georgia Baptist Association issued resolutions in the martial tenor of their northern brethren. These attained great popularity as prowar propaganda and were reprinted in Republican papers in many states. Exhorting their fellows in the fashion of the Philadelphians, the Georgians also counseled personal service in defense of America's violated rights. Their words left no room for equivocation:

> We, therefore, in this public and solemn manner, take the liberty of saying, that we have long viewed with emotions of indignation and horror, the many lawless aggressions committed on the persons, rights, and property of the people of these United States, by the corrupt, arbitrary, and despotic government of Great Britain, and its emissaries.[4]

By unanimous resolution the Georgians declared the war was "just, necessary, and indispensable." Madison had no greater apologists than these.

Like their fellow Georgians, the Ocmulgee association in their circular letter of 1813 took a definite stand on the war. They took this liberty of considering affairs of state because they addressed a people historically concerned with freedom:

> Your progenitors, brethren, from the Christian era, during the darkest as well as the most luminous ages of antiquity, and in all modern times, have been the asserters, the consistent and uniform asserters of civil and religious liberty—and very generally the most conspicuous sufferers for it. Do you, then, whose fathers have suffered so much for you, who have been so highly favored with its enjoyment, now deem it worth defending? [5]

This too was reprinted by Republican editors as a worthy example of Christian patriotism. When the Republican citizens of Savannah met in June 1812 to urge declaration of war and immediate occupation of the Floridas, it was entirely appropriate that their assembly hall was the Baptist meetinghouse in that city.[6]

The Dover association of Virginia, meeting in October 1813, considered whether music was permissible for Christians during their meals and, with a mind to the alcoholic excess common at festive banquets, declared that musical entertainment at table tended toward idolatrous and carnal practice. They then added a modification of their resolution: "We would not be understood to include the instruments of War-Music, &c. which may be thought necessary." [7] It was a nice distinction but an honest one. In the minds of most American Baptists, the War of 1812 was in no way carnal or idolatrous. On the contrary, it was, after a fashion, a vindication of their long struggle for the rights of man.

Such, at any rate, was the belief of prominent Baptist ministers. One of the most bellicose was William Parkinson of New York City, who, soon after the declaration of war, presided over the joint celebration of Independence Day by seven of the city's patriotic societies.[8] If his discourse on that occasion was at all like his fast sermon of the following month, it must indeed have been appropriate for a day of national jubilance. For Parkinson's sermon a month later was a thorough defense of both Madison and the war. Although he was sadly mistaken in predicting that his country would suffer no devastation in the conflict because it had no law-established religion, no American Baptist could mistake the implications of his address. An established church did exist in Canada, and there the horrors of war would be realized. It also existed in New England, and "what degree of trouble they may experience on account of it, I will not pretend to determine." Of one thing Parkinson was certain: all governments tainted by "that abomination" must suffer for their impiety. Britain, of course, was most notorious in this regard. It was, therefore, for the sake of true religion as well as for the sake of their country that Parkinson's congregation united their voices to seek benediction for their leader:

> Our *President* with wisdom crown,
> His soul with thy rich graces adorn;
> Resolve his heart, 'midst all his foes,
> "To launch the stream which duty shows." [9]

Their minister's martial sermon was soon being circulated as Republican propaganda for the forthcoming elections.[10]

Another proponent of the war was David Jones, septuagenarian chaplain in the United States Army. As a veteran of the Revolution, he bitterly hated Britain and contributed anglophobic material to prowar papers, in return for which he received the esteem of loyal Republicans, who praised his fervor and toasted "the patriotic chaplain." [11] Federalists scorned this "garrulous old fool," but a prominent antiwar editor perceived that Jones was both a religious and a political counterweight to New England's dissenting ministers:

Let Mr. Madison, and all his satellites, cease their clamourous, reviling rant against the learned and pious clergy of the East, for touching occasionally upon political subjects, while *they* pension with public money, and mount, even in the capitol, such loathsome old political crucibles, smoking with the hot cinders of Jacobinism.[12]

Like most politically active Baptists, Jones was crusading not only against Britain but also against Britain's domestic admirers. There were old scores to settle. The same antiwar preachers who extolled the enemy's piety were ancestral enemies to the varied sectarians within the Republican fold. Like Parkinson, Jones did not limit the power of antichrist to Napoleon and the Roman pontiff. Other minions of Babylon, more dangerous because nearer at hand, were the Congregationalist churches, based on infant baptism and guilty of the blood of Baptist saints. All Protestant prayers for the destruction of antichrist would, he warned, be in vain as long as the "dregs" of law-established religion persisted in the United States.[13] One suspects that Chaplain Jones wished Madison would hang treasonous dissenters [14] not only as a punishment for political disloyalty but also as a fitting retribution for their religious crimes. Madison himself could not have been surprised when Jones reported, "It would do your heart good to hear the Baptist clergy pray for you and the army. It would be well for us, if we were all Baptists." [15]

Madison had good cause to be comforted. Though his administration was short of funds, it was amply supplied with Baptist prayers. Presiding at the meetinghouse in Richmond, the Reverend Mr. Grigg celebrated the victory on Lake Erie and recounted America's blessings, foremost among which was religious liberty. When Grigg declared, "We sit, each one under our own vine and fig tree; none daring to make us afraid," [16] his congregation probably realized that their much abused president upheld their precious sectarian liberty.

Even in Massachusetts prayers were offered for the American army. The far-famed John Leland continued his long advocacy of Baptist beliefs and Republican politics, often championing both from his pulpit. It was from a borrowed pulpit, however, that Leland delivered one of his most impassioned political sermons. His clerical colleague, who had granted Leland the use of his church, was shocked to hear his guest's discourse on the Crucifixion suddenly become a political oration. Apparently some of the scenes of Calvary struck Leland as associated with events of the war; and although he tried to correct the tendency of his sermon, the surprise was too great for his audience to overcome easily.[17] Scarcely less surprising was Elisha Cushman's sermon to troops in Connecticut, who came to the Baptist church in Hartford to hear the whole of Christianity explained through military metaphors. It was a cleverly developed oration, if at times a little awkward, and must have well suited Cushman's hearers, who might have been comforted by his recounting of Christ's meeting with a Roman centurion: "By way of digression, I would here remark, that if wars are in no case admissible, still our Lord did not pronounce this man the culprit; he was under authority, accountable to higher powers, and, notwithstanding his employment, was pronounced, by holy lips, a man of faith." Thus Christians might oppose the present war but should not denigrate those who take up arms in it.[18]

Other Baptists offered more than prayers and sermons to the war effort. The distinguished William White served as commissioner of loans for the district of Pennsylvania, thus provoking Federalist sarcasm as to the Baptists' vaunted division of church and state.[19] The bitterly antiwar congressman from North Carolina, Archibald McBryde, was replaced in the Thirteenth Congress by John Culpepper, an ordained Baptist minister whose Federalist beliefs were of a milder sort than those of his predecessor.[20] A more raucous antiwar voice was temporarily silenced by the electoral defeat of John Randolph, who was replaced in Congress by John Kerr, another Baptist preacher.[21]

And so the catalog can be continued. Perhaps all the various contributions made by Baptists to the war effort can be encapsuled in the career of Spencer Houghton Cone, who participated in the conflict as editor, soldier, and Christian crusader and who later became one of the greatest figures in American Baptist history.

A former actor, Cone was general treasurer of the *Baltimore American* until he and an associate purchased the *Baltimore Whig* in 1814. He was an advocate of the war long before he entered the Baptist communion. When Federalist papers spread the news of mob violence against the *Baltimore Federal Republican*, Cone wrote to a shocked friend, "From my soul I believe Alexander Hanson and his associates [the mob's victims] enemies and traitors to their country." [22] He was particularly infuriated by

religious antiwar sentiment, which praised the moral character
of the oppressors of Ireland. "Oh! my blood curdles in my veins,"
he wrote, "when I hear reasonable creatures applauding that corrupt and nefarious government." [23] Obviously, Cone needed no
additional motivation for supporting the war against Britain. By
the time of his actual entrance onto the field of battle, however,
his political views were bolstered by renewed religious conviction.
While enemy marauding parties were terrorizing the Chesapeake
towns of Maryland, Cone experienced religious conversion and
was baptized in the Patapsco River after the ice had been broken
to allow his immersion according to the fullness of Baptist principles.[24]

Recalling many years later his acceptance of a lieutenant's commission in a company of sharpshooters, Cone was adamant as to
the correctness of his action. "I thought myself to be in the path
of duty then," he remembered, "and am of the same opinion
still." [25] In the interval between his military service and his later
justification of it, Cone had become exceptionally prominent in
his denomination and had been nine times elected president of the
National Baptist Convention. In the decentralized Baptist church,
his position came closest to possessing the stature of a denominationally representative figure. His biographer contended that
Cone's enthusiasm for the war against Britain explained his later
religious views and practices, "particularly with reference to the
independency and government of Baptist churches, which he
regarded as the perfect embodiment of development of the democratic principle." [26] Cone's son concurred. His father's defense of
the Republic had been undertaken, he was sure, in the belief that
the United States was to be "the grand theatre of His mercy to
His people, the peculiar place in which His truth expanded under
the benign influence of civil and religious freedom." With these
principles, characteristic of Cone's fellow Baptists, active participation in the war "seemed to him as much the duty of the Christian as the honor of the soldier." [27]

Cone's beliefs must have been shared by the members of the
Tammany Society of Newport, Rhode Island, who celebrated
the first Independence Day of the war with customary fervor
after prayers in the Second Baptist meetinghouse in that city.[28]
On the same day, Clark Kendrick led the Republicans of Poult-

ney, Vermont, in worship at the Baptist meetinghouse there.[29] In Bloomfield, Maine, John Cayford presided at the Baptist meetinghouse on similar occasions, as did Peter Griffing in the meetinghouse in Hartford, where the assembled faithful sang the seventy-fifth psalm, anticipating divine intervention in their country's cause.[30] Ariel Kendrick, pastor of the church in Cornish, New Hampshire, participated in many wartime celebrations and Republican rallies in which, as he later sadly recalled, he "drank into the war spirit, and delivered addresses and harrangues upon the awful conflict which swallowed up morals, men, and money, and fixed an indelible stain upon the Christian character of both nations." [31] But his repentance came many years later, when the war with Mexico had made him less ardent a patriot. During the War of 1812 he had no doubts as to the rectitude of his actions and publicly prayed that his Republican beliefs would sweep the entire country. For it was his ministerial duty to preach a crucified Savior "and in his holy name to urge my audience to submit to 'every ordinance of man for the Lord's sake.' " [32] Kendrick and his clerical brethren most eagerly performed this duty by counseling support for the national government. So eagerly did William Biddle do this that North Carolinian Federalists were outraged by his "turning aside from the Alter [sic] and serving the artillery of democratic slander." [33] And if, in rare instances, Baptist ministers were loath to perform that duty, their congregations were doubtless quick to rebuke them, as Elisha Andrews, pastor to the church in Templeton, Massachusetts, discovered. Although he had no sympathy with Federalism, he abhorred the war, earned the hostility of his flock, resigned his pulpit, and kept his position at Templeton only because no replacement was available.[34] Like any opponent of the war, he was out of place among the Baptist admirers of the president.

An archenemy of the Baptists in Massachusetts inadvertently testified to the relationship between that denomination and the war effort. It was not for rhetorical effect that Samuel Austin's sermon on the national fast day in 1812 was a personal defense of his clerical politics. His rabid Federalism had turned away several members of his congregation to the fledgling Baptist church of Worcester.[35] Nor was it accidental that Austin's bitter denunciation of the war was printed with appended footnotes, the first of which attacked the Baptists of Massachusetts, who, through their opposition to the tax for clergy support, "are the most clamorous for such a prostration of constitution and law." [36] One can only imagine the depths of Austin's dejection during the summer of 1812. Not only were his worst political fears confirmed by the war, but in addition the ordinance of baptism by immersion was for the first time being administered in Worcester. Accordingly, Austin divided his pulpit invective that summer between the national administration and local sectarians, who seemed to be in league against England, New England, and religious orthodoxy.[37]

The advent of peace was greeted with great enthusiasm by American Baptists, whose reaction differed from that of other Christians, who were thankful for the end of divine punishments against their guilty nation. Even when Baptists used the same jargon as antiwar religionists, their thanksgiving was of a different kind. The corresponding letter of the New York association, for example, was written during the ebullient spring of 1815 and played a significant variation upon the hackneyed theme of national guilt. Although the association perceived the goodness of God "in the restoration of that national peace which we had forfeited by our sins," it discovered great mercies mingled with past punishments. For although God "had a controversy" with America, "he did not intend to forsake us utterly. Hath he indeed smitten us as he hath smitten those whom he sent to smite us? Or have we been slain according to the slaughter of our enemies, whom God in his righteous providence hath slain?" [38]

The same sanguinary patriotism was evident in the corresponding letter of the Philadelphia association, which rejoiced that the enemy's arm was no longer lifted against "our beloved country, and garments rolled in blood are removed from the sight of our lately oppressed fellow-citizens." For this and for the preservation of civil and religious liberty the association offered thanks.[39] The Shaftsbury association also exulted at the return of peace and hailed the event "with rapture . . . in a land that freedom calls her own." [40] The Baptist Missionary Society of Kentucky proclaimed its program with a similar joy; for America's "combined adversaries" had been unable to defeat God's own new Canaan, and "the tree of liberty still flourishes and blooms in the fair fields of America." [41]

The Boston association also gave thanks for blessings bestowed upon "our beloved and highly favored country." This was in a circular letter written by Daniel Merrill, who, on the national thanksgiving in April 1815, presented the most complete single statement of the relation between wartime dissension and denominational conflict. Merrill was a "come-outer," a former Congregationalist minister who had graduated from Dartmouth at the head of his class and secured the pastorate of the church in Sedgwick, the largest congregation in Maine. Exposed to the forthright give-and-take of frontier religion, he together with most of his flock "came out" to the Baptists.[42] The phrase, of course, was scriptural, from the exhortation to the Hebrews to dissociate themselves from Babylon: "Come out of her, my people." The words had a literal meaning to Merrill and his congregation. The orthodox clergy who opposed his efforts to secure a charter for a Baptist seminary were, in his own words, "Babylonish ministers." [43] Accordingly, the war was heaven's instrument against New England's iniquity.

Despite his friendship with ministers and churches of his faith in Nova Scotia and New Brunswick, Merrill early in the war had exhorted his flock concerning their civic duties.[44] His text was Joel 3 : 10. "Beat your plough-shares into swords, and your pruning-hooks into spears: let the weak say, I am strong." Before the congregation at Nottingham-West on the day of national thanksgiving Merrill gave these sentiments full and eloquent expression. The historical introduction of his sermon was a true Baptist interpretation of world events. Persecuted first by the Roman harlot and then by her English daughter, their spiritual ancestors had fled to America, where they found grandchildren of the Roman whore, who soon showed "that it was not from religious tyranny they were averse, but from suffering the lash of it." [45] From these Congregationalist branches of Babylon came opposition to the war and calumniation of Madison,

for having prevented the flood-gates of law-religion from deluging his native State; for having been uniformly opposed

to an established religion, the most fruitful source of superstition and persecution; and for having resisted, stedfastly, the
haughty encroachments of Britain, declared war and vindicated the inestimable rights of our own nation against the
tyranny and cruelty of that government which may, for the
present, be styled the bulwark of national religion; that bane
of Christianity, and principle support of Babylon the great, the
mother of harlots, and abominations of the earth.[46]

On the same day, the Baptists of Colebrook, Connecticut, heard
Henry Bliss similarly condemn the alliance of corrupt Christianity
and "the vilest abominations of Kings and their authorized
agents." As if to make still clearer the application of his discourse,
he observed that if the Hartford Convention had been a truly
Christian assembly "the whole christian world might have fellow-
shipped their devotion." [47] When Orsamus Merrill some months
thereafter spoke in the Baptist meetinghouse in Bennington, the
former Republican clerk of Vermont's House of Representatives
showed that his fellow believers would not soon forget the sins of
the "standing order." They would remember Castine and East-
port, the towns which had collaborated with the occupiers of
Maine, "the Aholah and Aholibah of New-England" whose crime
was shared by the treasonous legislature.[48] Already some Christians had determined to separate themselves from the sinners, to
come out of Babylon, by detaching their land from the state of
Massachusetts. Their religious leaders presided while they toasted,
"District of Maine—Of full age; may she soon manage her own
affairs, and be no more under the control of an idolatrous parent,
who has so long worshipped the 'Bulwark.'" [49]
   As Daniel Merrill observed, the enduring bitterness was all
caused by Protestant establishments. "This is what the clergy are
now struggling for," he warned. "This is manifestly the root of
the present controversy, in this our otherwise happy country." [50]
This belief was as much a fact in the world view of American
Baptists as the horrors of impressment and the savagery of Indian
raids. It was, of course, assiduously supported by Republican
propaganda portraying the British "Goliah of religious persecu-

tion" and its Congregationalist imitators. Believing as they did, Baptists knew the war was more than justified; it was holy.

That the war was a holy endeavor was believed by most American Methodists too. Like many other ecclesiastical bodies in the spring of 1812, the Methodist General Conference addressed the church's members concerning national affairs. "We yet have abundant cause for deep humiliation before God and one another," they warned. "Our country is threatened, calamities stare us in the face, iniquity abounds, and the love of many waxes cold. O let us again resort to fasting and humiliation." [51] When news of the war declaration reached Lynn, Massachusetts, the New England Conference of the church was convened in its annual meeting. Preachers and people were greatly disturbed by the turn of events, but the reaction was not uniform. Some thought this war, whatever its political justification, was like all wars, contrary to the Gospel of peace. Others were so martial that their colleagues were taken aback at their exuberance.[52] Some expressed concern at the decline in religious practice and church membership usually attendant upon a state of war, an effect that was to be felt more or less by many churches. But in whatever degree American Methodists were affected by the excitement, there is no evidence that it impaired their Christian profession; for their faith and their nationalism were so harmonized that military involvement could even bolster their piety.

American Methodism had been born of a robust, expansive, independent religious mentality, at once the child of Wesley's theology, an interdenominational frontier environment, and the charisma of Francis Asbury, first bishop of the church in America. Older churches generally agreed that Methodist preachers were unlearned, if not illiterate, and that their camp meetings were often frantic, sometimes scandalous, and always "enthusiastic"— a pejorative term applied to any unrestrained and unorthodox religious activity. Moreover, the church openly boasted its Arminianism, the belief in a full, free, present salvation offered by God to all men. This pitted them against all Calvinists, who responded with unabated venom. "The enemies of the Methodists

. . . were not less abundant than the frogs in Egypt," remembered one itinerant, who suggested this as the reason for his church's political sentiments:

> The Republican party were zealous for a high state of civil and religious liberty, therefore the Methodists were generally of this party, and when the story of their joining the French became stale, then they were going to join Jefferson to overthrow our political institutions. When this also became stale, they said the people were spending so much time in following after these runagates that they would raise nothing, and would have to be maintained as paupers.[53]

Another circuit rider recalled that "anything like ministerial courtesy was scarcely looked for outside of one's own communion" during the decade of the war. He and his colleagues especially were treated as "blind leaders of the blind." [54]

To some extent the criticism was justified. Compared with the training available in eastern seminaries, the schooling of the church's itinerants was poor. But while the prudent plans of seaboard religionists produced eloquent preachers and learned debaters, Methodism took possession of the West. When Asbury arrived in the colonies as a Wesleyan missionary in 1771, his flock was small; but before his death in 1816 the bishop had traveled thousands of miles and had ordained many hundreds of preachers,[55] who brought in the sheaves of his sowing. The church's Western Conference—Kentucky, Tennessee, and the Northwest Territories—in its first twelve years increased from three thousand members to thirty thousand Christians.[56] It was no empty boast, which later Methodists would make, that their scorned itinerant founders had inaugurated the great missionary era of the nineteenth century.

The church's growth attested to its admirable adaptation to the New World, and opponents of Methodism had reason to be alarmed. One of them, refuting the charge that Congregationalists sought a union of church and state, warned in return, "should such an event take place, I give it to you as my deliberate opinion, that the religion established will be that of 'THE METHODIST EPISCOPAL CHURCH OF THE UNITED STATES OF AMERICA.' " [57] In light of the Methodists' antipathy toward governmental interference in religion, the statement was absurd at the time. It was ironic that even the anti-Methodist pamphleteer could not have foreseen the extent to which his warning would in a sense be fulfilled. Although not seeking state sponsorship, the Methodist communion was in the process of becoming a wealthy, socially prominent, and eminently respectable denomination. It was soon to be one of the most American of the American churches, in the sense that it reflected the values, ambitions, and mores of the mainstream of American culture.

The War of 1812 found the church approximately halfway in its development from primitive obscurity to social and political significance. Domestic wartime tensions, functioning as something of an endurance test for religious organizations, revealed the Methodist Episcopal church performing at its best. The church's role during the war provided the clearest evidence of its adaptation to its social environment and was indicative of what American Methodism was to become.

The catalog of ministers involved in the war effort is impressive; and in their support for the military effort they had an example in their venerable leader, Francis Asbury. During the Revolution he had found himself conscientiously unable to take an oath of allegiance to the rebel government of the colonies, and his sectarian opponents kept alive that stigma.[58] His reaction to his adopted country's second war with Britain was hardly eager, as he noted in his journal on June 21, 1812: "The proclamation of the president of the United States is out, to inform us that there is war between our people and the English people: my trust is in the living God." [59] Before the end of the fighting, however, he was to declare "most plainly and pointedly" on the floor of an annual conference that anyone refusing to pray for his country at such a time did not deserve the name of Christian or the title of Christian minister. For Scripture commanded Christians to honor all in authority "that we may lead quiet and peaceable lives, in all godliness and honesty." [60] Asbury did more than honor authority; he prayed for it, once at the request of the commanding officer of troops encamped at Uniontown on their way to the fighting around Lake Erie. One of his fellow circuit riders noted that, "though he was said to be a British subject, he did not pray for the English king, but he prayed most devoutly for the President of the United States—the cabinet—senate, and lower house." As the soldiers filed off the meeting ground, Asbury stationed himself where he could shake hands with the members of his martial congregation.[61]

Asbury's colleague in the episcopacy, William McKendree, shared his esteem for the American government. At a religious service on the day of national thanksgiving for peace, McKendree preached a sermon appropriate to what was both a national celebration and a Republican festival. "The Bishop was full of patriotism," a colleague recalled, "and with a national subject he was perfectly at home." [62] This facility with "national subjects" was typical of many Methodist preachers.

One of the most adept was Billy Hibbard, who championed James Madison as earnestly as he opposed John Calvin. He informed his fellows at the annual conference of 1814 that he would offer his services as a chaplain if the militia should be called out in any area where he was stationed. He soon secured appointment to a regiment at Boston, where he conducted daily services for the soldiers, who once volunteered to attack the enemy if "Father Hibbard" would lead them.[63] Their chaplain probably encouraged their belligerence against not only Britain but also the "false prophets" of New England, who used their influence over "superstitious mortals" to betray republican government. "I am ashamed of New England, the land of my fathers," he lamented. "Where is thy boasted goodness? How are thine altars (sacred to religion) polluted by the minister preaching his party politics and vehement invectives, slandering the best of men." [64] Although he condemned ministerial politics, Hibbard apparently saw no inconsistency in conferring with military officers at Boston, agreeing to turn their forces upon the Massachusetts troops should they fail to assist in repulsing a British attack.[65]

One must wonder whether Hibbard was at the time more a patriot attacking treason or an Arminian assaulting the Calvinist antiwar clergy. Methodists could crusade simultaneously against their country's internal enemies and their denomination's traditional foe, for in both cases the villains were the same. A decline

in the church's membership during the war indicated that the recollections of a pioneer preacher were partly accurate, that "the
people were so much taken up with war and politics, that they
lost their zeal in the cause of God." [66] But to a large extent such
a generalization is inaccurate, for the performance of Billy Hibbard and many of his colleagues made clear that their political
activity was not a substitute but a supplementary expression of
their religious devotion.

Ministering to Methodists scattered through the Maine wilderness, Timothy Merritt was angered by an antiwar sermon based
on the text, "This year thou shalt die." In refutation, he preached
by request to soldiers encamped at Hallowell, using as his text
Judg. 5 : 23. "Curse ye Meroz, said the angel of the Lord, curse ye
bitterly the inhabitants thereof; because they came not to the
help of the Lord, to the help of the Lord against the mighty."
Naturally his sermon was hailed by Republicans and scorned by
Federalists,[67] but it had a larger significance. The text he employed
had for generations been used by preachers in times of crisis,
sometimes during wars. Now it was once again taken up by ministers of many denominations and was used by the Republican
press, which frequently warned opponents of the war that punishment awaited those who abandoned Israel in its peril: "Curse ye
Meroz, curse ye bitterly." [68]

Preaching in Baltimore during the battle of North Point, Jacob
Gruber offered more than curses for the enemy. When the sound
of cannon broke up his service in the Light Street Church, he
loudly prayed that the Lord would bless King George, convert
him, give him a short life and a happy death, because they wanted
no more of him. Shortly after that, he remembered, defenders
marched off to meet the enemy and "prepared to give the king's
troops a warm salutation and reception, and send as many of them
as they could to heaven or hell without praying the Lord to convert them." Gruber's patriotic piety was so esteemed by the
townsfolk that they used his anglophobic prayer as a toast at their
consequent celebration.[69] Another Baltimorean Methodist awaited
the outcome of the battle, in which his stepson was fighting, with
confidence in divine protection for his city. After the British
retreat from the guns of Fort McHenry, he was sure that the

invaders could have taken the city, "but it would appear as if the Lord had intimidated them with fear." [70]

If the Lord had not intimidated them, perhaps Joshua Thomas had. The "parson of the islands," as he was called, ministered to British soldiers encamped on Tangier Island in the Chesapeake. When he was asked to preach to forces departing for the attack on Baltimore, however, he used the occasion to prophesy retribution awaiting Britain for her iniquity. "I told them," he recalled, "it was given me from the Almighty that they *could not* take Baltimore, and *would not succeed in their expedition.*" [71] Similarly reassured was Elder David Lewis at his station near the battle of Plattsburgh, who feared British victory and waited outside his house to hear better the noise of the fighting. Then, as he put it, "all was calm within. I trusted that the God of power, who sustained our fathers through the Revolutionary struggle, would give us the victory that day." [72]

There is no evidence of any substantial dissent among American Methodists from their church's support of the war effort. In an obviously autobiographical reference, the prominent Nathan Bangs recalled that some pious people on both sides of the Atlantic "deprecated this war as unnatural," kept aloof from partisan strife, and called on all to repent.[73] But this distaste for political activity was shared by few of his colleagues. One can only surmise the partisanship of William Theophius, assigned to the Jamaica circuit on Long Island in 1812, where his efforts to secure a revival were frustrated by political antagonists. He claimed they were charmed by British gold in exchange for their crops, while they cried, perhaps with ample reason, "We have a couple of war-hawks on our circuit." [74] Another war hawk was the future bishop Joshua Soule, who watched the fight between the *Chesapeake* and the *Shannon* from a coastal vantage point and wished he could contribute to the struggle.[75] Several circuit riders left their stations in Canada rather than take an oath of allegiance to the king.[76] And when the jubilant Republicans of Huntington, Long Island, gave thanks for the return of peace, they gathered in the Methodist meetinghouse to hear the farfamed Joshua Hart celebrate the climax of his long advocacy of the war.[77] For this Methodist preacher had contributed to the

war effort one of the most popular sermons, a savagely unsparing
attack upon antiwar Christians.[78] It goes without saying that there
were many more like him, preaching at community functions,
seldom publishing their speeches, but always serving in the fashion
of Martin Ruter, who delivered at an Independence Day rally in
Maine "such a supplication . . . as would have been made by
the Whig Clergy in 'the times which tried men's souls.' " [79]

The extent to which the war may have served to the denominational advantage of the Methodist church is a matter for conjecture. Surely the patriotism of its clergy must have been an asset
after the fighting stopped. When the infamous Elijah Parish
shortly after the war's end cast aspersion on the unlearned itinerants of Canada, a Methodist editor pointed to the apparent relationship between sedition and the church's Congregationalist
critics. Neither in Canada nor in America, he noted, did Methodists prostitute their pulpits on fast days by vituperating their own
government. "Were they to do these things," he continued, "we
believe the Doctor would have more cause, though less inclina-
tion, to censure them, than he now has." [80] It seems as if Asbury
too could not resist the opportunity to make the most of the
situation. During the Genesee Annual Conference in 1813, he
delivered a lengthy address concerning the polity of his church.
Restrained, prudent, politically inoffensive, it was typical of his
work, but it did recognize the facts of American ecclesiastical life.
He had never had a more opportune moment to vindicate the
legitimacy of the Methodist episcopacy, pointing out that "the
Methodist was the first church organized after the establishment
of peace in 1783, and that the Protestant Episcopalians were not
organized as a Church until after there was a law passed by the
British Parliament." [81] This was the species of criticism to which
the Episcopal church was especially sensitive during the war
years, and Asbury's deft use of it was probably particularly effective inasmuch as the Genesee Conference represented an area
greatly afflicted by the war against the land of Anglicanism. But
that was secondary to the bishop's real concern: that the Methodist Episcopal church was the firstborn denomination of the
American Republic.

The import of that heritage was made clear during a wartime

controversy between Methodist and Presbyterian spokesmen in Kentucky and Ohio, in the course of which the Calvinist advocate made an indefinite reference to the political inclinations of Asbury's church: "I have carefully avoided making this a political subject; hence many things have been suppressed, which were at the very nib of my pen. Let the western world slumber a little longer, and they will see and feel without the aid of my quill, the powerful influence of methodist policy." [82] A Methodist pamphleteer thereupon censured his opponent, cast contempt upon his charges, and argued no further. In a way, "the powerful influence of methodist policy" made further argument superfluous. For while the Presbyterian delivered his warning, the belligerently Republican *Fredonian* of Chillicothe, Ohio, announced plans for a new periodical, the *Religious Intelligencer*. This organ of theological enlightenment and depository for materials relating to the Methodist Episcopal church on the frontier was to be published from the offices of the *Fredonian*.[83] Asbury's description of his church was most apt in this case. It should not have surprised Presbyterians that the eldest ecclesiastical offspring of independence shared a printing and propaganda establishment with American Republicanism. Nor should it have surprised anyone that Methodism found a Republican war in accord with both its political interests and its religious profession.

No matter what opprobrium the "standing order" attached to the Baptists and Methodists, they were by no means the most despised of congregations. They were almost doctrinally respectable when measured against the membership of the more recently developed groups, dissident sectarians forming the most unorthodox creeds and the most democratic churches.

The Universalists, for example, had virtually no grounds of agreement with their religious neighbors, whether the comparison be with Calvinists or Arminians, hierarchs or congregationalists. As far as other Christians were concerned, only one Universalist tenet mattered: the denial of the existence of hell. To the orthodox, this was a worse impiety than the Romish invention of purgatory. The latter could be written off as a superstition; the former was a heinous evil. Stories were circulated in the press about men gone berserk, killing their families to carry them all guilt-free into a certain paradise. When a report of the Massachusetts Missionary Society related the encounter of a minister in Maine with sinners, despisers of the Gospel, blasphemers, and Universalists,[84] it accurately expressed the regard in which Universalists were held by other denominations. Even on their ministerial visits, Universalists drew taunts and occasional violence from more orthodox religionists. As one of them recalled, "every bigot or fanatic found an opportunity to display his zeal." [85] So disreputable was the new faith that it came to be something of an ultimate debating point for participants in theological controversies to accuse their opponents of Universalist sympathies.[86]

"I am not a Universalist," one opponent argued, "because this doctrine has a tendency to destroy the sanction of all law, both human and divine." [87] Here was the heart of the matter; remove the restraint of law, and civil society would be extirpated. Hosea Ballou, most prominent minister of his church, replied to this charge by denying that Calvinist eternal damnation could enforce any law, human or divine. "Here we see the scarlet colored beast," he proclaimed, "but thanks be to God, neither this beast nor his prophet, have much power." [88] Ballou's overwrought rhetoric was only a defensive response to the enmity of the American religious community, for Universalists did not have to refer to European history to explicate the Book of Revelation. Their persecutors were all about them; and the intolerant clergy, they claimed, could no more recognize the witnesses of Jesus than the Jewish scribes could see the features of Elijah in John the Baptist. Rather, the "standing order" would imitate their prototypes and "oppose the souls of those who were beheaded for the witness of Jesus, supposing them to be, what they are not, possessed of the devil." [89] All tyranny, whether civil or religious, the Universalists knew to constitute "mystical Babylon the mother of harlots." Conversely, the American government, fostering both civil and religious liberty, was regarded by them with a holy reverence.

When the General Convention of Universalists in the New England states undertook to revise Watts's hymnal, the most popular collection of church music in the United States, to bring

the sacred songs into agreement with Universalist tenets, they
found the task impossible. The lyrics were too tainted with concepts of eternal punishment and a vindictive Providence. They
therefore substituted for the intended revision a new hymnal of
original compositions, containing but a few reworkings of Watts's
least offensive songs.[90] The resulting songbook was consequently
much more than an instrument of Universalist piety. It was rather
a wide-ranging exposition of the world view of the church, and
it illustrated the essential relationship between the authors' faith
and their political affiliation.

One of the thanksgiving songs in the hymnal expressed the
author's religious patriotism:

> On a delightsome spot,
> From other nations free,
> Lord thou has't fix'd our lot;
> We owe, we owe, to thee
> The independence of our land;
> How happy does our nation stand! [91]

Nationalist diction was not inappropriate to Universalist hymns.
Wholehearted support for the American Republic was the natural
secular expression of a creed which could recognize no distinction
between "Gospel liberty" and Republican democracy. Accordingly, Universalists were emphatic in their support for the war,
praying for its success and lending their physical efforts for its
advancement.[92]

This support was vividly individualized in the person of Hosea
Ballou. On the national fast day in 1812, he preached to his congregation in Portsmouth, New Hampshire, from a seemingly
pacific text: "If my kingdom were of this world, then would my
servants fight." According to his exposition, however, the text
was virtually an endorsement of America's war, an implicit recognition that worldly kingdoms must indeed fight at times. Like
Esther, Americans had gone to war for the safety of their brethren on the frontier. Like Gideon, they fought to protect lawful
commerce. Like David, they fought to preserve national existence
itself. Even Abraham had resorted to warfare when Lot was
"impressed" by pagan banditti, whom British sea captains now

emulated.[93] It was no accident that Ballou's theological enemies, those minions of the "scarlet colored beast," were also the antiwar clergy. "Declaimers against the constituted authorities," he declared, were lost to the direction of the New Testament, which forbade rebellion against magistrates.[94] Like the Baptist Daniel Merrill and the Methodist Billy Hibbard, Ballou saw clearly that the opponents of the war were also the enemies of true religion.

After Ballou's sermon was noticed by partisan editors, "a bitter spirit became manifested toward me," because of which he accepted an invitation from the Universalists of Salem to serve as their pastor. His son recalled that Ballou never failed to evince his patriotism while always avoiding party politics.[95] The seeming inconsistency between a nonpartisan profession and an openly Republican practice was not real. For his martial attitude was the necessary complement to a religious creed which could scarcely have survived in a separated nation of New England—a creed which had good reason to sing the hymn of Abner Kneeland:

> Our rulers, may they all be blest,
>   And ruled subject be;
> While nought but vice our laws suppress,
>   The government is free.[96]

When peace was finally restored, another contributor to the Universalist hymnal assured his congregation that friends of religion had special cause for joy. Not only had politicians despaired of the Republic, said Edward Turner, but divines had doubted the viability of American religion because it lacked the force of law and penal coercion. They feared that the distractions of war would "break the hold which men have upon virtue and piety, if not strengthened by human power." [97] In a sense, the War of 1812 had vindicated not only Republican institutions but also Universalism's belief in the feasibility of unfettered religion.

Another writer of wartime hymns was Elder Abner Jones of the Christian Connection. His verses, inspired by the British blockade of Portsmouth, New Hampshire, offered "Thanks to the Lord, thou God of war, for thy protecting arm" and evinced a personal certainty that heaven favored his country's cause.[98] It was a persuasion natural to a man deeply involved in a brand of radical Christian republicanism that was one of the most powerful religious movements in American history—the rise and spread of heterogeneous elements that many years later would become the Disciples of Christ.

The new denomination was never meant to be one. Its disparate components originated at different times for varied reasons. A small group of western Presbyterian ministers, unwilling to submit to their synod's standards of doctrinal purity, formed in 1804 a separate Springfield presbytery, which thereupon dissolved itself as a sign of its rejection of sectarian divisions. Much the same end was reached by the Campbells, father and son, in their secession from the Associate church in 1811 to form the nucleus of the Disciples or Campbellites, as their opponents called them. Late in the eighteenth century, a small group of Methodists in Virginia and North Carolina, protesting the power of their church's episcopacy, sought a purer form of religion under the leadership of James O'Kelly. They assumed the name of Republican Methodists, which well expressed their democratic attitudes in both religion and politics. New England experienced a similar movement headed by Abner Jones and Elias Smith, who also renounced all denominational titles to subsume the Church's shameful divisions under the generic name of "Christian."

A union among some of these elements was not achieved until 1832. During the War of 1812, they had nothing in common in the way of organization but did share their most important tenet, a belief in the unity of Christians through the subordination of theological disagreements. They also shared a devotion to American democracy, incorporating its principles into their church structure. These "nondenominations" were in a way the logical application of democratic individualism to traditional Christianity. An early historian of what was eventually called the Christian church caught the spirit of the incipient movement when he described O'Kelly's dissident Methodists. They were "a new constellation of Republicanism" beaming in the southern sky, "and the Bible, God's Holy Book, was reflected from each individual star." [99]

The new religious units were widely reprobated. Their opponents charged that, while reducing religion to the lowest common denominator, they reduced it to nothing at all: no doctrines, no ministry, and little morality. It was not until long after the War of 1812 that the new faith's flourishing membership and tremendous evangelical accomplishments won the begrudging recognition of older churches. During the war, however, orthodox hostility was returned blow for blow by the *Herald of Gospel Liberty*, the crusading paper of Elias Smith. Smith was by no means representative of his religious brethren. Few of them could have been so vituperative, and none had his control of a major vehicle of public persuasion. Moreover, the individualism of the Christian Connection made it impossible for anyone to speak with denominational authority. The *Herald*, then, was no official publication. Smith spoke not for a sect but for a type, for the religionists at the very periphery of society's norms.

As the champion of what was considered, quite literally, the lunatic fringe of his day, Smith achieved a remarkable circulation for his ideas. The *Herald* originated many items that won great popularity with Republican papers, especially when Smith aimed his pen against British religion and the Anglican church.[100] The acceptance of this theological pariah by the prowar press is not surprising. As the historian of the church explained, "In almost any other country, the Christian religion would have been opposed to the political form of government; but, in this, it was synonymous with it." [101] The claim seems not at all pretentious when substantiated by the editorial record of Smith's *Herald*.

Like so many sectarians, Smith admired President Madison for his long advocacy of religious freedom and his scrupulous adherence to the separation of church and state. A tract printed at the office of the *Herald* in 1811 entitled *Madison and Religion* was practically a premature campaign document for the president's reelection.[102] Smith and his readers would have supported Madison's war under any conditions; but given the opportunity to do so and simultaneously be revenged on the antiwar clergy, the *Herald* responded to the crisis with an almost fanatic patriotism. Smithites railed against the false prophets who longed for "the leeks and onions of monarchy" and who vexed the souls of patriots "as much as Lot was vexed among the Sodomites." [103] Because the Christian Connection subscribed to that interpreta-

tion of history in which the role of Babylon was shared by Rome,
Britain, and New England, Smith was not surprised by the alliance
between Britain, her friends in America, and the pope. The
Herald sarcastically urged Congregationalists to fellowship with
the Catholics of Boston, damned individual ministers by name, and
awaited a Republican Armageddon.[104] Even the war's end could
not abate Smith's ire. For the British government had always
persecuted Christ's church; and only "when such governments
are destroyed, then, and not till then, will the world be at rest,
and wars cease to the ends of the earth." [105]

When Smith retired as editor of the *Herald*, his valedictory
summed up the faith of unnumbered nameless sectarians, who
knew the war had been a Christian conflict:

> To conclude—the things we have contended for, and pub-
> lished—viz: one God—one Mediator—one law-giver—one per-
> fect law of Liberty—one name for the children of God, to the
> exclusion of all sectarian names—A republican government,
> free from religious establishments and state clergy . . . the
> reign of Christ on earth one thousand years—the new heavens
> and earth at last.[106]

Expecting such a glorious outcome, Smith might have been forgiven the excesses of his wartime crusade. For his expectations
were by no means eccentric but were shared by other Republican
believers, among whom were the Freewill Baptists or, as they
preferred to be called, the United Churches of Christ.

The Freewillers' creed was somewhat akin to the beliefs of
Elias Smith, and Abner Jones accepted ordination at their
hands.[107] Their Arminian version of the Baptist faith made them
"the scum of the earth, the filth of creation" in the eyes of respectable Christians.[108] Along with the followers of Hosea Ballou
and Elias Smith, they were the "illiterate ministers" whom the
Theological Society of Maine charged with "subverting the Gospel of Christ, and leading immortal souls to destruction." [109] They
replied in kind, calling their opponents "Gog and Magog, viz. the
enemies of Liberty and Equality," dismissing the critics of their
revivals as "hireling priests, of all denominations." [110]

The coming of war surcharged this existing denominational

hatred with political antagonism. The Freewillers naturally would rally to defend "our beloved America, hitherto the Eden of the whole world, and an asylum for the oppressed," just as they naturally considered antiwar preachers public sinners for wickedly reviling the government. They were confident, after all, that the power which had delivered the first colonists from British persecution and later had established American independence under the best rule in human history would still protect the chosen people from their enemies, "who shall flee before us seven ways." [111]

Notions of a divinely assured victory were soon dispelled by the misfortunes of war, but the pattern of interchurch antipathy was not weakened by the worsening crisis. On the contrary, it was reinforced as the prowar churches again revealed the American symbiosis of politics and religion. Just as patriotism could be strengthened by one's faith, so too denominational ire could be inflamed by the knowledge that one's theological enemies were base traitors. Although dissension on the home front never developed into widespread violence, America's churches did enter into a veritable civil war, a conflict made all the more bitter because God seemed to be on everyone's side.

5 ✠ TERTIUM QUIDS

Our divine Master has commanded his ministers to be wise as serpents, and harmless as doves: and no ministers, that he has ever sent, have had more need than we of such prudence and innocency. We have to contend, not only with all the impediments and difficulties common to those who preach the Gospel; but, unhappily, with the prejudices of our Christian brethren, of other denominations.

Alexander Griswold, September 28, 1814

If wartime relations among America's churches formed a complex pattern of common goals, conflicting interests, and mutual antipathies, there were yet a few pieces to the pattern which fit conveniently into neither the prowar nor the antiwar category. A separate classification is due the Roman Catholic church, the Protestant Episcopal church, and the Society of Friends; for those denominations did not so much act as they were acted upon. That is, the war brought them not opportunities but challenges, because the position of each of them was vulnerable and was made more so by the state of war. They illustrated how disrepute in religious matters could have a political import and how America's churches failed or prospered according to their ability to harmonize private values and national goals. Their efforts to achieve that harmony were made both more necessary and more difficult by a climate of public opinion especially sensitive to unpatriotic disaffection.

Most vulnerable was Roman Catholicism, a hothouse exotic in Protestantism's most flourishing garden. The church was not only marked with the sign of the beast foretold in Revelation but was also handicapped by papal involvement in the Napoleonic wars, for Pius VII had been imprisoned for refusing to cooperate with the French emperor's ambitions. The gravity of the crisis was somewhat lessened in the United States by the limited autonomy which had developed in the American church because of usual difficulties in maintaining transatlantic direction. The American bishops issued a joint pastoral reaffirming their allegiance to papal authority in all ecclesiastical affairs and ordering prayers for the captive pontiff,[1] and there the matter rested until the force of British arms liberated Pius in the general restoration of "legitimate sovereigns." Faced with problems of such magnitude, the church in America successfully adapted to its awkward position. This was best demonstrated not by positive accomplishments but by the very absence of damaging controversy.

Official ecclesiastical involvement in wartime affairs was minimal. Archbishop John Carroll of Baltimore answered Madison's fast day message with a directive to the clergy for appropriate observances. At a later date he ordered Te Deums sung for the pope's deliverance, as did Bishop Benedict Flaget in Kentucky and Boston's Bishop Jean Cheverus, who ordered his cathedral illuminated as part of the city's grand celebration of the allied victory in Europe.[2] He saw in this final defeat of the French Revolution, which had driven him from his homeland, "the triumph of religion and of the church, and wished to demonstrate the joy which interests so dear must excite in every Christian heart."[3] The problem was that, to supporters of the war against Britain, the allied triumph and the freeing of Pius VII excited very little joy.

The Te Deums were unfortunately coincident with Federalist rejoicing at Napoleon's defeat, and the country's most hated anti-war editor applauded the Catholic service in Georgetown's Trinity Church. "This interesting solemnity," announced the *Federal Republican,* was ordered "in grateful acknowledgement for the special mercies vouchsafed by Almighty God to the Catholic world, by the restoration of the Sovereign Pontiff to the free exercise of his spiritual power and prerogatives."[4] To most American Protestants, papal restoration was abominable; and to all Republicans, any celebration of British victory was loathsome.

Even so, Republicans engaged in no anti-Catholic campaigns. Their reaction to religious services for the pope's liberation consisted of short references to Te Deums as shameful political spectacles.[5] Rarely was there any suggestion that participants in the Catholic religious festivals were not loyal citizens; nor were the celebrating Catholic bishops, who were so vulnerable to criticism as agents of the Man of Sin, threatened and damned as were the Congregationalist ministers who presided at similar religious observances. Indeed, the Catholic church in the United States enjoyed a strange immunity from political embarrassment during the war.

There is no simple explanation for that immunity. Certainly the church's leadership was partly responsible. Carroll's careful avoidance of controversy was typical. Republicans might have guessed his Federalist sympathies, for his family's politics were well known. They could not, however, fault his nonpartisan behavior. In the late summer of 1812, at a time when the *National Intelligencer* was ranting at the disloyal clergymen who had subverted the presidential fast day, that organ of the administration printed only two of all the resolutions and proclamations in observance of the day—the president's and Bishop Carroll's. The latter directed observance of the day by all the faithful, who "ought to feel an equal interest in the welfare of these United States, during the awful crisis now hanging over them." [6] On the national fast the next year, Carroll again ordered services, and his directions for the occasion implicitly defended Madison's fast proclamation from those antiwar critics who thought it an irreligious and deistic document. "With singular propriety" the president had called attention to the need to seek divine aid and protection,[7] and Carroll plainly approved of his much-maligned reasoning.

Carroll's colleagues in the episcopacy also conducted themselves with prudence. Like the Methodist prelate Asbury, Bishop Flaget prayed over military forces in the West before their departure for battle.[8] Bishop Cheverus himself pushed a wheelbarrow in the hurried building of fortifications at Boston. He had little worry about hostile neighbors; for in spite of his popery, he was one of the most respectable clergymen in New England, whose sermons were attended and praised by the religious and political leader-

ship of Puritan Boston.[9] The administrator apostolic of New
Orleans, William DuBourg, ordered prayers in the city's churches
to seek protection "while our brave warriors, led on by the Hero
of the Floridas, prepare to defend our altars and firesides against
foreign invasion." [10] The city's Ursuline nuns informed the hero
of their special prayers for his success, and General Andrew
Jackson must have approved of their pious assistance. After his
rout of the British invaders, he asked DuBourg to arrange a religious celebration of the event, attended the church services, and
was met at the door by his Catholic host, whose address to the
victor won applause from Republican editors.[11]

But the ecclesiastical superior of the American bishops, Pius
VII, was not immune to the venom of war-hawk journalists, who
were able to employ apocalyptic rhetoric much better than their
Federalist opponents. Republicans, after all, were fighting the
pope's British allies and could therefore take greater political advantage from traditional hatred of Jesuits, the Inquisition, and all
of Rome's infamies. The subjects of their attacks, however, were
always the institutions of European Catholicism. They abused
neither the leaders nor the creed of the American church. Any
incipient nativism was confined to an occasional Federalist orator
like Elijah Parish, who thought it fitting that the popish city of
Baltimore was the scene of a Republican massacre, or Arthur
Stansbury, who attributed the war in part to America's impiety
for allowing the "mother of abominations" to have five churches
in one city and sixteen thousand members in another.[12] Nothing of
this nature appeared in Republican papers, in which articles concerning Catholicism spoke as if only an accidental connection
existed between the church in America and the *bête noire* of
Protestant Christianity.

The church's relatively untroubled peace was not only evidence
of the tactfulness of its leaders. It also showed good sense among
Republican spokesmen, who avoided alienating the handful of
Catholic voters and the very useful Irish Catholic soldiers. Irish-
Americans approved of the war for reasons which require no
explanation. Half a year before the fighting began, one of their
number outlined a plan which was to be repeated for decades after
the war itself was a memory:

> Let not the eternal fiat of the humiliation of Ireland be pro-
> claimed by a conquering enemy, on the plains of Columbia—
> rather let the martial, the loyal, the zealous patriotism of Amer-
> icans and Irishmen proclaim, in the emancipated capital of
> Canada, that Ireland, like America, deserves and must be free,
> sovereign, and independent.[13]

When Republican papers bewailed the suffering of oppressed Ireland, it was impossible to separate the political issue from the
religious controversy of Catholic emancipation which then raged
in Britain. As one Irish-American editor pointed out, "We are
well aware that the distinguishing of the people into religious
classes is not congenial with republicanism, and we regret the
impossibility of reporting Irish affairs distinct from its religious
history. A vicious system of government has united the church
and state." [14]

It was something of a dogma in the antiwar creed that the
supposedly impressed American seamen were really Irish deserters
fleeing their rightful sovereign. Federalists never tired of blaming
the war on Irish renegades, who found it profitable to set up
Republican papers far away from the arm of British justice. When
the *Boston Patriot* urged Catholics in Ireland to take advantage of
Britain's distress, the editor's poetic conclusion was more likely to
terrify Protestant Federalists than to eliminate the British church
establishment. If armed uprising failed, he advised, they must pray
to their God,

> to *transplant* the little island of Hibernia to one of the American
> LAKES, under the benign influence of a free government, where
> the *Jew, Baptist, Dissenter, Catholic* and ALL *who believe in*
> GOD, (even the *church* and *king priests*) equally enjoy the
> rights of conscience, and the protection of government, and all
> the honors of the state.[15]

A more blatant appeal to the religious loyalties of American
Irishmen was made by the *New Hampshire Patriot*, which early
in the war published an address to "the Sons of Hibernia." With
a bold directness the author was identified as "D. C., a Catholic
lieutenant in 16th Regiment, U.S. infantry." No persecution, he

reminded his fellow Catholics, trampled them in the dust; no disqualifying law harried any sect; no church establishment plundered the labor of citizens in America. "You serve your God after the custom of your fathers," Irishmen were told, "or in the manner most congenial to your understanding and feelings." [16] If this denominationally aimed recruiting drive did not violate Madison's scruples concerning the separation of church and state, it certainly testified to a mutual adaptation of political interests and religious values in time of crisis.

The most important Republican paper in Baltimore, principal city of American Catholicism, naturally made an even greater adaptation to a political opportunity. *Niles' Weekly Register* pointed to a subtle sign of British influence in some parts of the country. "How does the blood recoil when a *Roman Catholic* is mentioned!" it declared, "What evil hath *he* done to us? Why attach terror to *his* religion? . . . Are not the *Catholics* men like ourselves; and in Maryland, and some other states, among the very best of our citizens?" [17] Anti-Catholic feeling, the editor explained, was "set in motion by rosy guilded priests and prostituted statesmen to keep the machine of monarchy a-going." Soon the same editor disclaimed the use of epithets like "whore of Babylon" to refer to the pope, "against whose religion *I* prefer no censure, further than it is, like that of *England,* connected with the state." [18] A Presbyterian war hawk, John Giles of Newburyport, made an even greater concession. He himself was a refugee from British rule and knew that the papacy was not Europe's only persecutor. It was law-support, not doctrine, which made a religion corrupt; for "here in America, a Catholic priest is a good citizen, a good character, and a good neighbor." [19] At a time when much of the American religious community was awaiting the imminent destruction of the Man of Sin and all his minions in the Roman church, Giles's statement was practically heretical. But Republicans could afford a little heresy to keep the support of American Catholics and to honor their party's general commitment to religious liberty. Perhaps there was at least a little truth to the claim that the most patriotic Christians in Boston were the Catholics of that city,[20] who thus proved the wisdom of Republican tolerance.

The many manifestations by Republican spokesmen of their willingness to accept domestic Catholicism as a reputable religion provide only indirect evidence of the adaptation of the church to its republican environment. The most important evidence was negative: the lack of editorial campaigns against an alien church, a minimum of political embarrassment, a remarkable disinclination among the clerical advocates of either party to associate the flock of John Carroll with its doomed leaders across the ocean. The course of European Catholicism, then, had little ill effect upon the church in America. One scholar has even suggested that the papacy's misfortunes were actually to the advantage of the American church, which was left on its own to deal with difficult problems involving the laity's control of property and authority over the clergy. Foreign direction could only have made those problems more complicated or insolvable.[21] As it was, the restoration of Pius VII proved to be a mixed blessing. For as soon as ecclesiastical contact across the Atlantic was renewed and Europeans again managed the church in America, a Tory subject of King George was made bishop of New York City.[22] American Catholics had no part in that appointment. As their wartime performance had shown, they were too much in harmony with the Republic's faith to be involved in such a fiasco.

Like Roman Catholicism, the Protestant Episcopal church was handicapped during the war. The very system of episcopacy was feared by many denominations, which considered that hierarchical structure a mark of ecclesiastical corruption. The titles and ceremony attendant upon an episcopal organization made it easy for opponents of the church to accuse it of aristocracy and monarchism. These accusations, of course, were tied to others based on historical enmities. The struggle immediately after the Revolution for disestablishment of the former Anglican church left deep impressions on the American religious psyche. The part played in that struggle by the Baptists and Presbyterians, for example, was proudly remembered by them and was often recounted for the edification of their membership. For the Baptists, the disestablishment movement had been one of their finest hours; and its veterans, like old John Leland, became almost folk heroes for their contributions to it.[23] Even after the War of 1812, when a Virginian Presbyterian defended his church from charges that it was seeking governmental sponsorship, the better part of his argument was a recounting of Presbyterian efforts in the disestablishment campaign of the last century.[24] The success of that campaign was an accomplishment in which almost all American Christians, whatever their internecine hostilities, could take satisfaction. When the Protestant Episcopal church in the United States was organized free of British jurisdiction, independent though it was and loyal though its members were, its ecclesiastical organization and transatlantic theological leanings made it vulnerable in times of controversy. Writing about the trials of his church during the American Revolution, Bishop William White made an observation which was applicable as well to the church's situation during the second war with Britain: "It is well known, that religious opinion has been often made by circumstances, the test and the instrument of a political party; when the views of the party had not any more natural connexion with the opinion, than with its opposite." [25] The Reverend William Wilmer of Alexandria testified to the wartime applicability of White's comment. In a letter to Richard Moore, his future bishop, Wilmer described the church in Virginia, which

> is in a very peculiar situation. Its having been once the established Church, the prevalence and virulence of other denominations, the sequestration of its glebes, the irregularity of the lives of its ministers, the various political causes have combined to swell high the tide of public opinion and indeed odium against her public form of service, her surplices, and all the paraphernalia of clerical costume.[26]

An anonymous pamphleteer of the Christian Connection demonstrated the sectarian use of political arguments against the Protestant Episcopal church. Its members were the supporters of "Sedition, Alien, Stamp Laws, Internal Taxation, Standing Armies, a large Navy, and the midnight Judges." "This is not all," he cautioned, "many of the Episcopalians in America take a malevolent pleasure in manifesting their hatred to our government, and to the men who zealously support it." [27] The most prominent clerical champion of the War of 1812, Alexander McLeod, was also one of the great bishop-baiters of his day; and his famous *Scriptural View* of the war was as much a Presbyterian tract against episcopacy as it was a patriotic defense of his country. Even the Swedenborgian *Halcyon Luminary* charged that Episcopalian clergymen were insufficiently attached to their country's welfare; for they recommended and circulated the *Christian Observer*, which was written and directed "by men of the English church and government, who send out fleets and armies to kill American citizens and burn their cities, because they will not permit their property to be robbed, and their people seized for military slavery." [28]

The eagerness with which such themes were exploited by many Republican newspapers is difficult to exaggerate. This was in addition to their propaganda against the Church of England, designed to influence sectarians who had suffered under that church. When the Federalist governor of Massachusetts called Great Britain the bulwark of the Christian religion, a Republican journalist in Vermont reminded Baptists and Quakers that the bulwark would protect no one but Episcopalians and Congregationalists, the only Americans who had ever desired state support of their religion.[29] Even the *National Intelligencer*, which usually avoided denominational controversy, insisted that Britain could be a religious bulwark only if New Englanders were all Episcopalians, yearning after their former pomp and lost clergy fees.[30] The *New Hampshire Patriot* early in the war employed a similar theme and continued it throughout the conflict, warning that British victory would establish an American Episcopal church: "No Congregationalist, Presbyterian, Baptist, Methodist, Universalian, or Free Willer, can so much as be a selectman in any Town. But still they must all pay one tenth of all their produce to satisfy the demands of the voracious national priests." [31] Every fault of the Anglican church—its persecutions, corruptions, and impiety—was easily applied to the Protestant Episcopal church in a clear case of guilt-by-association. Indeed, editorial vituperation of the English church often equaled the scathing attacks on papal religion. Throughout the ordeal, however, American Episcopacy performed with masterful tact.

In his charge to the clergy for 1814, Alexander Griswold, bishop of the eastern diocese, addressed himself to the dilemma. The "prejudice of our Christian brethren" concerning the nature of Episcopalian doctrines, he lamented, prevailed in most eastern states. Christ commanded his ministers to be as wise as serpents and as harmless as doves; "and no ministers, that he has ever sent, have had more need than we of such *prudence* and *innocency*." [32] Unfortunately, not all of Griswold's subordinates heeded that exhortation.

During the troubled war years, the official ranks of the church were most severely disarranged by the pulpit orations of John Gardiner, regular presiding officer of the Massachusetts Convention and pastor of the most prestigious congregation in the state. His parish numbered fully twice as many communicants as its nearest rival; and together with James Lloyd, the antiwar senator from Massachusetts, Gardiner represented his state in the General Convention of 1814 at Philadelphia. [33] His denunciations of the war were remarkable even among the antiwar clergy. He could threaten civil war and quote Juvenal, Cowper, Burke, and Shakespeare in the same sermons. His wartime fast sermons won him exceptional notoriety, especially for his declaration of July 23, 1812: "The union has long since been virtually dissolved, and it is full time that this portion of the *disunited* states should take care of itself." [34] On another occasion, he avowed that New England had nothing to lose by secession but Jefferson, Madison, Albert Gallatin, and Felix Grundy. [35] Gardiner was not alone in his partisanship. James Abercrombie, an Episcopal clergyman in Philadelphia, was involved in disputes with the city's Republican editors because of his opposition to the war. [36] Samuel Jarvis too used his pulpit to register disapproval of the president's policies. [37] The public involvement of these ministers in the politics of dissent was, however, directly contrary to the consistent prudence of their church's governing structure.

Gardiner's superior, Bishop Griswold, more accurately reflected the public position of the church. After Griswold's death, one of his clergy testified to the immense difference between the bishop and his most famous subordinate. They were like men of two different worlds, the cleric recalled; their personalities, like their habits of dress and modes of preaching, were at the extremes of forthright simplicity and labored elegance.[38] In the first year of war, one member of Griswold's flock angrily renounced his life-long affiliation with the church because of the clergy's false praise for British morality. The parishioner submitted his resolution to Griswold with the understanding that the action would be re-considered if the good bishop would convince him of its impro-priety.[39] The respect which even an angry patriot evinced for his bishop is perhaps explained by Griswold's own reminiscences. From his youth, he admitted, he had been as decided in his opin-ions as other men; but he early resolved to be "of no party in politics, or in sectarianism. In regard to the former," he added,

> it is, in my judgment, better for the clergy, and for their parishes, and indeed for their country, that they should leave civil government and the management of public temporal con-cerns to the laity. The history of the world well shews that politics and state affairs have seldom been well managed in the hands of priests.[40]

No Universalist or Baptist could have spoken more effectively on the subject. The extent to which Griswold followed his own ad-vice was indicated by the freedom from controversy which he enjoyed throughout the war.

Griswold's colleague in South Carolina, Bishop Theodore Dehon, also demonstrated the Church's adaptation to its Ameri-can environment. He was the embodiment of the socially respect-able Episcopal church in the South. On his way to the General Convention of 1814, he visited Jefferson and President Madison, whose aged mother was still devout in the bishop's faith. The Reverend Christopher Gadsden, his friend and traveling com-panion, recalled the bishop's displeasure with wartime dissension: "In the possibility of a separation of the union he had the solici-tude of a TRUE PATRIOT." [41] Gadsden himself was a fellow stu-dent with John Calhoun at Yale, and their intimate friendship continued until the latter's death.[42] Both Dehon and Gadsden represented their church more accurately than did their Boston colleague, John Gardiner, who attributed the war's carnage to "southern patriots, the slave-holding declaimers in favour of the rights of man." [43]

One of those "southern patriots" was the Reverend Philip Mathews of South Carolina, whose Independence Day oration in 1813 equaled Gardiner's sermons in vehemence. Mathews could not comprehend the clerical treason rampant in the country. He was sure that Elijah Parish was a maniac, perfectly in character with the church, government, and royal family of Great Britain. John Gardiner was "this clerical merryandrew," "this petty adventurer," "more devoted to the turf, than to the altar." Gardiner, it seems, had visited South Carolina, had been well entertained there, and was now repaying his fellow churchmen with invective. Mathews retaliated by suggesting that the Bostonian's sedition had placed him beyond the protection of the law.[44] His oration to that effect was a more meaningful expression of the church's wartime political attitude than were a few antiwar sermons from New England pulpits.

The twenty-seventh convention of the Episcopal diocese of South Carolina was meeting when news of peace arrived, and a motion was made to request the bishop's appointment of a thanksgiving day. This motion was quickly amended to specify observance of a presidentially appointed day, if such an occasion should be recommended by Madison.[45] Dehon's circular to the clergy, giving detailed instructions for the observances, is enduring testimony to how fully he understood the political environment in which American religion flourished. According to his direction, the day would celebrate the special joy of South Carolina, where under the dispensation of Providence, united patriots had preserved their land from foreign invaders. The services would offer thanks to the sovereign of all events, who was pleased "to prosper the efforts of the government of these United States." [46] For the morning service, Dehon ordered the reading of the eleventh chapter of Deuteronomy and the twelfth and thirteenth chapters of Romans. The former passage exhorted the Hebrews to remember the mercies of their God, who had protected them, like the Americans, for fully forty years of wandering in search of the promised land. The second reading contained

Paul's admonition to obey the civil powers, whose authority must be from heaven. Together the two passages formed the most accurate single statement of prowar American Christianity, expressing both support for James Madison and the fervent nationalism of the Republican Canaan.

When such diverse figures as Dehon, Griswold, and Gardiner gathered at Philadelphia in May 1814 for the Church's General Convention, Bishop John Henry Hobart delivered a sermon on the occasion of Richard Moore's consecration as bishop of Virginia. His address was a general defense of the Protestant Episcopal faith, a review of the condition of the American church, and a remarkable exposition of that church's allegiance to the Republic. Without referring to the war then raging, Hobart repeatedly made clear his denomination's loyalty to American institutions. Proud of the doctrinal heritage of Anglicanism, he was careful to distinguish between the English church and the British government,

> concerning which, wise and good men, and within the knowledge of him who addresses you, correct and exemplary churchmen entertain very different opinions; and your preacher would deprecate as unsound in principle and most impolitic in its results, any connexion of our church, as a religious communion, with the principles and views of political parties.[47]

Hobart suggested that gratitude for former British assistance could best be shown by fidelity to the principles of the mother church, "so far as those principles maintain primitive faith, order and worship distinct from secular influence and local arrangements." And as if to remove all doubts as to the purpose of his sermon, Hobart asserted that the supposedly aristocratic structure of the church was, on the contrary, parallel to American constitutional government. Both possessed a unified executive authority in the office of bishop and president, a bicameral legislature, the right of judgment by one's peers, and an independent judiciary.[48] This same point—the similarity of their church government and American republicanism—was made by Presbyterians, Baptists, Methodists, and others. But in light of the vulnerable position of his church, Hobart's sermon was less a propaganda tract than a pledge of allegiance. It was treated as such by the church's only wartime periodical, the *Churchman's Magazine*. Minimal notice was given to the doctrinal aspects of the address, and greatest approval was reserved for Hobart's deprecation of political involvement on the part of ministers. The *Magazine* quoted this at great length and appended its own emphatic agreement: "Whenever a clergyman displays the views and feelings of a political partisan, his influence among those whose spiritual good should be his supreme object, will be seriously injured; and it will be well, if he does not thereby endanger the general reputation and interests of the church." [49]

Examples of this same sort of caution are easily multiplied. Hobart himself demonstrated the application of his own advice in his handling of a controversy concerning the New York City fast day in February 1814. That observance was ordered in consequence of an American defeat in upper New York and was announced by the city corporation without previous consultation with the clergy, who thereupon refused to participate. They objected to a special fast day for one particular defeat after the nation had recently observed a general fast for all the calamities of war. The ministers' notice to this effect was drawn up at a meeting chaired by Alexander McLeod, whose mere presence was itself sufficient to remove from the proceedings any stigma of antiwar sentiment. Nevertheless, several New York papers soon reported that the clerical unanimity in the controversy was not perfect, inasmuch as the meeting had not been attended by the bishop and clergy of the Protestant Episcopal church. This information, it was explained, "is given with a view to prevent the impression that they concurred in the resolutions passed at this meeting; it being their usual practice to observe *all* the days of public humiliation and thanksgiving recommended by the civil authorities." [50]

The standing committee of the church in the diocese of New Jersey demonstrated the same prudence with regard to another fast day. Some of the state's congregations, in accord with prevailing sentiment in the neighboring states of New York and Pennsylvania, had proposed to observe July 30, 1812, as a day of prayer and humiliation on account of the recent resort to arms.

The committee disapproved of this suggestion and advised "that the third Thursday in August (being the day appointed by the President of the United States) be observed for these purposes, instead of the last Thursday aforesaid." [51] This message was given to several papers in the state, and New Jersey's Episcopalians were thereby advised of their church's effort to avoid even the occasion of political dissent.

Bishop Thomas Claggett responded to the same presidential fast day by ordering church services throughout the diocese of Maryland. The scriptural readings he prescribed—the third chapter of Jonah and the fourth chapter of James—were far from martial, calling for repentance, sincere fasting, and reformation so that the country might be spared further punishment. The presidential fast of the following year gave Claggett an opportunity to demonstrate more plainly his dissociation from opponents of the war. His instructions for religious observances on September 9, 1813, seemed to take an implicit notice of the boycott of those services repeatedly proposed to residents of Maryland and the District of Columbia by an antiwar editor. "Trusting that a call thus sanctioned by God, by the Church, and by the Civil authority, will not be lightly regarded," Claggett directed parishioners to attend their local churches on the occasion.[52]

Bishop William White of Pennsylvania also had difficulty concerning a fast observance, and his reaction demonstrated the same solicitude for the public image of his church. Soon after the declaration of war, he wrote to a friend in New York, inquiring whether the "Prayer in time of war and tumult" was being used in that city's religious services. He feared that if it were not soon employed in the services of his own diocese "it will give occasion to those who seek occasion." As for his own opinions, the bishop added, the individual should submit in his conduct, if not in his judgments, "to the public voice of his country. In the prayer itself there is nothing that any can in conscience object to: and yet I confess there is something in me rendering the use of it the reluctant yielding to duty, because of the very improper views which I conceive to have occasioned the present war." [53] That White's own opposition to the war was subordinated to his regard for the social situation of his church was yet another illustration of the narrow course which American Episcopacy steered through wartime political turmoil.

In his capacity as presiding bishop of the church in the years preceding the war, White had authored the church's first two national pastorals. The second pastoral letter, that of 1811, showed deep concern at the danger that the American Episcopal succession might become extinct. The three bishops required to consecrate a new prelate had not been able to meet at the General Convention of that year. In view of the difficulties the church had experienced after the Revolution, White's letter was an understatement. "It would be extremely unpleasant," he warned, "to be under the necessity of having recourse again to the episcopacy of our mother church. Neither do we know what civil considerations might interfere, to impede reiterated recourse of this description." [54] The War of 1812 was such a "civil consideration." Fortunately, the church maintained its hierarchy and required no ecclesiastical interference from America's military enemy. More fortunately, the leadership of the church was careful to avoid political controversy, lest any association with opponents of the war make its position "extremely unpleasant."

The strongest statement of the dissociation between the Protestant Episcopal church and the Church of England was made by the General Convention of 1814. That assembly was faced with the continuing problem of its disputed title to certain lands held before the Revolution by the Anglican church in the colonies. The convention asserted its inheritance of Anglican property while insisting upon its total independence from foreign jurisdiction. Lest they take upon themselves the enemies as well as the property of Anglicanism, the delegates warned that it would be erroneous to infer "that the discipline exercised in this church, or that any proceedings therein, are at all dependent on the will of the civil or of the ecclesiastical authority of any foreign country." [55] This defensive posture was only prudent in light of the denominational hostilities which would exploit any seeming relationship between American Episcopalians and their country's military foe.

The war had a limited beneficial effect upon the church. The antiwar clergy, Federalist admirers of Great Britain, the grandchildren of Puritan saints, made some concessions to the theological respectability of Episcopacy. On the national thanksgiving day for peace, John Lathrop, venerable patriarch of the New England clergy, addressed himself to the anti-Anglican propaganda circulated by Republican journalists. "It would be unjust," he asserted, "and base, and wicked, to impute to the present inhabitants of Great Britain, the bigotry and the persecuting spirit of their great grandfathers." [56] Even the *Connecticut Evangelical Magazine*, stalwart guardian of New England's ancestral faith, made its peace with the church of Bishop Laud. It argued that Anglicanism's Thirty-nine Articles of faith would be accepted as theologically correct by most churches in New England. It was only "certain forms" and "ceremonial observances" to which the first colonists of Massachusetts had objected. American Episcopalians must have been surprised to discover that "The Episcopal Church in England is the parent church from which the present dissenters of England, and the Presbyterians and Congregational churches of New-England originated." [57] The reconciliation was remarkable. Little wonder, then, that the war's end brought a "great swelling" of the Episcopal church in Connecticut, because of an increased appreciation of its merits.[58]

The same day on which John Lathrop explained his affection for British churchmen saw Bishop Hobart turn his attention to the political state of his country. True to his past performances, Hobart emphatically disclaimed clerical involvement in political affairs. It would be, he said, "inconsistent both with my duty and my feelings" to allude to particular men or measures from the pulpit, because "general political truth alone should be inculcated from this sacred place." [59] He wished only to impress his hearers with the "general truth" that political dissension undermines a nation's happiness. American Episcopacy thereby celebrated the war's end as it had endured the conflict's domestic strife: with prudence, loyalty, and a patriotic aversion to political involvement.

Like it or not, the Society of Friends could hardly have avoided political involvement when their country went to war. Even so, they experienced less difficulty with the civil authorities during the War of 1812 than during the Revolution. Several factors contributed. Most important was the commitment, albeit inexactly defined, of the national government to freedom of religion. Then too, the devastation wrought by the second war with Britain was localized and less severe than that caused by the War of Independence; and public antipathy toward nonparticipants was correspondingly less harsh. This was especially true in light of the politically inspired pacifism of five governors in New England, which caused them to withhold their state militias from federal control. Compared with their partisan scruples, a truly religious pacifism was quite respectable. Finally, the Quakers were in powerful political company. They could hardly be treated as an inconsequential minority when their antiwar bedfellows were feared to have power sufficient to dissolve the Union.

Pacifism did provoke some retaliation by local authorities. They took everything from teaspoons to haystacks from Friends in Burlington, New Jersey.[60] In Bedford and Campbell counties, Virginian Quakers suffered similar losses: a forty-dollar watch, a two-dollar counting reel, four-dollar saddlebags, and fines of several dollars.[61] These expropriations were hardly ruthless, however, since most states allowed payment of a fine in lieu of military service. It was the refusal to conscience even that payment, connected as it was with the perpetration of war, which brought about the seizure of property. In a few instances, Quakers without goods of value were imprisoned instead of fined; but these were certainly exceptions.[62] The experience of other Quakers was probably more representative. Although William Evans claimed that the war let loose a wickedness against those who were unwilling to participate, he himself did not greatly suffer from it. Summoned to a hearing for his failure to perform militia duty, he explained his beliefs, left the courtroom, and never again heard from his judges.[63] When Elias Hicks bewailed the "encroachment of the secular powers," it was clear that his main complaint was wartime taxation.[64] Shopkeeper Isaac Martin stopped selling imported goods to avoid the war tax imposed on them. Although this hurt his business, he believed the testimony "worth suffering for, if thereby the peaceable government of the Messiah may be promoted." [65]

Not all Quakers were as faithful to their beliefs as Evans and Martin. Although the yearly meetings of the Society had long advised members against participating in the "deceitful spirit of party, by joining with political devices or associations," and warned that viewing military parades implied approval of blood-letting,[66] wartime pressures limited the observance of this advice. One Friend sadly noted that "some who assume the name of Christians" were beginning to find excuses for military measures,[67] while another lamented that some brethren in New York City had joined in the festive launching of a new frigate. It was, he complained, "an evil thing for those who profess to have a testimony against war, to give their company on such occasions." [68] Some Friends in Philadelphia participated in the city's illumination to celebrate the triumph on Lake Erie, although their acquiescence was in part explained by the activities of other celebrants, who occasionally smashed unlighted windows as retribution for the unenlightened politics of their owners. The Friends in Burlington were more steadfast; they declined to illuminate their homes even to celebrate the news that peace had been restored.[69]

Apparently the scruples of the Burlingtonians were not shared by all the members of the meeting in Alexandria, Virginia, which appointed a committee to consider the challenge presented to the faith; for it was feared some might compromise their principles in the face of military necessity.[70] Although the itinerant Joseph Hoag provoked no opposition in a southern meeting by condemning slavery, when he began his censure of the war "a number straitened themselves up, and stared me full in the face, with all the defiance of confident countenance they could; so much so, that I stopped, and thought to sit down, and give up any further attempt to preach to them." At length he reaffirmed the gospel of peace with apparent success: "the last head came down; many of them wept much." [71] Although Charles Osborn's pacifist witness met no vocal challenges when he traveled through the country in 1813, he suspected hidden disagreement in the various meetings to which he spoke. But the Spirit so attended his testimony, he thought, that advocates of the war remained silent.[72] Even a Quaker apologist, upholding his faith, expressed his concern "that the religious society of which I am a member, may look well to its conduct in all respects on this subject. My fears have been, that many are in danger of departing from the true ground of this testimony." Many Friends supported defense measures, he lamented, perhaps to protect their possessions from invading armies; and they thus opposed the purposes of "Him who regards with an equal eye all the nations of the earth." [73]

No Federalist politico could have more clearly repudiated the war; and in fact, no American Quaker was so much involved in partisan controversy as the author of that censure, Jesse Kersey. His personal dilemma illustrated the plight of the Society as a whole. Refusal to participate in military activities was condoned, tolerated, or only lightly punished by the law; but refusal to forswear political action in support of the Federalist party provoked a vindictive fury among Republicans.

When a Friend early in the war rebuked his brethren "who imbibe the spirit of political parties," he had good reason to warn that the faithful "should dwell alone, and not be reckoned among the nations." [74] His fellows did not always heed that advice, and the consequences were often unpleasant. When the Society's Annual Assembly in New England urged Congress to end the war on religious grounds, its petition unfortunately sounded much like innumerable statements drawn up by men who made no claim to pacifism.[75] And whether their motives were moral or partisan, Quaker devotion to peace often seemed indistinguishable from Federalist sympathy for Great Britain. An extreme example was provided by the encounter between a British blockade vessel and a band of Nantucket merchants, who informed the enemy that they were Quakers,

> and of the description of Pease makers and have not at any period been enemies to Great Britain and her dependencies, neither have we in any point injured her subjects. In consequence we feel imboldened to solicit thy lenity towards the Inhabitance, being perswaided that the well informed and most correct part of the Inhabitance are solicitous and ever have been for Pease with G. Britain.

Their neutrality was respected by neither Republicans nor the enemy officer, who informed his petitioners that he was "of the

description of pease breakers called Sailors" and would demand
supplies from them because the sloop *Mariner* was a dependency
of Great Britain.[76]

Even though the enterprising merchants of Nantucket may not
have been representative of all American Quakers, their somewhat unpatriotic attitude must have been sufficiently common to
outrage martial editors. If Republicans early in the war really
believed that Quakers would rally to Madison as a champion of
religious freedom and would scorn the Federalist admirers of
William Penn's persecutors,[77] they were soon disappointed. It was
only natural that pacifists would use what little power they had,
their votes, to end the fighting, even if this aligned them with one
party to the outrage of the other. An angry Republican went so
far as to blame the war itself on the Quakers, who had opposed
Jefferson's peaceful embargo and now consorted with those who
would rend apart the Union. "How will you answer to our country," he asked them, "your consciences or your God, for the ruin
and distress brought upon your fellow-citizens and yourselves,
by your blindness and obstinacy?" [78] A propagandist in Maine,
invoking the same specter of civil war, praised Quaker principles
but accused the Society of betraying them: "If you in all cases
excite the animosity of one party, by uniformly appearing at the
polls, and perseveringly opposing them; how can you in times
of ruin, bloodshed and conflagration (which many men think at
hand) expect to be exempted from the common calamity." [79] A
Maryland wit urged the clergy of Baltimore to preach on the text
of Jer. 48 : 10 and added satirically, "The Society of Friends are
also requested to take the text into their consideration." [80] The
lines spoke for themselves: "Cursed be he that doeth the work of
the Lord deceitfully, and cursed be he that keepeth back his sword
from blood." Another Baltimorean lauded his fellow citizens for
their fervent observance of the national fast in January 1815 and
claimed there was "but a single class of beings in our community,
who did not observe the day as a *holy one;* and that class do nothing like other, or, as they please to say, 'like the world's people.' " [81]

Anti-Quaker arguments, whether mild or bitter, had one common denominator. They were notable for what they did not say.

There seems to have been no serious objections to the principle of pacifism, nor was the supremacy of individual religious beliefs questioned. Whatever hardships Quakers may have feared or actually endured, Republican editors faulted them not for their faith but for their political activities. An exception might be made in the case of a letter from "an aged Quaker" printed by the *National Intelligencer*, asserting that "nothing but groveling enthusiasm, treachery or cowardice, could dissuade American freemen at this time, whatever might be their religious creed, from arming against the Prince Regent." [82] But this was apparently not an editorial opinion, and the administration's newspaper did not return to the theme. For there were numerous Federalist editors all too ready to cast Madison in the role of persecutor and to champion anyone who opposed the war for any reason.

In the *Federal Republican*, for example, Alexander Hanson indignantly, and perhaps accurately, called the aged Quaker's letter "a remarkable and barefaced example of the imposition which is attempted to be practiced upon the ignorant and incredulous," an insult to both the public and "that reputable society." [83] Widely reprinted in the Federalist press was a speech by Joseph Lewis, one of Virginia's three antiwar congressmen, who criticized militia laws forcing Quakers and Mennonites into service or confiscating their property in fines.[84] During the presidential campaign of 1812, a Clintonian paper in Quaker Pennsylvania went so far as to publish recent correspondence between English Friends and the prince regent, who assured his pacifist subjects of his continued protection and expressed his hope for peace as soon as Yankee belligerence subsided.[85] Even on the frontier the *Ohio Federalist* could show support for Quaker scruples by publishing a declaration of the Philadelphia meeting, which a Republican editor had recently accused of treason. Although the beleaguered Friends insisted that "subjects of a political nature make no part of the deliberations of our religious assemblies," their pacifist statements could by chance provide antiwar propaganda for Federalist journalists, who clearly had other than altruistic reasons for their interest.[86] The *Federal Republican*, for example, charged that Pennsylvania's Quakers, had they voted according to their religious beliefs, could have kept their state's congressional delegation from casting eighteen votes for war.[87] And when the same paper published in 1813 a Quaker petition to the Virginian legislature defending the practice of pacifism, readers might have noticed that the document had been presented three years previous and that it was now resurrected not to defend religious liberty but to berate the federal government.[88] In that way it typified Federalism's newly developed concern for the rights of conscientious objectors.

Quaker opposition to the war, then, became propaganda material for both parties. This was evident in what was probably the most heated controversy involving the Society, occurring in the Quaker heartland of Chester County, Pennsylvania, where the *Downington American Republican* made Quaker-baiting a regular part of the news coverage. From the first months of the war until well after its end, it attacked Friends for alleged hypocrisy and sedition but never challenged the right to practice pacifism. Doctrine, however, had little to do with the membership of prominent Friends in the Washington Benevolent Society. That association's charitable activities naturally interested humanitarians, but its scarcely concealed Federalism made it a suspiciously partisan fellowship for the county's pacifists; and General Washington was a strangely martial hero for the disciples of George Fox. The inconsistency was "too palpable. No rhapsody of blackguardism and nauceating and worn-out epithets can hide it." [89] Matters worsened when Jesse Kersey led a delegation to the capital city, called on Madison to end the fighting, and noted that the president "seemed to feel the weight of my concern for the return of peace to our land." [90] Republicans told a different story. According to their version, Madison asked whether any of the delegation had voted in the last election, dismissed all those who had done so, and allowed the others to confer with him, inasmuch as they were truly bound to avoid partisanship. Which of the reports was more accurate is a moot point, but the *American Republican* discussed the encounter in a way that epitomized all its anti-Quaker tirades: it objected to the Friends' partisan involvement without challenging their pacific testimony. The local Federalist newspaper of course hurried to defend the political activities as well as the religious profession of the Society.[91] Unfortunately for the Society, its political enemies were as numerous

as its theological foes, while its political defenders objected not so
much to war as to a war against Britain.

The Quakers' wartime witness may have served them well after
the Peace of Ghent. When the *Connecticut Evangelical Magazine*,
faced with the dissolution of its millennial prospects, buried its
enthusiasm for the Hartford Convention under a stream of pacifist articles, the Quakers won a new respect from their traditional
opponents in New England. The Friends were, after all, proof
that a warless world was possible; and they were expected to take
a major part in recently devised programs for international
peace.[92] Even Jedidiah Morse and Elijah Parish joined in the
reconciliation. When a third edition of their *Compendious History of New England* appeared in 1820, like most new editions of
the period it was largely a verbatim reprint of earlier versions.
Its few changes were significant. A revised history of the Reformation was prefixed, for the three-hundredth anniversary of
Luther's revolt had recently been celebrated. A new section was
added to include New Jersey and New York, states which now
seemed godly and respectable enough to be linked to New England, especially when compared with the South and West. Ex-
planatory passages were inserted to make clear that the settlers
of New England, unlike frontiersmen of the nineteenth century,
had purchased, not stolen, the Indians' land. Most important,
every section dealing with the early American Quakers was substantially revised. No longer did the authors justify the punishments inflicted on early Friends because of their crude and pro-
fane disruption of the social order.[93] They instead substituted
pleas for understanding the fathers of New England, whose
punitive measures, if harsh, were always sincere. Morse and
Parish were in part reacting to wartime mockery of New England's religious traditions; for more than a few Republican ministers, orators, and editors had ridiculed the land of witch trials,
blue laws, and Quaker-whippings. The crimes of Puritanism had
become standard ammunition in attacking Federalist leaders. If the
revised edition of the *Compendious History* recorded the effects
of the War of 1812 upon the beliefs of its authors, then the
principal change wrought upon their theology was a new appreciation of the Quakers' ancient testimony to peace.

Just as the war confronted Catholics, Episcopalians, and

Quakers with certain challenges, which they met with varying success, so too in each case political partisans discovered corresponding opportunities, which they exploited with diverse results. This was basic to the American social equation. Just as theological matters could be politicized, so too the getting and keeping of civil power could become a moral endeavor. The entire process was apt to turn opponents into sinners, elections into crusades, and to suffuse wartime politics with that righteous fervor more fittingly characteristic of conviction, awakening, and conversion to truth.

EPILOGUE

After a quarter of a century of violent commotion among the nations, universal peace ensued, which has been of longer duration than any other that has existed since the commencement of the Christian era. God was pleased before the close of those troublous times to pour out his Spirit upon ministers, churches, and people very extensively, and greatly to revive his work, especially in this land.

John Fiske, October 26, 1846

Like the Peace of Ghent, the state of American religion in 1815 seemed to be summed up in the phrase, *status quo ante bellum*. Churches, sects, and individuals still bickered one with another over matters of doctrine, liturgy, governance, morals, and personnel. The ended war was still wicked to those who had always deemed it so, justified to those who had originally cheered it. Like the military denouement, heaven's final verdict was annoyingly ambiguous. If the clash at New Orleans demonstrated that God had blessed Republican arms, the burning of Washington rebuked wicked rulers and wayward citizens, especially the government workers who regularly abused the Sabbath.[1] If Allied triumphs in Europe finally smashed the horrific infidelity that for twenty years had poisoned the Atlantic community, the victors seemed as adept as Napoleon in extinguishing liberty and smothering conscience. No wonder that Americans agreed no more about the meaning of peace than they had about the need for war.

That did not mean that nothing had changed in two and a half fearful years. It is by now trite to say that the war stimulated nationalism, that thereafter the American people indulged themselves in a binge of cultural pride, sometimes grandiose and occasionally chauvinistic. While the symbolic framework of republican glory was pieced together through successive celebrations of Independence Day, while the *North American Review* boosted artistic independence from the Old World's regimen, American religion too was caught up in the patriotic resurgence. It may be that of all the forms in which postwar nationalism was expressed, this religious variety would weigh most heavily in deciding the country's future. For literary nationalism was the plaything of a relative few, and economic nationalism would be limited by conflicting interests and foreign events. The stirring of national messianism, however, rooted in the prewar years, invigorated by the crisis, emboldened by the fighting's end, seemed to be leading Americans to a still greater identification of religion with their destiny. Somehow sparked by wartime experience, the long-amassed evangelical kindling would soon blaze up and down America, throwing Gospel lights into dark and hidden places, occasionally burning those who handled it recklessly.

Thus did the machinery of American society, to repeat a metaphor, function under the stress and abuse of war, revealing its strengths and weaknesses, although it might be difficult to say with certainty which was which. For example, the facile interworking of religion and politics that was so boisterous during the war foreshadowed continued intermingling of the two, so that shortly it would be impossible to identify them as separate components of the American world view. The power of this compound would soon be evident, but perhaps more intoxicating than tonic. For just as the heat and pressure of war had fused a religious sanction to national success, so too it had revealed how a Christian ethos, wedded to unyielding militance in a sectional or partisan faction, could transform political disputes into moral crises and could turn crises into civil war.[2] But that was no worry in the peaceful spring of 1815. March and April and each succeeding month made the ended war seem more glorious and surely successful.

Before all that would become clear, however, the last few months of fighting would see Republicans despondent at the capture of the capital, outraged by the Hartford Convention, and justifiably exultant in the victory at New Orleans. They were as yet unaware of the Treaty of Ghent when the president proclaimed yet another fast day on January 12, 1815; and most of them were sure, as Joshua Hart told the Methodists of Long Island, that their only course was "to lay low the bulwark of governor Strong's religion, that arm of the beast. It is a folly at this stage of the business to contend about the justness or necessity of the war, both of which have been proven an hundred times and more." [3]

Many disagreed, among them the Unitarian society in Philadelphia, which refused to observe the recommended fast.[4] Critics saw no improvement in Madison's fast messages and suggested that he himself should be leading the people in explicitly Christian prayer.[5] A Presbyterian in Kentucky put it more bluntly, explaining that citizens were now called to repent "because they have committed their dearest earthly interests into the hands of men who are so generally inimical to the government of God, or at least totally indifferent as to the prosperity of the kingdom of Immanuel." [6] Even an anglophobe like John Romeyn, hungering for vengeance upon Britain and the papist Bourbons, could warn his parishioners in New York City that their atheistic Constitution would continue to provoke judgments upon them until it was amended to include religious tests for officials and an explicit mention of a Christian deity.[7]

Even after diplomats ended the shooting, there was no one to stop partisan sniping, especially when antiwar Christians celebrated the national thanksgiving for peace by reaffirming their contempt for the federal government. Reporting this last perfidy of antiwar religion, the *Boston Yankee* charged that the city's Federalists "neither rejoice nor pretend to rejoice" for their country's good fortune.[8] This was not quite correct. Many could celebrate peace but not the supposed vindication of America's past behavior. This attitude could be found even in the South, where a Federalist editor summed up the meaning of recent events with his customary piety:

> The Supreme Governor of the Universe, in compassion to a suffering people, hath mercifully interposed and arrested the

progress of a war, which, though not unproductive of glory
to our country, has cost rivers of precious blood unnecessarily
shed; involved the nation in an enormous debt; reduced it to
the verge of bankruptcy, and brought distress and embarass-
ment into every house.[9]

Farther north, where such sentiments were more common than
in Carolina, Federalists knew who were the real heroes of the
peace and hailed them in their celebrations: "The Clergy—May
they dispense the Gospel of peace and continue to declare the
whole truth." [10]

Their ministers did not disappoint them. Typical of the clergy's
attitude was Samuel Blatchford's address to the Presbyterian congregations of Lansingburg and Waterford, New York. Although
he could proudly declare that "the American eagle tore with his
talons the cross of St. George," he felt compelled to add, "still
war is a dreadful scourge, call it by what name you please." [11]
His colleague in upstate New York, John McDonald, observed
the thanksgiving day with gratitude for the destruction of foreign
and domestic infidelity but apparently saw no reason to delight
in military success.[12] More forcefully, William Miltimore told
his flock that if they expected boastful words about the number of
enemy slain they could hire another to fill his pulpit. For it was
not American prowess that routed the invaders at New Orleans
but rather divine vengeance upon those sinners who had opened
fire upon the Sabbath.[13]

When John Popkin led his congregation in Newbury, Massachusetts, in thanksgiving service, he too could not be induced to
celebrate the glory "of thousands killed and wounded, and thousands destitute, distressed and ruined. I cannot find a christian
joy in destroying even our enemies." But he could find in past
trials a lesson for the future and warned that henceforth only
pious men should be honored with public office, lest the country
again be brought to ruin.[14] Venerable Seth Payson told the people
of Rindge, New Hampshire, that the reelection of infidels would
provoke a renewal of America's suffering.[15] The same threat was
implicit in Humphrey Moore's thanksgiving sermon when he
castigated the foreigners—Swiss-born Albert Gallatin, perhaps—

whose corruption had exposed the capital city to British invasion.[16] Still another Hampshire pastor reaffirmed the "first inquiry respecting a candidate for public office. . . . *Does his life prove, that he is actuated by the true principles of Christianity?*" [17] The criterion was strangely reminiscent of the fast sermons of 1812. It had not, however, won the presidency for DeWitt Clinton then and would not do so for Rufus King in 1816, as Jesse Appleton was perceptive enough to foresee.[18] For just as the president of Bowdoin College confessed himself unable to relish military success, so too voters generally were unwilling to repudiate their Republican chief. They still cheered Madison, even though his thanksgiving proclamation was condemned, as usual, for failing to cite Scripture, mention the Redeemer, and confess national guilt.[19]

Indeed, the coming of peace only emboldened Republican vengefulness toward those who had opposed the war. They hailed Theodore Dwight, secretary of the assembly at Hartford, as a Yankee pope, an office befitting his bigotry, and mocked the pious Federalists who had joined him in praying, "Our Mother who art in Europe, adored be thy name. Thy kingdom come: Thy will be done in New-England as it is done in Ireland and its dependencies." [20] When Napoleon resurged briefly in the spring of 1815, wits noted that the Jesuits might again need a place of refuge and suggested that, "as their labors had the same object with regard to mankind, would it not be well if the *three commissioners* from *Hartford* were sent to *condole* with them, and offer them an asylum among the descendants of the *Pilgrims*." [21] "How applicable to this faction," they warned, "is the denunciation of GOD in the song of Deborah and Barak, who saved Israel from the hands of their enemies—Curse ye Meroz, said the angel of the Lord, curse ye bitterly the inhabitants thereof; because they came not to the help of the Lord, to the help of the Lord against the mighty." [22] As if to affirm that damnation, Madison's most effective propagandist informed the world "that a large proportion of the clergy of the town of Boston, are absolute Unitarians" and "that the present principal of Harvard College was known to be a Unitarian when he was elected." [23] For years the antiwar clergy had been pointing to America's suffering as punishment for the war, but now the kicking shoe was on another foot. When parts of New England suffered greatly in the hurricane season of 1815, the damage seemed to be most extensive in the three states which had held the Hartford parley, less severe in the two that had been involved only unofficially, while New York, faithful to the Union, had been spared entirely. More than agreements among diplomats, that single fact showed what the War of 1812 had settled and who had really emerged victorious.[24] All in all, there seemed little reason for Republicans to doubt

> that the war was just and necessary, and we have abundant evidence to believe it was a holy war, for the Lord has fought for us the battles, and given us the victories which have been signal and marvellous on water and on land. In how much then ought we to have confidence in the political opposers, who have declared the war unholy and unjust? [25]

The victors were obviously gloating, and their cockiness was understandable. The stigma of past disaffection would not soon leave the antiwar clergy, or the Federalist party as a whole, especially when Republican leaders did their best to make it permanent. An editor in Missouri could in 1816 still berate New England's missionaries in the West by rehearsing their opposition to what now could be called a glorious war; and as late as July 4, 1823, a Baptist preacher could cast aspersion on those admirers of Czar Alexander who had not always observed Independence Day "in a manner the most judicious, and the most 'becoming a moral and religious people.' " [26] Perhaps the most popular abuse of the clergy was reprinted from William Cobbett's *Weekly Register* in England. His address to "The Cossack Priesthood of Massachusetts," another allusion to their esteem for the Russian, was as vicious an attack as any written in America and won such popularity that editors gave up advertising space to print it in full. Toasters used its title to mock Federalist religion, and the Congregationalist ministers were warned that several thousand copies of the pamphlet had been purchased by Americans who would no longer be willing to subsidize pulpit treason.[27] Before long Connecticut's established order, political and religious, was swept away in the constitutional changes of 1818, while a separationist spirit rose among the Republican Christians of Maine, who urged Massachusetts, "Go Ye to the Bulwark, and We Will Turn

TO THE UNION." [28] Their fellows in New Hampshire used the same handy brush to tar their opponents in the Dartmouth College controversy in 1815; and as if to prove how little popular concerns had changed with the coming of peace, Republicans continued to bewail Juggernaut and its British sponsors.[29]

The rhetoric, as it usually does, lingered after the crises were passed. When New England's wartime children grew to maturity, they would still hear Isaac Hill, venomous editor of the *New Hampshire Patriot*, defending Jackson as he had defended Madison and damning the Second Bank of the United States with the same apocalyptic phrases, the same millennial jargon he had used against the antiwar clergy. Young people in upper New York and on the northern frontier who reached voting age in the next decade would still be called to battle in the sometimes paranoid patois of Universalists and Freewillers, but those later campaigns would rage against the Masonic order and in the process help to revolutionize American politics. Youthful members of the Reformed Presbyterian and kindred communions, nurtured in the fiery absolutism of their elders, would in time turn Alexander McLeod's draconian anger from the British beast to the Slave Power. And their hungering after righteousness would not be satisfied by facile compromises, not that of 1820 concerning Missouri, not those of later years.

Thus, although the war itself was soon wreathed in the pleasantly obscuring haze of patriotic memory, the hatreds and terrors and hopes it had revealed among American Christians were not ephemeral but remained acute, cutting, driving forces. They had not been generated by the war but were concentrated by it, focused more sharply, and perhaps can show us, better than contemporaneous political events, what was brewing, maturing, transforming in the potent distillation that became Jacksonian America and soured into tragedy.

Welcome as the Peace of Ghent was to antiwar Christians, the outcome left them a profound, a distracting dilemma. For years they had assured one another that their country was being punished for its sins and would continue to suffer until it repented, turned away from evil men and infidel policies, and enthroned Jehovah in the place of the Virginian dynasty. They had hoped

to save themselves and their own states from divine retribution by
electing godly rulers, shunning the war, and, in a few cases,
breaking the political fellowship that tied them to a corrupt
Union. They had made of the war years one long jeremiad. They
had repeatedly knotted together the need for national reform and
the hope of peace. They had warned, threatened, pleaded, castigated, condemned their countrymen in the belief that America's
guilt had caused the war and that only America's sorrow could
end it. And they had failed. For several more terms, deists would
foul the presidential chair, while New England remained within
the unrepentant union, tied to slave states ever bolder in their
infamy. Mail would still be delivered on the Sabbath in spite of
Christian protest. The Constitution would not be amended to
recognize the Trinity, nor would religious tests for public officials
be required. And yet—a great puzzle—heaven's justice would not
overtake America. On the contrary, the wicked war would end
reasonably well; and the escape from doom would, with increased
distance, look more and more like a decided victory. How could
this be? Either God's vengeance did not fall upon sinful nations,
which was impossible; or New England's leaders in church and
state had aligned themselves with the devil's side in the late conflict, which was not impossible but was too devastating to consider
seriously.[30]

Foreign affairs were equally awry. A millennium was not imminent, neither the Federalist vision of a world evangelized by
Britain and America nor the Republican hope of a future without
kings or established churches. Events in Europe put a cruel end
to what now seemed to have been only fantasies, as the world
ran again in its ancient course. Bourbon monarchs, Pius VII, the
Inquisition, a congress at Vienna plotting death to republics, even
plans for a renewed slave trade—it was all too much for the most
optimistic millenarian to endure. There was a time, too painfully
brief, when it seemed an apocalyptic climax might be in the
offing. Reading about Napoleon's escape from Elba to lead another French army against the allies, Americans could for a while
again believe

> That grand anti-christian usurper, the Pope—
> The Lord by his power shall wholly destroy,

> While nations which long under darkness have groped,
> Shall hail the first dawn of the gospel with joy.[31]

But after this last seizure of chiliastic fever there was nothing for disappointed Christians to do but wonder how their dogmas had failed them, or how they themselves had failed the responsibilities of their covenant.

There was another explanation for the conundrum. God's hand might have been stayed temporarily. His mercy toward his children of the New World had always been bountiful, and perhaps he had not brought them through so much to abandon them now. Many after all had remained faithful, even if they had not succeeded in quickly stopping the war. This was the hope of the authoritative *Panoplist*, voice of the New England establishment, which had long been assuring the public that "whatever opinions may be entertained as to the origin and immediate causes of the war in which we are involved, no well-informed and conscientious man will deny, that the procuring causes have been our national sins." A month after those words were written, an understandably confused editor, stunned by the news of peace, confessed,

> We had intended to devote a column to this subject; but, in the first moments of joy, it seems hardly possible to say anything, which shall make a deeper impression than the bare news of this happy event. Let us all receive so great a blessing, as becomes those who are favored with the Gospel of peace, and who are accountable to God for the use which they make of this new instance of the Divine benignity.[32]

That explained everything. The "Holy Remnant," like that of ancient Israel, might with the return of peace be given another chance to make the most of divine mercy, to be the leaven in America's loaf.

The implications were staggering. As a Vermonter put it, "We may venture to hope, that the judgments of God have not been visited upon us in vain; that they will, to no small extent, cause us to learn *righteousness*." [33] For failure to do so would surely provoke even greater punishment. That was the pervasive assumption of a great many Americans as they celebrated the end of the fighting, and it was little wonder that they did not share the jubilance of their Republican neighbors. That was why William Miltimore, John Popkin, Seth Payson, Humphrey Moore, and so many of their colleagues used the national thanksgiving day in April 1815 to call Americans back to their ancestral covenant. That was why editorialists continued to carp against Madison's impiety. They were not being petty. They feared for the safety of their unrepentant country. And if Republicans did not appreciate the way they observed the thanksgiving day, their blindness was inexcusable. They should have understood that the wars of the Lord had, in a sense, only begun.

It was as simple as this: if the war had been heaven's judgment against America and if that affliction was suddenly lifted from the sinful people, then, if the Republic were to avoid future punishment, the most pressing business for a Christian was national reform, the rooting out one by one of every vice that might provoke divine vengeance.

But so narrowly escaped, the nation—or at least a large part of it—seemed not to realize that they had received not a pardon but a stay of execution. Samuel Jarvis caustically asked whether Americans had yet formally proclaimed themselves a Christian people: "Where is the instrument, where the decree, where the solemn writing, by which we have announced it?" [34] Even if the Republican Baptists, good Calvinists in the tradition of the covenant, celebrated peace correctly by remembering "the great goodness of God towards us, in the restoration of that national peace which we had forfeited by our sins," they presumably would not carry reformation to the point of abandoning their leaders for more pious politicians.[35] An anonymous "American layman" could reasonably bemoan an entire world ripe for destruction. The victorious European allies were as corrupt as the defeated French; all had persecuted the saints; Orthodox Russia and Anglican England were but children of the Roman whore. And the children of the covenant, to whom so much had been given, still enslaved blacks and mistreated Indians. Who then could argue with the layman when he asked,

But has not America greatly departed from her original principles, and left her first love? Has she not also many amongst her chief citizens, of every party, who have forsaken the God of their fathers, and to whom the spirit may justly be supposed to say, "ye hold doctrines which I hate, repent, or else I will come unto you quickly, and will fight against you with the sword of my mouth." [36]

This was not the raving of a backwoods visionary but the informed judgment of the learned Elias Boudinot, who knew whereof he spoke.

Living under a Damoclean sword, never knowing when America's cup of iniquity might brim over, a Christian patriot like Boudinot must now interpret his covenanted obligations in a new way. No more would a specific calamity call for peremptory reform to get things, as it were, back on the right track. Now the day-to-day life of the country might become one long jeremiad, if the faithful could endure the moral tension of desperate lifelong reform. Thus antiwar journalists chorused the maxims of their cause: "Righteousness exalteth a nation, but sin is a reproach to any people" and "True national honor is a virtuous people." [37] Thus community organizations sprang up, repeating those mottoes or ones very like them and operating on a set of hypotheses which were to characterize the myriad aspects of American reform for many decades. "The experience of other nations proves to us unequivocally, that virtue is the only basis on which republican governments and institutions can rest," declared the newly formed Moral Society of Madison County, New York,

> and that whenever this ceases to characterize the motives of citizens, they are ripe for the ambitious grasp of some aspiring demagogue, who will fasten upon them the iron bands of despotism. We believe that "pure religion, and undefiled," is that which can alone secure our individual happiness, both for time and eternity; and that in proportion as this prevails in any nation, that nation is blessed and happy. [38]

There may have been few prominent or powerful men among Madison County's moral reformers, but the future was theirs in a way that they themselves could not have imagined. They would soon be joined by more prestigious groups with more ambitious

projects. The Massachusetts Peace Society, for example, num-
bering in its ranks much of the antiwar elite, still praised Czar
Alexander, whose postwar Holy League renewed their hopes and
aroused their energies. The war had taught them a lesson, however, as to the need for activism as well as orthodoxy; for now
they cautioned, "But let us never indulge the thought, that those
predictions which involve the agency of men, will ever be ac-
complished without that agency. Having put our hands to the
plough, let us never look back. Having enlisted as soldiers of the
Prince of Peace, let us quit ourselves like men." [39]

That must have been the thinking of many thousand citizens,
honestly concerned with their country's welfare, who poured
out upon their rulers in the first months of 1815 hundreds of
petitions seeking an end to Sabbath desecration by the Post Office.
The same principles that engendered antiwar fervor explain also
the protests of many towns in New Hampshire shortly before
the fighting's end. Civil institutions rested upon public morality,
they reminded Congress, and the Sunday mail was thus a threat
to both. They wanted peace, and "the surest way to obtain this
blessing will be for the nation to respect the ordinances of
Heaven." [40] The District of Maine offered Congress the same
threatening promise, "that the smiles of Heaven on a community,
are to be expected then only, when regard is extensively paid to
His commands, on whose good pleasure depends the prosperity
both of nations and individuals." [41] It does not matter if the men
in the Capitol did not take seriously this theological algebra that
equated probity with prosperity and sin with national disaster.
Voters did; and from upright Connecticut, raw Ohio, boisterous
Tennessee and North Carolina, Delaware, Maryland, and the
capital city they sent identical petitions, a few crudely copied by
hand, throwing in their rulers' faces full responsibility for whatever doom awaited America in February 1815. Repeatedly groups
of Christians sent these futile sheets of paper to warn their representatives that "the profanation of the Sabbath is calculated to
awaken the displeasure of God, and bring down his judgments." [42]
Ardor like theirs in such an essential mission had to survive the
war's end. No wonder, then, that their cause outlived the crisis as
peace drove them to greater exertion.

"The petitioners at least have done their duty," one of them observed, "and will no longer be chargeable with the guilt of those national sins, which have brought down on us the judgments of Heaven." [43] But were there not greater sins than Sabbath-breaking for which America had suffered the war and in which Americans wallowed still? Were there not greater evils to be assaulted by those who petitioned Congress, by the Madison County reformers, by men like Elias Boudinot, by all those who realized what a close call America had had in the war and knew that divine vengeance had been postponed, not prevented? One such cancer at the Republic's heart had been laid open by the fast sermons of 1812, as it was dissected by the peace sermons of 1815. During the war it had been diagnosed as "a sin that pleads with fearful eloquence for that Divine vengeance which sooner, or later, visits upon the oppressor the injuries of the oppressed; and it holds a conspicuous rank in the catalogue of offences, for which this nation now bleeds, and groans." [44] Those who wished to save America in 1812 or 1815 or later, therefore, had to excise the malignancy, had to end human slavery in their land.

It had been no coincidence that the few western voices critical of the war were also apt to criticize slavery. Thus the *Weekly Recorder* had printed a circular letter of the Kentucky Abolition Society, which, though moderate, must have outraged many citizens, from whom the society pleaded for help "at this awful crisis, while the cause of the only remaining republick is at issue in the high court of Heaven: and if that cannot be granted, we pray their forbearance, while we discharge our duty to God and our country, in using our feeble efforts to remove this crying sin of the nation." [45] So too the *Almoner*, while disclaiming a belief in "civil emancipation," insisted "that the present situation of blacks in these states is pregnant with danger. The land groans under a vast load of guilt on their account." Accordingly the journal's antiwar editor pleaded for repentance, lest the guilt be washed away by blood some day.[46] That was not a popular warning in Kentucky; but then neither was the antiwar piety of the two Presbyterian publications, which seemed to represent a culture awkward and alien in the Mississippi Valley.

Granted that these wartime jeremiads were ineffective, that

they expressed a minority viewpoint, it is still important that what they said would be said later in peacetime, and said by a great many people. Once one is familiar with the moral controversy of the war years, it comes as no surprise that the *Panoplist*, adamant as ever, condemned any compromise regarding Missouri's entry into the Union and called slavery the continuing evidence of national criminality.[47] When chastised sinners balked at this gratuitous sermonizing, true to form the *Panoplist*, and with it the whole social apparatus it represented, only struck harder at the sins that could bring upon the Union the fate of the Dead Sea cities.

Needless to say, the antislavery movement in America would develop in many forms, change directions, leadership, tactics; but it would never lose this sense of desperate necessity in the face of national guilt. When the president of Washington College on Independence Day, 1823, pleaded with his countrymen to end slavery and so save their country, all his presuppositions, the flow of his logic, the sources of his evidence, his outraged tenor of immediacy, all these matched the antiwar sermons of earlier years.[48] And perhaps we do wrong even to make the distinction. For in a way the same subject concerned Andrew Wylie on that July festival as had provoked Elijah Parish's notorious protest against the war declared by "southern *Heroes*," "inflicting the bloody lash on more than ten hundred thousand *African* slaves." [49] Neither man was addressing himself to an isolated political problem, to the war only or to just the Missouri Compromise. Both were part of a broader censure of the comfortable majority's sins, a continuing protestation that transcended each of the many crises from which its fervor was drawn. And its driving motives, as well as many of its arguments, would form a continuum of righteousness, with one end rooted in the disgusted rejection of national normalcy by antiwar Christians in 1812.

The way in which antiwar Christians adapted to peacetime opportunities was, therefore, inevitable. To be faithful to America's covenant with the Lord (even if their rulers ignored it), to save their land from renewed punishment (even if their neighbors mocked their efforts), they would act politically to secure pious rulers. They would organize an array of clubs, associations, committees, and devote spare time and surplus funds to the cause of national reform. Even if their country's ills were too profound and numerous to be wiped out easily, a second generation, schooled in their mission, might with sufficient organization make the world marvel at their success. Rightly might their program be called theocratic.[50] And well might some of its proponents refuse compromise with national sins, having that incontrovertible purpose and assured sense of leadership which David Donald has so controversially analyzed.[51] It was to be expected that, decades after Elijah Parish damned the sins of "southern heroes," his namesake with equal fervor would whip the consciences of slavers. When the very salvation of his country was at stake, the Reverend Mr. Lovejoy had no choice but to wipe out America's wickedness or die trying.

It remains true that the great effusion of evangelical activity which historians are wont to call an age of reform was underway well before the Peace of Ghent so confused the prophetic calculations of antiwar Christians. Covenanted Americans had for some time been organizing to protect and improve their neighbors' morals. But even if the war's unexpected outcome did not begin this domestic crusade, it certainly strengthened it. One may argue that "the ferment of reform" was part of the nation's psychic chemistry and that sooner or later it would have set corks to popping. One would thereby ignore the catalytic experience that gave American reform its peculiar urgency, its almost demonic drive. The jeremiad tradition had aborted. At war's end those who had opposed it could not assure themselves that there had indeed been a reformation and that they were, for a time at least, out of danger. On the contrary, their safety was all too tenuous, as the citizens of Cambridge must have realized when they gave thanks for peace by singing a reaffirmation of their wartime principles:

> Long hast thou stretched the avenging hand,
> And smote thy people in thy wrath;
> Hast frowned upon a guilty land,
> While storms and darkness veiled thy path.[52]

And it makes a great deal of difference whether the Christians of 1815 and afterward set about improving America to accomplish certain worthy goals or whether they did so to extricate their country, or at least themselves, from mounting national guilt and its sure punishment. For the "Holy Remnant" of Cambridge and other towns were not becoming meddling do-gooders. They were in fact desperate Lots, who knew just what would happen if they could not find or educate or rehabilitate ten just men in Sodom.[53]

How that may have shaped their hopes, pointed their politics, or colored their relations with other citizens is perhaps a matter more amenable to imagining than documenting. But it suggests that America's symbiotic union of religion and politics not only developed into crusading nationalism but also provided the rationale for fervid, and continuing, reform. In this respect it may be helpful to our understanding of the decades after 1815 to take seriously the apocalyptic mentality of Boudinot and other antiwar Christians, who, if they had lived to see it, would have had good reason to consider later bloodshed along the Mississippi, in the Pennsylvanian countryside, and across the face of Virginia as the Armageddon of their hopes. They would have found still applicable the public address issued by the Philadelphia Bible and Missionary Society late in the War of 1812: "Still, in the midst of this mighty and sanguinary conflict; Zion lives and is safe: for lo! one like unto the Son of man passes with her through the fire, and she comes forth, not only unhurt, but purified." [54] For such was the happy fate promised to those who were faithful and to the nation which, like it or not, would be reconciled to its Lord by their efforts.

Thus the bumpkin petitioners who somewhat pathetically warned Congress that continuing the Sunday mail service would prolong the war were prototypes of later citizens who, if they could not stop the Sabbath posts, could outlaw liquor in their towns, keep papists from their neighborhoods, and drive slaveholders out of the national government. Because of their determination, while America rollicked in prosperous peace and Federalism waned and old issues faded, the war's domestic battles continued, sporadic and haphazard. Perhaps James Madison never understood that the antiwar Christians of his tortured presidency had struggled to control not only Congress and foreign policy but also the nation's soul. Contests like that take generations, and victories fall more often to the determined than to the numerous. In this sense, the record of American religion during the war was a rough-draft scenario for ensuing decades of conflict.

One man embodied all that had happened to antiwar religion: Timothy Dwight, president of Yale College, grandson of the great Edwards, scourge of Jeffersonian infidelity. As an exuberant student in the heady days of 1776, he had told the senior class of Yale that the immediate future would be a critical period for mankind, in which each of them would have wonderful roles to play. For although they might not see the summit of American glory, it would surely be their task to lay its foundation.[55] Grandiose though his vision was, it was largely accurate, especially when applied to the young orator himself. Forty years later, suffering from the cancer that would soon take his life, Dwight stood as an intermediate figure, handing over to a new generation of orthodox leadership the traditions of the past he so fittingly had come to embody. Although his opposition to Madison's war was now discredited and his Federalism would before long waste away in America's burgeoning democracy, his grander religious ambitions won adherents who would keep them alive long after his death in 1817.

With much reason did one obituary of the patriarch recall that he had been "very early aware of the rapid growth of this country, and of the importance which the American states would soon possess in the affairs of the world," and that he accordingly prepared his students for tasks far beyond the ken of lesser men.[56] And no projects concerned him more than those "which had reference to the wants of all mankind; which contemplated the universal diffusion of the Gospel,—the conversion of the world. As earnests of this great consummation, he received with pious joy and gratitude all accounts of the triumphs of the cross in the benighted regions of the earth." [57] Testifying to the truth of that encomium, Dwight's colleagues on the American Board of Commissioners for Foreign Missions eulogized the devotion to missionary efforts with which "he probably did not less than anyone of his survivors in this country has done towards the advancement of this holy cause." [58] Even if these accolades seem stilted

and extravagant, we do well to give them a hearing; for they cut
through all the controversy that surrounded Dwight, much of it
of his own making, to indicate one reason among many why the
man was elevated to demigod status among the true believers of
New England. For if later students of Dwight's lifework would
not share that esteem for him, generations of eastern Christians
would indeed do so, along with émigrés in New York's burned-
over district and settlers planting their crops and traditions in the
Middle West. He spoke the thoughts of that multitude and never
more than when he eloquently, and always at great length, protested America's social ills and proposed religious remedies. That
was the context of his antiwar sermons; and that was the emotive
engine for his supranational fervor, directing his country into
paths of reformation that transcended the continent's secure ocean
limits.

Many years earlier, while Captains Gray and Kendrick charted
a western river named after their ship, *Columbia*, Dwight had
envisioned the Republic's expansion to the Pacific and the exten-
sion of its influence across the seas:

> Soon shall thy sons across the mainland roam;
> And claim, on far Pacific shores, their home;
> Their rule, religion, manners, arts, convey,
> And spread their freedom to the Asian sea.
>
> . . . .
>
> The long, white spire lie imag'd on the wave;
> O'er morn's pellucid main expand their sails,
> And the starr'd ensign court Korean gales.
>
> . . . .
>
> And tartar desarts hail the rising day;
> From the long torpor startled China wake;
> Her chains of misery rous'd Peruvia break.[59]

Ironically in 1815, at the very nadir of Federalist religion,
Dwight's dream began to be realized, as legions of Christians—
Federalists and Republicans alike—vowed that

Thus, thro' all climes, shall Freedom's bliss extend,
The world renew, and death, and bondage, end;
All nations quicken with th'ecstatic power,
And one redemption reach to every shore.[60]

This would be called evangelism by some, republicanism by
others; but a global mission was being outlined for America by
those who considered the Peace of Ghent a God-given opportunity to advance his kingdom.

This too was part of the war's religious aftermath. The Christians, presumably Congregationalists, who had united to aid the
Hartford Convention by their conjoined devotions could now
turn their concert of prayer to other worthy causes.[61] As the
Panoplist explained,

> Since the proposal above alluded to was made public, it has
> pleased God, in the abundance of his mercy, to restore to us
> the blessings of peace. On many accounts this is a most joyful
> event; but the Christian will not fail to acknowledge it to be
> preeminently desirable, as it opens the world to missionaries,
> and to all benevolent exertions.[62]

On this point even many Republicans concurred. It quickly became something of a bipartisan dogma that Americans had a
special role to play in Christianizing the world and that the sudden return of peace called for heroic endeavors in gratitude to
that God who seemed especially to favor their nation. Dwight
was vindicated. While his countrymen seemed to turn away from
his values, they rushed headlong toward his goals. In the process
they were beginning the drama of American evangelism overseas,
the importance of which has been emphasized in a recent presidential address to the American Historical Association.[63] And
John K. Fairbank's advice, that America's religious role in Asia
had implications far greater than have been recognized, should
help us appreciate the importance of that postwar activity.

Like domestic reform, this enterprise abroad antedated the war.
It was in 1810 that the American Board of Commissioners had set
up their standard "around which the young soldiers of the cross
might rally, who were panting for the honor of being sent forth,

to invade the empire of pagan darkness, and wear out their lives
in the service of their KING." [64] With an exalted mission like that,
the irrepressibly optimistic commissioners may be forgiven if, one
month after the burning of Washington, they attended to really
important matters, "advancing the progress of the millenium, not
only within our own borders, but extensively also in foreign lands.
How noble will be the distinction, should we be known as a people, to the inhabitants of distant continents and islands, not as
covetous of territory—not as ambitious of political dominion,—
not as engrossed by commerce and swallowed up by the cupidity
of avarice;—but as the liberal dispensers of unsearchable riches." [65]
And peace would make it all possible. Peace would remove the
most serious obstacle to America's transpacific mission. That
explains why the members of the Pacific Congregational Church
in Providence, Rhode Island, for example, turned their attention
from mundane political affairs to their minister's prophecy of
world progress, established by Britain and the United States
through their bible societies and missionaries.[66] That explains why
the *Panoplist* cheered Thomas Williams's happy vision in the certainty that true peace could be won by "the publication of the
Gospel through the whole earth, and the effusion of the Holy
Spirit on all nations." [67]

Such was the hope of many citizens on the national thanksgiving day in April 1815. India was opened to them, and they
looked forward to catechizing the Indians of their own continent
while extending their "evangelizing armies" to South America.[68]
The sudden calm the world enjoyed that year reminded them of
the Augustan peace, "when the Son of God made his advent. . . .
Shall such an interesting crisis as the present, pass unnoticed and
unimproved by the friends of the Redeemer?" [69] Republicans too
felt the impulse and longed to repay divine favor with world missionary activity.[70] It would take generations of effort and literally
millions of widow's mites from the female brigades that were
joining the Lord's forces, foreshadowing the future involvement
of women in reform campaigns. "The silver trumpet of PEACE"
was only the herald of nobler joys for the Boston Female Society
for Missionary Purposes, whose devout oratory was to have
longer lasting effects than its members might have imagined. "Is

the faithful Missionary waiting," they asked, "impatiently waiting, to set his foot on the benighted shores of Asia? to unfurl the
banner of 'the Prince of Peace,' and proclaim salvation by
grace?" [71] He was indeed, and behind the missionary were ever
more organizations like Boston's Female Bible Society, the dis-
taff side of the town's best families, including among its members
the wives of Jedidiah Morse, Jeremiah Evarts, and Senator James
Lloyd. Like their husbands, they knew the war had been "directed
by the chastening hand of a Parent, to remind us of the duties we
had neglected," and urged the only proper tribute of thanksgiving: renewed zeal in bringing the Gospel to all men. [72]

Incited by the missionaries' letters that filled their reading
matter and the pulpit eloquence that filled their churches, [73]
Americans were redefining their country's role in the world.
From Africa they thought they heard the ancient plea to come
over into Macedonia and began to train ministers to liberate the
Guinea shore, while the folks back home, like the women of Bath,
Maine, collected pennies to make real the promise that "Ethiopia
shall stretch forth her hands unto God." [74] The Female Mite
Society of Pittsfield recognized its duty, as did the Female
African Good Intent Society of Newport, while Americans again
and again repeated the prophecy of Africa's conversion as if their
belief would make it come true. [75] Their faith would shine as from
the mountaintop to that continent, whither they could carry the
Gospel in reparation for past crimes against the luckless inhabitants. [76] Here was an especially critical obligation, because "our
land is polluted with slavery. A mighty debt is due from us to
injured Africa. Nothing short of sending the Gospel to that
continent will cancel it." [77] Hence the frenzy to act, meet, collect,
contribute, dedicate and reaffirm, encourage the timid and emulate
the heroic. This was no pastime but a life's work, and by it
America's overseas presence would be rooted in righteous fervor
and driven toward apocalypse.

That was at least the rhetorical tenor every time a congregation gathered to send off young warriors of the cross to foreign
lands, usually the Orient, and poured out its heart in expressions
that tell us much about America's overseas involvement in the succeeding decades. Philadelphians bade farewell to their heroes with

a determined spirit that was to appear many times in the future,
whether the departing stalwarts carried Bibles or rifles for mankind's salvation:

> Go, then, to Pagan Burmah's shore,
>   God calls you from above;
> Go—and Christ send a thousand more
>   To join your work of love.[78]

Bostonians too instructed their young men:

> Go, ye heralds of salvation,
> Go proclaim "redeeming blood";
> Publish to that barb'rous nation,
> Peace and pardon from our God;
>   Tell the Heathens
> None but CHRIST can do them good.[79]

Those who remained at home could be part of the endeavor by
financing the missionary enterprise, while vicariously feeling the
grandeur of it all as they read monthly or weekly the latest verses
on the subject, assuring them that,

> Tho' now almost alone ye stand,
>   Expos'd to slander and abuse,—
> Yet sure a Saviour's last command
>   His foll'wers dare not long refuse.[80]

The legacy of Claudius Buchanan was paying high interest. His
books "all operated with living energy to kindle a fire never to be
extinguished." Reading his *Star in the East,* young Adoniram
Judson was led to dedicate his life to the Oriental cause, and after
Judson came legions more.[81] Juggernaut still terrified Americans,
as if it reflected badly on them that such evil continued to exist
in their world, almost as if longer tolerance of Asia's sins would
make them guilty too. Purge it they would, while their missionaries emulated Buchanan's literary style as well as his fervor. "We
also visited the awful temple of Juggernaut (Calc.), and were per-
mitted by the priests to see the horrid monster, and his detestable
CAR! Horrid indeed he is!" one of them reported.[82] Meanwhile,

Americans sang impatiently of the future they were all together
making:

> When will the idol gods
> At Jesus' presence move,
> And cruelty's abodes
> O'er flow with pard'ning love? [83]

When Lyman Beecher preached an ordination sermon in September 1817 for six young ministers, it was somehow fitting that
one of the newly commissioned was Sereno Edwards Dwight,
true son of his illustrious father. For although the Reverend Mr.
Dwight would remain at home, his fellow novices were being sent
"to erect and sustain the standard of the cross in the benighted
regions of Asia, and one of their number at least to devote himself to the instruction of the Indians in our own country." [84] That
was, after all, just what the recently deceased president of Yale
had expected of his people.

Even the restrained Episcopalians, who seldom rushed into anything, partook of great expectations. While diplomatic and military pressure forced Spain to disgorge Florida, Bishop William
Kemp of Maryland urged Christians to continued labor "until we
carry the joyful tidings of salvation to the wilderness and the
solitary places—till the dominion of Christ extend from sea to
sea." [85] The Gospel, it seems, would be made manifest, and with
it America's destiny. That at least seemed to be the belief of
American orthodoxy as its representatives gathered in New York
City to form the United Missionary Society in 1817. The spokesmen of the northern elite were there in force: Romeyn, Spring,
McLeod, Rensselaers and Livingstons, Proudfit, Milledoller,
Bethune, Rutgers, Lenox. These names mattered, and what they
thought they were doing matters even more. When an enthusi-
astic delegate, carried away with the glory of it all, portrayed
"twenty or thirty million who are groping in Pagan darkness, or
Popish superstition" right there on America's own continent, all
must have agreed that Providence had prepared the Western
Hemisphere, torn by revolts, for the Spanish and Portuguese
Scriptures that were the ultimate weapons of the American Bible
Society. "A great day is preparing for the benighted nations of the

South," the orator continued. "Ere long we shall see a heavenly light capping the tops of the Andes, and rivers of salvation flowing through the plains of La Plate. Millions, who are not strangers, but Americans, will be the happier for this day, and will eternally bless God for your existence." [86]

Seconding the adoption of the society's constitution was the eminent Alexander Proudfit, announcing the enrollment of his entire family in its ranks and expecting all Americans to be equally generous. For did not the sudden return of peace plainly foretell the imminent coming of Christ, if not in physical glory at least in the universal spread of the Scriptures? Was it not equally plain that his countrymen were assigned a great role in preparing for that event? No wonder the United Missionary Society marked out for its own "the Indians of North America, the inhabitants of Mexico, and South America," the pagans and papists living in "the whole region of death from the river Del Norte to Cape Horn." [87] At the same time, the newly organized Baptist General Convention for Missionary Purposes was planning "the triumphs of redeeming grace, in the regions where the policy, avarice and ambition of Cortez and Pizarro, strewed the plains with desolation and mortality." [88] Both organizations were still promulgating the ancient Black Legend, the basis for Anglo-American superiority over Latin Catholic peoples; but in the process they were claiming a special responsibility for their inferior neighbors while expecting the rest of the world to leave the Western Hemisphere alone. Soon James Monroe would announce his own version of their fiat; but even he had not already detached Texas from Latin degeneracy, as the United Missionary Society did by implication when it began its crusade at the Rio Grande.

Even the New World was not America's fair share of responsibility, considering what British Christians were doing with their resources.[89] But if Britain was fully occupied with Africa and India, there were yet other lands for Yankees to win for Christ: "Burmah, Siam, several other Indo-Chinese nations, the great empire of China, Japan, thence north indefinitely, and southward, the numerous Malayan isles" where "the British are suspected and feared; but not the Americans." [90] A concurring view would be accidentally expressed some years later, when Edmund Roberts,

America's first official diplomat in the Far East, was instructed to assure the king at Hue that "we never make conquests as the English, the French, and the Dutch have done, in the East Indies." [91] But the kind of conquests contemplated by the United Missionary Society in 1817 and by later generations of like-minded crusaders would dwarf the schemes of imperialists, outrun the vision of powers and principalities. One may disagree with the assembled Baptists of 1817 who thought that "it is providence that has placed before us the wretched natives of Burmah, and inspired the cry—'Christians of America, come over and help us!'" [92] But there can be no doubt as to the vigor of their belief, especially when it fused with nationalism, as in a widely reprinted Independence Day speech which the Connecticut Baptist Missionary Society offered its pious readers. "Let us manifest that love of liberty, of which we make such high professions," declared the orator in the best style of 1822, "by using exertions to break the shackles which hold the heathen world in cruel bondage. Let us take the only effectual method, and send them that proclamation of liberty which Christ has made, and then they shall be free indeed." [93] Because America was the land of liberty, her missionaries would carry with them more than one kind of good news; "and then, in whatever breeze the star-spangled banner of the union floats, it will remind all who see it of the blessings pronounced on those who turn many to righteousness." And John Holt Rice was not the only influential clergyman who envisioned the flag-wrapped cross freeing foreign peoples from moral slavery. Nor was this the last time a large part of American Christendom would gird itself for battle in the vain folly that, as Rice put it, "all nations shall rise up and call us blessed." [94]

The country was, then, indeed different after the war: burgeoning economically, somewhat rambunctious, and more truly a nation than ever before. And the changes certainly extended to matters of the spirit, for Christians could not forget what they had learned in the past several years. They could not be idle while Asians died needlessly in pagan rites and the Pawnee murdered children to honor the morning star. They dared not shirk their national calling to topple idols, just as their republican example made dynasties tremble. And some Americans could not rest until, by purging their country's sins, they restored the Republic to its covenanted faith and saved it from disaster.

Despite all their angry, even fratricidal dissension during the war, most Americans remained united in the belief that religious truth and Christian duty were inseparable from national policy. Believing that, they could disagree about all else, as they had disagreed about the war. They had called it sinful and sanctified, boldly pagan and militantly Protestant. But even those who had considered it an antichristian adventure appeared convinced by the end of 1815 that somehow America had made another advance toward the republic of New Jerusalem. They knew that "the politician will find abundant materials for his contemplation" in reviewing the war,

> but the Christian will raise his thoughts to the Governor of the world, by whose wise and holy counsels all the unexpected changes of our times have been produced, who has in view the promotion of a greater cause and higher interests than are directly involved in the erection or overthrow of any temporal empire; and whose determinations will all be carried into full effect, notwithstanding any violent opposition or adverse appearances. In the great political events of the last five and twenty years, the Christian will see an unexampled preparation for the spread of pure religion.[95]

Observing the American churches during the War of 1812 may be a first step in heeding that advice by trying to interpret a dangerous and wonder-filled era in terms recognizable to the men of that time. It may help us reopen sympathetic communication with the men and women, patriarchs and schoolboys, great and inconsequential, who could pore over the finely printed pages of Jedidiah Morse's *Universal Geography*, thrill to its account of Christianity's worldwide advance, and exult that "the long established imposture of the Koran, is retiring before the blaze of divine truth; the gigantic empire of paganism is mouldering away, and its defenders retiring before the soldiers of the Cross." [96] It is still possible for us to enter their world, share their thoughts, tremble with their indignation or joy, if only we do not let the wisdom of our hindsight blind us to how accurately old Jonas Galusha of Vermont, in the rich simplicity of his fast and thanksgiving proclamations of 1818, expressed all that the Republic had learned through its trials, all that it would make of its opportunity:

> Let that charity which begins at home, enlarge its sphere till it encompass the world of mankind; and teach us to pray that iniquity and its consequent misery every where cease; that the shackles of tyranny may fall from off the oppressed, ignorance be banished from the abodes of men, and the bloody rites of Idolitry abolished forever.[97]

Farmer, innkeeper, captain of militia at the battle of Bennington in the first war with Britain, Republican governor of his state during the second, Galusha led his people in praying for both their rulers and their missionaries. And it was the very heart of the American situation that hardscrabble farmers in the Green Mountains, artisans in the Winooski River towns, and antique patricians in drawing rooms could all pray with Galusha that "he would cause the rights of man, every where, to be regarded; tyranny and oppression to be done away; superstition and bigotry forever to cease, and that the peaceable kingdom of the Redeemer may prevail throughout the habitable world." [98] For whatever the shortcomings of their piety, it nurtured the seeds of nationhood; it drew from the past its direction; it made day-to-day events comprehensible. Without it they could have explained neither themselves nor their world, neither the joy of peace nor their recent war. And if the mawkish naïveté of the Vermonters makes them suspect witnesses for those who collect the testimony of the past, then that perhaps reveals, not how far we have come, but how much we have lost in the moving.

NOTES

INTRODUCTION

1 The extensive literature on the war is partially surveyed by Warren H. Goodman, "The Origins of the War of 1812: A Survey of Changing Interpretations," *Mississippi Valley Historical Review* 28 (1941–42): 171–86. An annotated bibliography is provided in Reginald Horsman, *The Causes of the War of 1812*, pp. 269–92.
2 Ralph Henry Gabriel, *The Course of American Democratic Thought*, p. 39.
3 Resolutions of the Legislative Council and House of Representatives of Mississippi, June 1812. This and other petitions to Congress concerning the embargo, the war, and Sabbath mail service are in the Legislative Branch of the National Archives, Record Group 233, files of the Twelfth and Thirteenth Congresses.
4 Memorial of Inhabitants of Anne Arundel County in the State of Maryland.
5 Petition to Congress from a meeting on Jan. 6, 1814, of delegates from several towns in the county of Saratoga, at the courthouse in the town of Ballston.
6 *Delaware Gazette*, in the *Weekly Recorder*, Nov. 1, 1814.

CHAPTER I

1 *Baltimore Whig*, Jan. 14, 1813.
2 *Speech of the Hon. George Sullivan, at the late Rockingham Convention, with the Memorial and Resolutions, and Report of the Committee of election*, p. 16.
3 *Declaration of the County of Essex, in the Commonwealth of Massachusetts, by its Delegates, assembled in convention at Ipswich*, pp. 3, 10, 15, 16.
4 *Proceedings of a Convention of Delegates from forty one towns, in the County of Worcester*, p. 5.
5 Several dozen printed petitions submitted to Congress in spring 1812.
6 Resolutions of Boston Town Meeting, sent June 15, 1812, to Congress.
7 Petition of a meeting in the County of Philadelphia, May 1812.
8 Memorial from Citizens of Cumberland County, Pennsylvania.
9 Memorial of Inhabitants of Anne Arundel County, Maryland.

10 *An Address of Members of the House of Representatives of the Congress of the United States to their Constituents, on the subject of the War with Great Britain*, pp. 9, 16, 32. The Federalist Congressman and Presbyterian minister, Samuel Taggart, expressed privately the same moral objections to the war. "Letters of Samuel Taggart, Representative in Congress, 1803–1814," *Proceedings of the American Antiquarian Society* 33 (1923–24) : 425.

11 Memorial of the Inhabitants of Richmond, Manchester, and Vicinities, convened at the Capitol, Saturday, May 30, 1812.

12 Resolutions of the Citizens of the First Congressional District of Pennsylvania, convened May 20, 1812, in the State-House Yard.

13 *Extracts from the Minutes of the General Association of the Presbyterian Church in the United States of America, A.D. 1812*, pp. 15–16.

14 *The Acts and Proceedings of the General Synod of the Reformed Protestant Dutch Church in North America*, 1 : 440.

15 *The Constitution of the Reformed Dutch Church in the United States of America*, p. 191.

16 *Panoplist* 5, no. 1 (June 1812) : 47–48.

17 Irving Brant, *James Madison, Commander in Chief 1812–1836*, pp. 27–28.

18 Freeman Parker, *A Sermon delivered at Dresden, July 23, 1812; the day appointed by the governor and Council for a State Fast; and at Wiscasset, on the 20th of August following: the day recommended by the President of the United States for a National Fast.*

19 John Fiske, *A Sermon delivered at New-Braintree, August 20, 1812*, pp. 12, 17.

20 *Boston Gazette*, in the *Washingtonian*, Aug. 24, 1812.

21 Nathaniel Thayer, *A Sermon delivered August 20, 1812*, p. 4.

22 Samuel Austin, *The Apology of Patriots, or the heresy of the Friends of the Washington and peace policy defended*, p. 26.

23 John Lathrop, *The present war unexpected, unnecessary, and ruinous*, p. 38.

24 Henry Ware, *Memoirs of the Rev. Noah Worcester*, pp. 64–65. See also *New Hampshire Patriot*, Aug. 4, 1812.

25 *Martinsburg Gazette*, June 17 and Aug. 21, 1812.

26 James Richardson, ed., *A Compilation of the Messages and Papers of the Presidents 1789–1902*, 1 : 532–33.

27 *Baltimore Patriot*, in the *National Intelligencer*, Aug. 14, 1813.

28 *National Intelligencer*, Sept. 9, 1813.

29 *Federal Republican*, July 30, 1813.

30 *Federal Republican*, Aug. 27, 1813.

31 *American Commercial Advertiser*, in the *New Brunswick Guardian*, Aug. 19, 1813.

32 *Portsmouth Oracle*, in the *Pittsburg Gazette*, Aug. 21, 1812.

33 *National Intelligencer*, Mar. 8, 1813; *Baltimore Patriot*, Mar. 16, 1813.

34 *Washingtonian*, Mar. 8, 1813.

35 *Washingtonian*, Sept. 21, 1812.

36 *Boston Chronicle*, in the *National Intelligencer*, Apr. 19, 1813.

37 *Columbian Phenix*, Nov. 20, 1813.

38 Jedidiah Morse and Elijah Parish, *A Compendious History of New England* (2d ed.), pp. 332-33.

39 Elijah Parish, *A Protest against the War, a Discourse delivered at Byfield, Fast Day, July 23, 1812*, p. 16.

40 Peter Vanpelt, *A Discourse, delivered on the Fourth of July, in the North Brick Church*, preface.

41 *American Mercury*, in *Rhode Island Republican*, Dec. 17, 1812.

42 Isaac Hilliard, *A Wonderful and Horrible Thing is Committed in the Land*, p. 47.

43 *Niles' Weekly Register*, June 25, 1814.

44 Mathew Carey, *The Olive Branch: or, faults on both sides, federal and democratic* (2d ed.), p. 310.

45 Jedidiah Morse, *A Sermon delivered at Charlestown, July 23, 1812*, passim.

46 A Layman [William Plumer], *An Address to the Clergy of New England, on their opposition to the Rulers of the United States*, p. 21.

47 Parish, *A Protest against the War*, p. 9.

48 Nathan Strong, *A fast sermon, delivered in the North Presbyterian Meeting House in Hartford, July 23, 1812*, pp. 5-6.

49 Samuel Austin, *Sermon preached in Worcester, Massachusetts, on the occasion of the special fast, July 23, 1812*, p. iii.

50 Austin, *Apology of Patriots*, p. 8.

51 Ibid., p. 9.

52 Nathan Beman, *A Sermon delivered at the meeting house of the Second Parish in Portland, August 20, 1812, on the occasion of the National Fast*, p. 4.

53 Lathrop, *The present war*, pp. 23-24.

54 Morse, *Sermon, July 23, 1812*, pp. 19-21.

55 David Osgood, *A Solemn Protest against the late declaration of war, in a Discourse, delivered on the next Lord's Day after the tidings of it were received*, p. 11.

56 Noah Worcester, *Abraham and Lot, A Sermon on the Way of Peace, and the Evils of War, delivered at Salisbury, in New-Hampshire, on the day of the National Fast*, pp. 31-32.

57 Micah Stone, *Danger and Duty pointed out, in a Discourse, delivered at Brookfield, South Parish, July 23, 1812*, p. 21.

58 Stephen Rowan, *The Sin and Danger of Insensibility under the calls of God to Repentance. Two Sermons, delivered in the Reformed Dutch Church at Greenwich, in the city of New York, on Thursday, July 30, 1812*, p. 3.

59 Brown Emerson, *The Equity of God's dealings with Nations, A Sermon, preached in Salem, July 23, 1812*, p. 21.

60 Timothy Dwight, *Discourse, in Two parts, delivered August 20, 1812, on the National Fast, in the chapel of Yale College*, pp. 31-32.

61 Parish, *A Protest against the war*, p. 17.

62 Moses Dow, *A Sermon preached in Beverly, August 20, 1812 . . . and again at the Tabernacle in Salem, April 8, 1813*, pp. 9-10.

63 Samuel Worcester, *Courage and Success to the Good, A Discourse delivered at the Tabernacle in Salem, August 20, 1812 . . . and the*

Substance of a Discourse, delivered Sabbath Day, August 9, 1812, p. 16.

64 S. M. Worcester, *Life and Labors of Rev. Samuel Worcester*, 2 : 226.
65 Lathrop, *The present war*, p. 4.
66 Reuben Holcomb, *A Discourse in Two parts, delivered at Sterling, Massachusetts, Thursday, July 23, 1812, at the State Fast*, p. 18.
67 John Church, *Advantages of Moderation, A Sermon delivered at Pelham, N. H. August 20, 1812*, passim.
68 Holcomb, *Discourse, July 23, 1812*, p. 22.
69 Parker, *Sermon, July 23, 1812*, p. 14.
70 Stone, *Danger and Duty*, p. 6.
71 Thayer, *Sermon, August 20, 1812*, p. 15.
72 Jeremiah Evarts, *An oration delivered in Charlestown, (Mass.) on the fourth of July 1812, in commemoration of American Independence*, p. 26. The moderation of all but a few ministers does not substantiate the findings in James Banner, *To the Hartford Convention: The Federalists and the Origins of Party Politics in Massachusetts, 1789–1815*, p. 166.
73 Austin, *Sermon, July 23, 1812*, p. iii.
74 Evarts, *Oration on the fourth of July*, pp. 10, 27.
75 William Channing, *A sermon preached in Boston, July 23, 1812*, p. 19.
76 Morse, *Sermon, July 23, 1812*, p. 52.
77 Timothy Dwight, *A Discourse, in two parts, delivered July 23, 1812, on the Public Fast in the Chapel of Yale College*, p. 27.
78 Lyman Beecher, *Sermons, delivered on various occasions*, 2 : 102. The ideological context of the ministers' antiwar rhetoric is usefully explored by James Banner, *To the Hartford Convention*, passim, and Linda Kerber, *Federalists in Dissent. Imagery and Ideology in Jeffersonian America*.
79 Stone, *Danger and Duty*, pp. 17–19.
80 James Abercrombie, *Two Sermons; The first, preached on Thursday, July 30; the second, preached on Thursday, August 20, 1812*, p. 38.
81 Ibid., pp. iii-iv; *Aurora*, July 27, 1813.
82 Lathrop, *The present war*, p. 28.
83 Thayer, *Sermon, August 20, 1812*, pp. 15–16.
84 Rowan, *Sin and Danger of Insensibility*, p. 50.
85 S. M. Worcester, *Life and Labors of Samuel Worcester*, p. 231.
86 *New York Columbian*, July 18, 1812.
87 *New York Columbian*, July 22, 1812.
88 Jonathan French, *Sermons, delivered on the 20th of August, 1812 . . . to which are added Observations on the Propriety of preaching occasionally on Political Subjects*, pp. 20–21.
89 *New York Columbian*, July 13, 1812.
90 For example, *Touchstone to the people of the United States, on the Choice of a President;* True Republican, *Jefferson against Madison's War; The Republican Crisis; Address of the Republican Committee of the City of New York.*
91 *Hornet's Nest*, Oct. 8, 1812.
92 *Eastern Argus*, Nov. 26, 1812.
93 James Renwick, *Life of DeWitt Clinton*, p. 286.
94 *Extracts from the Minutes of the General Association of the Pres-*

byterian Church, 1812, p. 44. For consideration of the somewhat confusing response of Presbyterianism to the war, see my "The War of 1812 and American Presbyterianism: Religion and Politics during the Second War With Britain," *Journal of Presbyterian History* 47 (1969): 320–39.

95 Cuyler Staats, *Tribute to the Memory of DeWitt Clinton*, p. 104.

96 Alexander Proudfit, *The Agency of God in the Elevation of Man*, pp. 21–22.

97 James Milnor, *Sermon occasioned by the death of his Excellency De-Witt Clinton*, pp. 16–17.

98 *Columbian Phenix; Rhode Island Republican*, issues of Mar. 1812.

CHAPTER 2

1 Channing, *Sermon, July 23, 1812*, p. 13.

2 For example, Gustaf Koch, *Republican Religion: The American Revolution and the Cult of Reason*, pp. 239–84; Vernon Stauffer, *New England and the Bavarian Illuminati*, pp. 103–41.

3 *Panoplist* 4, no. 4 (Sept. 1811) : 184.

4 *Panoplist* 4, no. 6 (Nov. 1811) : 246.

5 *Vermont Evangelical Magazine* 5, no. 2 (Feb. 1813) : 58.

6 *Panoplist* 5, no. 6 (Nov. 1812) : 253.

7 Charles Foster, *An Errand of Mercy: The Evangelical United Front, 1790–1837* is a thorough account of Britain's activities in spreading the Gospel.

8 *Evangelical Record and Western Review* 1, no. 1 (Jan. 1812) : 1–7.

9 *Almoner* 1, no. 2 (July 1814) : 93.

10 Hugh Pearson, *Memoirs of the Life and Writings of Rev. Claudius Buchanan*, 1 : 394.

11 Claudius Buchanan, *Christian Researches in Asia: with notices of the translation of the Scriptures into the Oriental languages*, p. 34.

12 *Christian Disciple and Theological Review* 2, no. 2 (Feb. 1814) : 61–62.

13 *Vermont Evangelical Magazine* 4, no. 7 (July 1812) : 205.

14 *Panoplist* 9, no. 2 (July 1813) : 86.

15 *Columbian Phenix*, Nov. 7, 1812.

16 *Columbian Phenix*, Nov. 28, 1812.

17 *New Hampshire Patriot*, Mar. 2, Sept. 21, 1813; Aug. 16, 1814.

18 *Rutland Herald*, June 9, 1813.

19 *Centinel of Freedom*, Jan. 19, 1813.

20 *Niles' Weekly Register*, Jan. 30, 1813.

21 *Columbian Phenix*, Aug. 21, 1813.

22 *Connecticut Evangelical Magazine* 7, no. 1 (Jan. 1814) : 23–24.

23 *Panoplist* 9, no. 7 (Oct. 1813) : 322.

24 *Christian's Magazine* (New York) 4, no. 7 (July 1811) : 405.

25 *Christian Disciple and Theological Review* 2, no. 8 (Dec. 1814) : 241.

26 Fred Engelman, *The Peace of Christmas Eve*, p. 142.

27 Quoted in Henry Adams, *History of the United States during the Administration of Jefferson and Madison*, 9 : 13.

28 *Almoner* 1, no. 3 (Sept. 1814) : 158–61.

29 *Almoner* 1, no. 2 (July 1814) : 109.

30 *Weekly Recorder*, May 17, 1815.
31 *Churchman's Magazine* 1, no. 3 (May, June 1813) : 204. Foster, *Errand of Mercy*, p. 105, calculates the total British donation to various American Bible societies between 1809 and 1817 as approximately £5,000.
32 Beman, *Sermon, August 20, 1812*, p. 15.
33 Jesse Appleton, *A Sermon delivered at Brunswick, April 13, 1815, appointed as a day of National Thanksgiving*, p. 8.
34 *Extracts from the Minutes of the General Association of the Presbyterian Church in the United States of America, A. D. 1814*, pp. 119–20.
35 Holcomb, *Discourse, July 23, 1812*, p. 20.
36 Benjamin Bell, *A Sermon preached at Steuben, April, 1813, in which are shewn the evil effects of war and when it may be lawful to go to war*, p. 69.
37 Thomas Andros, *The place of the church in the grand chart of scripture prophecy, or the great battle of Armageddon*, p. 46.
38 Morse, *Sermon, July 23, 1812*, p. 18. It should be noted that, like his colleagues in pulpit and press, Morse praised the virtue and zeal of Britain's people but did not applaud the character and conduct of her rulers. Thus they could sincerely admire British religion without undue attachment to a foreign government.
39 *Christian Visitant* 1, no. 6 (July 8, 1815) : 42.
40 *Christian Monitor and Religious Intelligencer* 1, no. 2 (June 27, 1812): 28–29.
41 *Evangelical Record and Western Review* 1, no. 7 (July 1812) : 219.
42 *Christian Disciple and Theological Review* 1, no. 4 (Aug. 1813) : 127.
43 *Vermont Evangelical Magazine* 5, no. 2 (Feb. 1813) : 60.
44 *Connecticut Evangelical Magazine* 7, no. 6 (June 1814) : 238–39.
45 *Vermont Evangelical Magazine* 7, no. 2 (Mar., Apr. 1815) : 183.
46 *Niles' Weekly Register*, June 24, 1815.
47 *Somerset Whig*, June 28, 1815.
48 *Panoplist* 11, no. 12 (May 1813) : 552.
49 *Federal Republican*, June 9, 1813.
50 *Federal Republican*, Apr. 26, 1813.
51 *Charleston Courier*, in the *Federal Republican*, Aug. 18, 1814.
52 Samuel Jarvis, *The duty of offering unto God thanksgiving. A Sermon, preached in St. Michael's Church, Bloomingdale, on the Second Thursday in April, A.D. 1815*, p. 10.
53 *Connecticut Evangelical Magazine* 7, no. 4 (Apr. 1814) : 152.
54 *Massachusetts Baptist Missionary Magazine* 4, no. 1 (Mar. 1814) : 13.
55 *Connecticut Evangelical Magazine* 7, no. 10 (Oct. 1814) : 383–90.
56 *Churchman's Magazine* 2, no. 6 (Nov., Dec. 1814) : 426–27.
57 *Second Report of the New-Hampshire Bible Society*, p. 11.
58 [Asa McFarland], *A Defence of the Clergy of New-England, against the charges of interfering in our political affairs, and condemning the policy of the present war*, pp. 37–38.
59 *Federal Republican*, May 14, 1813.
60 Jarvis, *Sermon, April 1815*, p. 11.
61 *Weekly Recorder*, Sept. 6, 1814.

62 Lucius Stockton, *An Address before the Convention of the Friends of Peace of the State of New-Jersey, July 4, 1814*, p. 7.
63 *Address of the Convention to the free electors of New-Jersey*, p. 18.
64 Joseph Tufts, *Oration, pronounced before the Federal Republicans of Charlestown, Massachusetts, July 4, 1814*, p. 6.
65 Andros, *The place of the church*, p. 40.
66 *Massachusetts Baptist Missionary Magazine* 3, no. 4 (Dec. 1811) : 100.
67 *Military Monitor and American Register*, Apr. 12, 1813.
68 *Vermont Evangelical Magazine* 3, no. 3 (Mar. 1811) : 75.
69 See below, chap. 3, p. 68.
70 *Panoplist* 4, nos. 1 and 2 (June, July 1811) : 32–38, 75–84.
71 *Connecticut Evangelical Magazine* 4, no. 9 (Sept. 1811) : 357–60.
72 Parker, *Sermon, July 23, 1812*, p. 11.
73 An American Layman [Elias Boudinot], *The Second Advent, or coming of the Messiah in Glory*, p. iv.
74 *Connecticut Evangelical Magazine* 7, no. 1 (Jan. 1814) : 6–7.
75 *Christian Monitor* (Maine) 1, no. 1 (Jan.–Mar. 1814) : 4.
76 *Panoplist* 10, no. 7 (July 1814) : 319.
77 *Connecticut Evangelical Magazine* 7, no. 7 (July 1814) : 272.
78 *Connecticut Evangelical Magazine* 7, no. 11 (Nov. 1814) : 405.
79 *Panoplist* 10, no. 3 (Mar. 1814) : 137–38.
80 *Vermont Evangelical Magazine* 6, no. 4 (Apr. 1814) : 126.
81 *Almoner* 1, no. 4 (Nov. 1814) : 197.
82 *Weekly Recorder*, Mar. 30, 1815.
83 John Holt Rice, editor of the *Christian Monitor* (Virginia), Dec. 30, 1815.
84 *Connecticut Evangelical Magazine* 8, no. 9 (Sept. 1815) : 337–45.

CHAPTER 3

1 Fiske, *Sermon, August 20, 1812*, p. 12.
2 Beman, *Sermon, August 20, 1812*, p. 14.
3 French, *Sermons, delivered on the 20th of August, 1812*, pp. 24–25.
4 John Giles, *Discourses delivered to the second Presbyterian society in Newburyport, August 20, 1812 . . . with a copious appendix*, p. 26.
5 For example, Bradford Perkins, *Prologue to War*, p. 420; Brant, *Commander in Chief*, p. 24; Adams, *History of the United States*, 6 : 400; Samuel Eliot Morison, "Our Most Unpopular War," *Proceedings of the Massachusetts Historical Society* 80 (1968) : 41–42; Banner, *To the Hartford Convention*, p. 307.
6 Bell, *Sermon preached at Steuben, April, 1813*, p. 86.
7 "Diary of Archelaus Putnam of New Mills," *Danvers Historical Collections* 6 (1918) : 27.
8 David Benedict, *A General History of the Baptist Denomination in America, and other parts of the world*, 1 : 84, 474–78.
9 *Massachusetts Baptist Missionary Magazine* 3, no. 1 (Mar. 1811) : 21.
10 L. K. Greene, *The Writings of the Late Elder John Leland*, p. 355.
11 *Herald of Gospel Liberty*, May 8, 1812.
12 *Herald of Gospel Liberty*, Dec. 11, 1812.
13 *Religious Magazine* 1, no. 1 (Jan. 1811) : 33.

14 *Religious Magazine* 1, no. 4 (Oct. 1811) : 131.
15 *Massachusetts Baptist Missionary Magazine* 3, no. 10 (May 1813) : 320.
16 Henry Clarke, *A History of the Sabbatarians or Seventh Day Baptists in America*, p. 16.
17 Billy Hibbard, *Memoirs of the Life and Travels of Billy Hibbard*, p. 339.
18 *Long Island Star*, July 26, 1815.
19 *Aurora*, Oct. 14, 1812; *Liberty Hall*, Nov. 10, 1812; and others.
20 *Baltimore Patriot*, Apr. 28, 1813.
21 *Baltimore Patriot*, Apr. 28, 1813.
22 *Niles' Weekly Register*, July 15, 1815.
23 *Boston Patriot*, in the *Long Island Star*, May 17, 1815.
24 *New Hampshire Patriot*, Nov. 1, 1814.
25 *Columbian Phenix*, Dec. 25, 1813.
26 *Niles' Weekly Register*, Jan. 8, 1814.
27 *Boston Yankee*, Jan. 13, 1815.
28 *Niles' Weekly Register*, Oct. 30, 1813.
29 *Rutland Herald*, June 9, 1813.
30 *Rhode Island Republican*, July 15, 1813.
31 *New Hampshire Patriot*, Oct. 6, 1812.
32 *Niles' Weekly Register*, Jan. 30, 1813; *Baltimore Patriot*, Sept. 15, 1813.
33 *New Hampshire Patriot*, Aug. 16, 1814.
34 *Baltimore Patriot and Evening Advertiser*, Mar. 23, 1815.
35 *Albany Argus*, Dec. 23, 1814; *Farmer's Repository*, May 4, 1815.
36 *Centinel of Freedom*, Dec. 13, 1814.
37 *Rutland Herald*, Nov. 1, 1815.
38 *Herald of Gospel Liberty*, Mar. 18, 1814.
39 Alexander McLeod, *A Scriptural View of the Character, causes, and ends of the present war*, pp. 44-45.
40 *Baltimore Patriot and Evening Advertiser*, Nov. 5, 1814.
41 *Aurora*, Mar. 9, 1813.
42 *Washingtonian*, July 13, July 27, 1812.
43 *Rutland Herald*, Apr. 29, 1812; also Mar. 6, Mar. 11, Apr. 1. See also William A. Robinson, "The Washington Benevolent Society in New England: a Phase of Politics during the War of 1812," *Proceedings of the Massachusetts Historical Society* 49 (1915-16) : 274-86.
44 *Washingtonian*, May 4, May 28, 1812; *Rutland Herald*, May 20, 1812.
45 *Vermont Republican*, July 27, 1812; *New Hampshire Patriot*, in the *Eastern Argus*, June 4, 1812.
46 *Rutland Herald*, May 20, 1812.
47 *Pittsfield Sun*, in the *Boston Yankee*, July 7, 1815.
48 *Walpole Republican*, in the *Columbian Phenix*, Dec. 5, 1812.
49 John Kirkpatrick, *Timothy Flint, Missionary, Author, Editor, 1780-1840*, p. 47.
50 "Notes from Memorandum Book of John Stone, Deacon of the First Church, Salem," *Essex Institute Historical Collections* 61, no. 2 (Apr. 1925) : 100.
51 Asa Cummings, *Memoir and Select Thoughts of the late Rev. Edward Payson*, pp. 355-56.
52 *Eastern Argus*, Sept. 17, 1812.

53 *Voice of the Yeomanry! Proceedings of the York Convention, holden at Alfred, Sept. 10, 1812,* p. 8.
54 *Rhode Island Republican,* Aug. 13, 1812.
55 *Military Monitor and American Register,* Aug. 2, 1813; *Long Island Star,* July 12, 1815; *New York Columbian,* July 7, 1813.
56 *American Advocate,* July 16, 1814; *New Hampshire Patriot,* July 12, 1814; Mar. 16, July 13, 1813.
57 *Aurora,* Feb. 28, 1815.
58 *Rutland Herald,* July 29, 1812; Apr. 5, 1815; *Long Island Star,* Aug. 23, 1815.
59 *American Advocate,* Jan. 28, 1812; *Eastern Argus,* Oct. 22, 1812.
60 *Rutland Herald,* Sept. 1, 1813.
61 *New Hampshire Patriot,* Oct. 20, 1812.
62 *New Hampshire Patriot,* Oct. 27, 1812.
63 *New Hampshire Patriot,* Oct. 31, 1812.
64 *New Hampshire Patriot,* Sept. 27, 1814. For complete account of the controversy, see Lynn Turner, *William Plumer of New Hampshire 1759–1850,* pp. 227–30.
65 *Trenton True American,* Dec. 12, 1814.
66 *Aurora,* July 21, 1812; *Rutland Herald,* July 8, July 15, 1812; *New Hampshire Patriot,* July 21, 1812.
67 *Eastern Argus,* July 9, 1812.
68 *Eastern Argus,* July 16, July 23, 1812.
69 *Centinel of Freedom,* July 28, Aug. 4, July 21, 1812.
70 *Centinel of Freedom,* Aug. 11, Sept. 22, 1812.
71 *Lexington Recorder,* Aug. 1, 1812.
72 Vanpelt, *Discourse, delivered on the Fourth of July,* p. 16.
73 John Giles, *Two discourses delivered to the second Presbyterian society in Newburyport, August 20, 1812;* Samuel Knox, *A Discourse, delivered in the Second Presbyterian Church, in the City of Baltimore, on Thursday, the 20th of August, 1812.*
74 Sermon of Cornelius T. Demarest to workers building fortifications at McGowan's Pass near Harlem, *New York Columbian,* Sept. 6, 1814. Other examples in *New York Columbian,* Sept. 21, 1814; G. D. Bernheim, *History of the German Settlements of the Lutheran Church in North and South Carolina,* p. 418.
75 *New York Columbian,* Sept. 2, 1812.
76 *Lansingburg Gazette,* Oct. 6, 1812.
77 Elisha Cushman, *Christian Fortitude, A Discourse, delivered at the Baptist Meeting-House, in Hartford, May 30th, 1813,* p. 15.
78 Charles Hay, *Memoirs of Rev. Jacob Goering; Rev. George Lochman, D.D.; and Rev. Benjamin Kurtz, D.D., LL.D.,* pp. 96–102.
79 William Sprague, *Annals of the American Pulpit,* 9 : 128. Each section of this volume, covering several small churches, has separate pagination. See also Abdel Wentz, *History of the Lutheran Church of Frederick, Maryland, 1738–1938,* p. 208.
80 Sprague. *Annals,* 9 : 158.
81 Ibid., p. 34. John Dunlap, *The Power, Justice and Mercy of Jehovah, exercised upon his Enemies and his People. A Sermon, delivered on Board the Fleet, at Whitehall, December 18, 1814,* p. iii.

82 Clifford Drury, *The History of the Chaplain Corps, United States
    Navy*, 1 : 255.
83 "Journal of Nathaniel Pierce of Newburyport, Kept at Dartmoor
    Prison, 1814–1815," *Essex Institute Historical Collections* 73, no. 1
    (Jan. 1937) : 33, 34, 36, 42. *Journal of Joseph Valpy, Jr. of Salem,
    Nov., 1813–April, 1815*, p. 19.
84 *Federal Republican*, Mar. 10, 1814.
85 Cullen Carter, *History of the Tennessee Conference*, p. 55.
86 George Peck, *Early Methodism within the bounds of the old Genesee
    Conference from 1788 to 1828*, p. 349.
87 Hibbard, *Memoirs*, pp. 323–25; Sprague, *Annals*, 7 : 449, 211–12, 316,
    504, 506.

CHAPTER 4

1   Sprague, *Annals*, 6 : 454.
2   *Minutes of the Philadelphia Baptist Association, Held, by appointment,
    in Philadelphia. October 5th, 6th, and 7th, 1813*, pp. 7–14.
3   *Columbian Phenix*, Aug. 22, 1812.
4   Jesse Campbell, *Georgia Baptists, Historical and Biographical*, p. 223.
    Used as Republican propaganda in, for examples, *Baltimore Patriot*,
    Nov. 20, 1813; *New Hampshire Patriot*, Dec. 28, 1813.
5   *American Advocate*, Mar. 18, 1813; *New Hampshire Patriot*, Jan. 19,
    1813; *Lexington Reporter*, Dec. 19, 1812.
6   Petition of the Republican Citizens of Savannah to Congress, June 3,
    1812.
7   *Minutes of the Dover Association held at Hopeful Meeting-House . . .
    October ninth, tenth, & eleventh, 1813*, p. 12.
8   *New York Columbian*, July 2, 1812.
9   William Parkinson, *A Sermon preached in the meeting house of the
    first Baptist Church in the city of New York, August 20, 1812*, pp. 19,
    27.
10 *Long Island Star*, Oct. 14, 1812.
11 *Boston Yankee*, Jan. 20, 1815; *Aurora*, Feb. 28, 1815.
12 *Federal Republican*, Mar. 10, 1814.
13 David Jones, *Peter Edward's Candid Reasons examined and answered*,
    pp. 173–74.
14 Sprague, *Annals*, 6 : 88.
15 Quoted in Brant, *Commander in Chief*, p. 341.
16 *Richmond Enquirer*, in the *Trenton True American*, Oct. 18, 1813.
17 Sprague, *Annals*, 6 : 185–86.
18 Cushman, *Christian Fortitude*, pp. 13–14.
19 *Trenton Federalist*, June 8, 1812.
20 Leonard Richards, "John Adams and the Moderate Federalists: the
    Cape Fear Valley as a Test Case," *North Carolina Historical Review*
    43 (Winter 1966) : 30.
21 Sprague, *Annals*, 6 : 445.
22 Edward Cone, *Some Account of the Life of Spencer Houghton Cone*,
    p. 79.
23 Ibid., p. 82.

24 Thomas Armitage, *The Funeral Sermon on the Death of Rev. Spencer Houghton Cone*, p. 12.

25 Ibid., pp. 31–32.

26 Ibid., p. 32.

27 Cone, *Account of the Life of Cone*, pp. 117–18

28 *Rhode Island Republican*, July 1, 1812.

29 *Rutland Herald*, Aug. 12, 1812.

30 *American Advocate*, July 16, 1814; *New York Columbian*, July 12, 1814.

31 *New Hampshire Patriot*, July 21, Oct. 6, 1812; July 12, 1814. Ariel Kendrick, *Sketches of the Life and Times of Elder Ariel Kendrick*, p. 36.

32 In letter to *Vermont Republican*, in *New Hampshire Patriot*, Sept. 21, 1813.

33 *Carolina Federal Republican*, Sept. 12, 1812.

34 Sprague, *Annals*, 6 : 272. The Baptists of Londonderry, Vt., carried political conformity so far as to excommunicate their fellows who joined the local Washington Benevolent Society. See David Fischer, *The Revolution of American Conservatism*, pp. 127, 225.

35 B. D. Marshall, *Historical Sketches of the First Baptist Church of Worcester*, p. 8. On the subject of Federalist preaching, William Bentley observed, "The other Sects profit from this indiscretion & threaten the extirpation of the Cong. Churches if this zeal continues" (*The Diary of William Bentley, D.D.*, 4 : 114–15).

36 Austin, *Apology of Patriots*, p. 28.

37 Isaac Davis, *An Historical Discourse on the Fiftieth Anniversary of the First Baptist Church in Worcester, Mass.*, p. 11.

38 *Christian Visitant* 1, no. 5 (July 1, 1815) : 35–36.

39 *Minutes of the Philadelphia Baptist Association, held in the Meeting House of the First Baptist Church in Philadelphia. October 3d, 4th, and 5th, 1815*, p. 13.

40 *Christian Visitant* 1, no. 9 (July 29, 1815) : 68.

41 *Weekly Recorder*, Apr. 27, 1815.

42 *Minutes of the Boston Baptist Association, held at the Meeting-House of the Third Baptist Church in Boston, September 20 & 21, 1815*, p. 12. Daniel Merrill et al., *Centennial of the First Baptist Church of Sedgwick, Maine, June 11–18, 1905*, pp. 40–41.

43 Daniel Merrill, *Centennial*, pp. 55–56.

44 Sprague, *Annals*, 6 : 509.

45 Daniel Merrill, *Balaam Disappointed. A Thanksgiving sermon, delivered at Nottingham-West, April 13, 1815*, p. 7.

46 Ibid., p. 9.

47 Henry Bliss, *An Oration, delivered at the Baptist Meeting-House in Colebrook, (Con.) on the National Thanksgiving*, pp. 9–10.

48 Orsamus Merrill, *An Oration, delivered at the Meeting House in Bennington, Vermont, on the sixteenth of August, anno domini 1815*, p. 19.

49 *American Advocate*, July 15, 1815.

50 Daniel Merrill, *Balaam Disappointed*, p. 28.

51 Nathan Bangs, *A History of the Methodist Episcopal Church*, 2 : 329.

52 D. W. Clark, *Life and Times of Rev. Elijah Hedding, Late senior bishop of the Methodist Church*, pp. 221–22.

53 William Strickland, ed., *Autobiography of Dan Young, a New England preacher of the Olden Time*, pp. 102–3.

54 Peck, *Old Genesee Conference*, p. 356.

55 L. C. Rudolph, *Francis Asbury*, pp. 71–79.

56 William Sweet, *Circuit-Rider Days Along the Ohio*, p. 27.

57 Francis Brown, *Reply to Rev. Martin Ruter's Letter, relating to Calvin and Calvinism*, p. 32.

58 *Herald of Gospel Liberty*, Oct. 25, Nov. 22, 1811.

59 Elmer Clark et al., eds. *The Journal and Letters of Francis Asbury*, 2 : 701.

60 Bangs, *History*, 2 : 356.

61 Jacob Young, *Autobiography of a Pioneer*, pp. 292–94.

62 Henry Boehm, *Reminiscences, historical and biographical, of sixty-four years in the ministry*, p. 423.

63 Sprague, *Annals*, 7 : 301.

64 Hibbard, *Memoirs*, p. 339.

65 Ibid., p. 325.

66 Young, *Autobiography*, p. 309.

67 Sprague, *Annals*, 7 : 274–75.

68 *Albany Argus*, Feb. 10, 1815; *New Hampshire Patriot*, Feb. 21, 1815.

69 William Strickland, *Life of Jacob Gruber*, p. 98; Sprague, *Annals*, 7 : 346.

70 William Hawkins, *Life of John H. W. Hawkins*, pp. 11, 12, 14.

71 Adam Wallace, *The Parson of the Islands; a biography of the Rev. Joshua Thomas*, p. 146.

72 David Lewis, *Recollections of a Superannuate: or, sketches of life, labor, and experience in the Methodist itinerancy*, p. 99. James Quinn was also stationed near the fighting along the Canadian border and ministered to sick and wounded soldiers in Chillicothe, Ohio. Elijah Sabin, first Methodist to be chaplain to the House of Representatives, was a victim of the fighting in Maine, lost his property to British plunder, and was confined to a prison ship until a fellow Mason among the captors secured his release (Sprague, *Annals*, 7 : 310, 316).

73 Bangs, *History*, 2 : 359–61. The case of Henry Bailey, converted by Asbury himself but expelled from a Methodist meeting in Delaware because of political dissension, was an exception proving the rule of Methodist support for the war. His side of the affair is set forth in Henry Bailey, *A Federal Call to the People of the United States to come forward at the ensuing elections and save their country*.

74 Daniel Kidder, *Recollections of William Theophius, a Pilgrim of Fourscore*, p. 119.

75 Horace DuBose, *Life of Joshua Soule*, p. 99.

76 Sprague, *Annals*, 7 : 426, 524, 540.

77 *Long Island Star*, Apr. 16, 1815.

78 Joshua Hart, *A Sermon, prepared for the General Fast, shewing the lawfulness of defending ourselves and our leaders by the sword, at the risk of our lives, when attacked. Delivered at Huntington, Long-Island, Jan. 12, 1815*.

79 *Eastern Argus*, July 9, 1812.
80 *New England Missionary Magazine* 1, no. 2 (1815) : 46–47.
81 Clark, *Journal and Letters of Francis Asbury*, 3 : 477.
82 Joshua Wilson, *Episcopal Methodism or Dagonism Exhibited*, p. 78, quoted in Barnabas M'Henry, *Remarks on some passages in a periodical work, printed in Lexington, K., entitled "The Evangelical Record and Western Review,"* p. 6.
83 *Fredonian*, Mar. 22, 1813.
84 *Gospel Visitant* 1, no. 1 (June 1811) : 50–51.
85 Stephen Smith, *Historical Sketches and Incidents, illustrative of the establishment and progress of Universalism in the state of New York*, p. 59.
86 For example, Elisha Andrews, *A Brief Reply to Bickerstaff's short epistle to the Baptists*, p. 5; Martin Ruter, *A Letter, addressed to Rev. Francis Brown . . . containing an answer to his defence of Calvin and Calvinism*, p. 50.
87 John Kelly, *Solemn and Important Reasons against becoming a Universalist*, pp. 17, 19.
88 Hosea Ballou, *Divine Benevolence: being a reply to a Pamphlet, entitled Serious and Important reasons against becoming a Universalist*, p. 37.
89 *Gospel Visitant* 1, no. 4 (Mar. 1812) : 225–26.
90 *Hymns composed by different authors, at the request of the General Convention of Universalists of the New England states and others*, pp. iii–v.
91 Ibid., p. 252, Hymn 302 by S. Ballou.
92 Thomas Whittemore, *Life of Rev. Hosea Ballou*, 1 : 375.
93 Hosea Ballou, *A Sermon delivered at Portsmouth, N. H., appropriate to the occasion of a day of Humiliation and Prayer*, pp. 5–11. For a full account of Ballou's years in Portsmouth and his opinions on public issues, see Ernest Cassara, *Hosea Ballou, the Challenge to Orthodoxy*, pp. 82–85.
94 Ballou, *Sermon*, p. 15.
95 Whittemore, *Life of Ballou*, p. 379. Maturin Ballou, *Biography of Rev. Hosea Ballou*, pp. 94–95.
96 *Hymns composed by different authors*, pp. 256–57, Hymn 307 by Abner Kneeland.
97 Edward Turner, *The Substance of a Discourse, delivered at the Universalist Meeting-House in Charlestown, Mass. April 13, 1815*, p. 13.
98 Abner D. Jones, *Memoir of Elder Abner Jones*, pp. 186–88.
99 J. R. Freese, *A History and Advocacy of the Christian Church*, p. 23.
100 For example, *Shamrock*, Feb. 3, 1813; *Columbian Phenix*, June 13, 1812; Jan. 29, 1814.
101 Freese, *History and Advocacy of the Christian Church*, p. 23.
102 Themistus, *Madison and Religion: or a Warning to the People of the United States of America*, passim.
103 *Herald of Gospel Liberty*, July 17, 1812; Apr. 16, 1813.
104 *Herald of Gospel Liberty*, Apr. 29, 1814.
105 *Herald of Gospel Liberty*, Apr. 28, 1815.
106 *Herald of Gospel Liberty*, Dec. 22, 1815.

107 I. D. Stewart, *The History of the Freewill Baptists, for half a century*, p. 339.

108 Kirkpatrick, *Timothy Flint*, p. 48, quoting the Massachusetts Society for Promoting Christian Knowledge.

109 *Panoplist* 5, no. 4 (Sept. 1812) : 188.

110 *Religious Magazine* 1, no. 1 (Jan. 1811) : 31; 1, no. 3 (Aug. 1811) : 107.

111 *Religious Magazine* 1, no. 7 (July 1812) : 249–50.

CHAPTER 5

1 Peter Guilday, *The Life and Times of John Carroll, Archbishop of Baltimore*, 2 : 594–95; see pp. 805–14, involvement of Catholics in the war.

2 John G. Shea, *Life and Times of the Most Reverend John Carroll*, 2 : 657–58; Martin Spalding, *Sketches of the life, times, and Character of the Rt. Rev. Benedict Joseph Flaget, First Bishop of Louisville*, p. 133.

3 J. Huen Doubourg [André Hamon], *Life of the Cardinal de Cheverus*, pp. 102–3.

4 *Federal Republican*, July 15, 1814.

5 For example, *New York Columbian*, June 30, 1814; *American Advocate*, Aug. 14, 1813.

6 *National Intelligencer*, Aug. 13, 1812.

7 *National Intelligencer*, Aug. 30, 1813.

8 Spalding, *Sketches of Flaget*, p. 130.

9 Annabelle Melville, *Jean Lefebvre de Cheverus*, pp. 139–45, 157.

10 Shea, *Life of Carroll*, pp. 671, 673. Although foreign born, DuBourg had already shown himself adept at harmonizing his faith and patriotism, insisting that Catholicism was consistent with republicanism and suggesting that papal government was in its own way democratic, inasmuch as the pope's decisions required general approval from the bishops of the world (William Dubourg, *The Sons of St. Dominick: A Dialogue Between a Protestant and a Catholic*, p. 29).

11 A detailed account of the victory celebration in all its Gallic pomp is in Marquis James, *Andrew Jackson, the Border Captain*, pp. 228, 274–75.

12 Parish, *A Protest against the War*, p. 9; Arthur Stansbury, *God Pleading with America, a Sermon delivered on the late fast day*, p. 10.

13 *New York Shamrock*, Dec. 14, 1811.

14 *New York Shamrock*, June 18, 1814.

15 *Boston Patriot*, in the *Baltimore Patriot*, May 7, 1812.

16 *New Hampshire Patriot*, quoted in the *New York Shamrock*, Sept. 26, 1812.

17 *Niles' Weekly Register*, Sept. 14, 1813.

18 *Niles' Weekly Register*, Apr. 23, 1814.

19 Giles, *Two discourses, August 20, 1812*, p. 9.

20 Doubourg, *Life of Cheverus*, p. 55. Catholic participation in the war effort is detailed in Benjamin Blied, *Catholic Aspects of the War for Independence, the War of 1812, the War with Mexico, the War with Spain, Four Essays*.

21 Guilday, *Life and Times of Carroll*, 2 : 556.

22 Shea, *Life of Carroll*, 2 : 665–67.

23 *Massachusetts Baptist Missionary Magazine* 2, no. 12 (Dec. 1810) : 374–76; pp. 110–20 are reprinted, largely unchanged, from *Historical Magazine of the Protestant Episcopal Church* 38, no. 1 (Mar. 1969) : 25–36, with permission.

24 John Rice, *An illustration of the character and conduct of the Presbyterian Church in Virginia*, pp. 20–38.

25 William White, *Memoirs of the Protestant Episcopal Church in the United States*, p. 55.

26 John Henshaw, *Memoir of the Life of the Rt. Rev. Richard Channing Moore, D.D.*, pp. 129–30.

27 Themistus, *Madison and Religion*, p. 92.

28 *Halcyon Luminary* 2, no. 9 (Sept. 1813) : 393–94.

29 *Rutland Herald*, July 29, 1812.

30 *National Intelligencer*, Aug. 28, 1813.

31 *New Hampshire Patriot*, Oct. 20, 1812.

32 Jesse Stone, *Memoir of the Life of the Rt. Rev. Alexander Viets Griswold, D.D.*, pp. 618–19.

33 *Journals of the Conventions of the Protestant Episcopal Church in the Diocese of Massachusetts, from the year 1784 to the year 1828*, records for 1805–14 passim, and p. 118.

34 John Gardiner, *A Discourse delivered at Trinity Church, Boston, July 23, 1812, on the day of Publick fast in Massachusetts*, pp. 18–19.

35 *Aurora*, Aug. 31, 1812.

36 Abercrombie, *Two Sermons*, pp. iii–iv.

37 Jarvis, *Sermon, April 1815*, passim.

38 Sprague, *Annals*, 5 : 421.

39 Jesse Stone, *Memoir of Griswold*, pp. 208–9.

40 Ibid., pp. 176–77.

41 Christopher Gadsden, *A Discourse . . . on the occasion of the Death of Bishop Dehon*, pp. 21–22.

42 Sprague, *Annals*, 5 : 513–14.

43 Gardiner, *Discourse, July 23, 1812*, p. 8.

44 Philip Mathews, *An Oration, delivered on the 5th of July, 1813*, pp. 28–31.

45 Frederick Dalcho, *An Historical Account of the Protestant Episcopal Church in South Carolina*, p. 539.

46 Christopher Gadsden, *An Essay on the Life of the Right Reverend Theodore Dehon, D.D.*, pp. 240, 337–39.

47 John Hobart, *The Origin, the General Character, and the Present Situation of the Protestant Episcopal Church in the United States of America*, p. 11.

48 Ibid., pp. 13–14.

49 *Churchman's Magazine*, n.s. 2, no. 4 (July–Aug. 1814) : 291.

50 *New York Gazette*, in the *Long Island Star*, Feb. 2, 1814.

51 *Journal of the Convention of the Protestant Episcopal Church of the State of New Jersey, 1785–1816*, p. 445.

52 *Federal Republican*, Aug. 9, 1813.

53 Bird Wilson, *Memoir of the Life of the Rt. Rev. William White, D.D.*, p. 390.

54 *Pastoral Letters, from the House of Bishops to the Clergy and Members of the Protestant Episcopal Church in the United States*, p. 45.

55 *Journals of the General Conventions of the Protestant Episcopal Church in the United States, 1785–1835*, 1 : 431.

56 John Lathrop, *A Discourse, delivered in Boston, April 13, 1815, the day of Thanksgiving appointed by the President of the United States in consequence of the Peace*, p. 25.

57 *Connecticut Evangelical Magazine* 5, no. 11 (Nov. 1812) : 431–32.

58 E. Edwards Beardsley, *The History of the Episcopal Church in Connecticut*, p. 118.

59 John Hobart, *The Security of a Nation. A Sermon, Preached in Trinity Church . . . April 13, 1815*, p. 10.

60 Amelia Gummere, *Friends in Burlington*, p. 72.

61 Mrs. Douglas Brown, *A History of Lynchburg's Pioneer Quakers and Their Meeting House 1754–1936*, p. 77.

62 Peter Brock, *Pacifism in the United States from the Colonial Era to the First World War*, p. 340. For additional material on Quakers and the war, see pp. 339–42, 353, 356–58, 360, 365–66. This study also discusses the wartime experience of other pacifist groups: pp. 393–96 (Mennonites); 407–8 (Church of the Brethren); 416 (Rogerenes); 428–34 (Shakers). For the ethical problems of wartime pacifism, such as payment of militia fines and war taxes, its treatment is excellent.

63 Charles Evans, *Journal of the Life and Religious Services of William Evans*, pp. 28–32.

64 Elias Hicks, *Journal of the Life and Labours of Elias Hicks*, p. 197.

65 Isaac Martin, *A Journal of the life, travels, labours, and religious exercises of Isaac Martin*, p. 114.

66 *Christian Advices: published by the Yearly Meeting of Friends, held in Philadelphia*, p. 109.

67 Evans, *Journal of William Evans*, p. 32.

68 William Kite, *Memoirs and Letters of Thomas Kite*, p. 82.

69 Ibid., pp. 71, 83.

70 William Stabler, *A Memoir of the Life of Edward Stabler*, p. 54.

71 Joseph Hoag, *Journal of the Life of Joseph Hoag, an eminent minister of the Gospel, in the Society of Friends*, pp. 186–88.

72 Charles Osborn, *Journal of that faithful Servant of Christ, Charles Osborn*, p. 71.

73 Jesse Kersey, *A Treatise on the fundamental doctrines of the Christian Religion: in which are illustrated the profession, ministry, worship and faith of the Society of Friends*, pp. 93–95.

74 Joseph Tallcot, *Memoir of Joseph Tallcot*, p. 85.

75 Petition from the Society of Friends, of New-England, in Annual Assembly on Rhode Island (June 17, 1813).

76 Walter Whitehill, ed., *New England Blockaded in 1814. The Journal of Henry Edward Napier, Lieutenant in H. M. S. Nymphe*, pp. 39–40.

77 *New Hampshire Patriot*, Oct. 13, 1812.

78 *Trenton True American*, Mar. 8, 1813.

79 *American Advocate*, Jan. 7, 1815.

80 *Baltimore Whig*, Apr. 28, 1813.

81 *Baltimore Patriot and Evening Advertiser*, Jan. 13, 1815.

82 *National Intelligencer*, Sept. 29, 1812.
83 *Federal Republican*, in the *Carolina Federal Republican*, Oct. 17, 1812.
84 *Franklin Repository*, Jan. 10, 1815.
85 *Cumberland Register*, Aug. 26, 1812.
86 *Ohio Federalist*, Nov. 30, 1814.
87 *Federal Republican*, Oct. 19, 1812.
88 *Federal Republican*, May 31, 1813.
89 *Downington American Republican*, Sept. 6, 1814. See also Apr. 26, 1814; Aug. 4, Nov. 17, 1812; Aug. 23, 1814. Some anti-Quaker articles were extracted from other papers, like John Binns's *Democratic Press* in Philadelphia, further evidence of the extent of such sentiment.
90 Jesse Kersey, *A Narrative of the early life, travels, and gospel labors of Jesse Kersey, late of Chester County, Pennsylvania*, p. 195.
91 For this controversy and continuing abuse of the Quakers, see *Downington American Republican*, Mar. 7, Apr. 11, Sept. 19, Sept. 26, 1815.
92 *Connecticut Evangelical Magazine* 8, no. 4 (Apr. 1815) : 127; 8, no. 5 (May 1815) : 164–65. Even Shakers were included in plans for world peace. That sect, however, did not share Federalism's esteem for the Quakers, whose political activities, officeholding, and ownership of private property made their pacifism fraudulent. To this extent Shakers agreed with Republicans, for both insisted that pacifism included a disavowal of partisanship. *A Declaration of the Society of People (commonly called Shakers) shewing their reasons for refusing to aid or abet the cause of war and bloodshed by bearing arms, paying fines, hiring substitutes, or rendering any equivalent for military services*, pp. 15–16.
93 Jedidiah Morse and Elijah Parish, *A Compendious History of New England* (3d ed.). Compare chap. 11, pp. 143–44, with former chap. 12; chap 18, p. 196, with former chap 19.

EPILOGUE

1 *Christian Monitor* (Maine) 1, no. 4 (Oct.–Dec. 1814) : 121.
2 "This sense of duty, this sensitiveness to the promptings of conscience, had been the main precept in the education of a large proportion of those who in the fifties were at years of maturity" (Roy F. Nichols, *The Disruption of American Democracy*, p. 22).
3 Hart, *A Sermon, prepared for the General Fast*, p. 16.
4 Elizabeth Geffen, *Philadelphia Unitarianism 1796–1861*, p. 91.
5 *Almoner* 1, no. 5 (Jan. 1815) : 232.
6 *Weekly Recorder*, Feb. 16, 1815.
7 John B. Romeyn, *Sermons, in two volumes*, 2 : 337–39, sermon 13, "The Duty of America in the Present Crisis," preached Jan. 12, 1815. Other jeremiads on the crisis were delivered by John McDonald and Azariah Clark, both Presbyterians in New York. See *Christian Visitant* 1, no. 8 (July 22, 1815) : 59–60; *Columbian Magazine* 1, no. 7 (Mar. 1815) : 195–96.
8 *Boston Yankee*, Apr. 14, 1815.
9 *Charleston Courier*, Mar. 2, 1815.
10 *Washingtonian*, Feb. 27, 1815.

11 Samuel Blatchford, *A Sermon, delivered to the United Presbyterian Congregations of Lansingburg and Waterford, April 13, 1815,* p. 18.
12 *Christian Visitant* 1, no. 3 (June 17, 1815) : 18–19.
13 William Miltimore, *A Discourse, delivered at Falmouth, March 1, 1815, on the ratification of peace, between America and Great Britain,* p. 8.
14 John Popkin, *A Discourse delivered on the day of National Thanksgiving for Peace, April 13, 1815,* p. 10.
15 Seth Payson, *An Abridgment of Two Discourses, preached at Rindge, N. H. at the Annual Fast, April 13, 1815,* pp. 13–15.
16 Humphrey Moore, *An Oration, delivered at Milford, N. H. March 9, 1815, occasioned by the Treaty of Peace, made and ratified, between Great-Britain and the United States,* p. 6.
17 Jonathan Curtis, *Two Sermons, delivered at Epsom, New Hampshire . . . April 13, 1815,* p. 28.
18 Jesse Appleton, *A Sermon delivered at Brunswick, April 13, 1815, appointed as a day of National Thanksgiving,* pp. 15–18.
19 *Weekly Recorder,* Mar. 23, 1815.
20 Hector Benevolus, *The Hartford Convention in an Uproar! and the Wise Men of the East Confounded! together with a short history of the Peter Washingtonians; being the first book of the Chronicles of the Children of Disobedience; otherwise falsely called "Washington Benevolents,"* pp. 26, 28.
21 *Aurora,* in the *Rhode Island Republican,* May 17, 1815.
22 *New Hampshire Patriot,* Feb. 21, 1815.
23 Mathew Carey, *The Olive Branch* (7th ed.), pp. 275–76.
24 *Columbian Phenix,* Oct. 14, 1815.
25 *Rutland Herald,* Aug. 23, 1815.
26 *Missouri Gazette,* Apr. 6, 1816, quoted in Colin Goodykoontz, *Home Missions on the American Frontier,* p. 145. Charles Train, *An Oration, delivered in Hopkington, (Mass.) on the forty-seventh anniversary of our National Independence, July 4, 1823,* p. 5. The phrase which Train used in quotation marks is of course a sarcastic reference to the refusal by the Federalist legislature of Massachusetts to celebrate wartime victories because such festivals were not "becoming a moral and religious people."
27 *Farmer's Repository,* May 4, 1815; *Boston Yankee,* May 5, June 16, July 14, 1815.
28 *Boston Patriot,* in the *American Advocate,* Feb. 25, 1815.
29 *New Hampshire Patriot,* Aug. 1, Sept. 5, Sept. 12, 1815; *Long Island Star,* July 12, 1815.
30 This dilemma is discussed in William Gribbin, "The Covenant Transformed: The Jeremiad Tradition and the War of 1812," *Church History* 40, no. 3 (Sept. 1971) : 297–305, parts of which are incorporated here with permission.
31 *Vehicle, or Madison and Cayuga Christian Magazine* 1, no. 5 (June 1815) : 242.
32 *Panoplist* 11, no. 1 (Jan. 1815) : 2; 11, no. 2 (Feb. 1815) : 64.
33 *Vermont Evangelical Magazine* 7, no. 1 (Jan.–Feb. 1815) : 2.
34 Jarvis, *Sermon, April, 1815,* p. 14.
35 *The Christian Visitant* 1, no. 5 (July 1, misdated June 24, 1815) : 36.
36 An American Layman, *The Second Advent,* pp. 528–31.

37 Repeatedly in the *Weekly Recorder,* e.g. Jan. 19, 1815, reprinting the rules of the Steubenville Moral Association. *Christian Disciple* 3, no. 3 (Mar. 1815) : 86.

38 *Utica Christian Magazine* 2, no. 12 (June 1815) : 377.

39 *Christian Disciple and Theological Review* 5, no. 1 (Jan. 1817) : 29.

40 New Hampshire Petitions to Congress Concerning Sabbath-Delivery of Public Mails. Sixteen copies, all identical, presented to Congress late in 1814 and early in 1815.

41 Petition Concerning Delivery of Mails on the Sabbath, from about fifty towns in Maine, presented to Congress in Jan. and Feb. 1815.

42 Petition Against Sabbath-Day Delivery of Mails, all from early 1815.

43 *Christian Monitor* (Maine) 1, no. 4 (Oct.–Dec. 1814) : 119–20.

44 Joel Linsley, "An oration on the moral history of the United States, pronounced at commencement of Middlebury College, 17 August 1814," in *Vermont Evangelical Magazine* 7, no. 1 (Jan.–Feb. 1815) : 38.

45 *Weekly Recorder,* June 7, 1815.

46 *Almoner* 1, no. 6 (May 1815) : 276.

47 *Panoplist* 16, no. 1 (Jan. 1820) : 15–24; 16, no. 6 (June 1820) : 241–45; 16, no. 11 (Nov. 1820) : 480–94.

48 Andrew Wylie, "Praise to God for Independence, a sermon, preached on the fourth of July, 1823," in *Evangelical Witness* 2, no. 4 (Nov. 1823) : 145–57.

49 Parish, *A Protest against the War,* p. 16.

50 John Bodo, *The Protestant Clergy and Public Issues, 1812–1848,* pp. viii–ix.

51 David Donald, "Toward a Reconsideration of Abolitionists," in *Lincoln Reconsidered,* pp. 19–36.

52 *Christian Disciple and Theological Review* 3, no. 3 (Mar. 1815) : 96.

53 Samuel Walker of the Second Church in Danvers, Mass., was not the only deliverer of wartime jeremiads to make explicit use of the analogy between covenanted Americans and unsuccessful Lot, vainly trying to prevent national disaster. *Two Discourses delivered July 23, 1812.*

54 *Weekly Recorder,* Mar. 23, 1815.

55 *Analect Magazine* 9, no. 4 (Apr. 1817) : 269.

56 *Analect Magazine* 9, no. 4 (Apr. 1817) : 268.

57 *Panoplist* 13, no. 1 (Jan. 1817) : 43.

58 Report of the Prudential Committee of the A.B.C.F.M. in *Panoplist* 13, no. 10 (Oct. 1817) : 459.

59 Timothy Dwight, *Greenfield Hill,* p. 52, lines 709–12, 718–20, 737–40.

60 Ibid., p. 158, lines 311–14.

61 *Connecticut Evangelical Magazine* 7, no. 12 (Dec. 1814) : 475–76.

62 *Panoplist* 11, no. 3 (Mar. 1815) : 62.

63 John K. Fairbank, "Assignment for the '70's," *American Historical Review* 74, no. 3 (Feb. 1969) : 877–79.

64 *Panoplist* 14, no. 2 (Feb. 1818) : 59.

65 *Connecticut Evangelical Magazine* 7, no. 12 (Dec. 1814) : 462.

66 Thomas Williams, *A Discourse, occasioned by the Proclamation of Peace between Great Britain and the United States of America,* pp 22–23.

67 *Panoplist* 11, no. 6 (June 1815) : 169.

68 *Massachusetts Baptist Missionary Magazine* 4, no. 5 (Mar. 1815) : 136–37, 159.
69 *American Baptist Magazine and Missionary Intelligencer* 1, no. 1 (Jan. 1817) : 4.
70 *Christian Messenger,* May 10, 1817.
71 *Massachusetts Baptist Missionary Magazine* 4, no. 6 (June 1815) : 175.
72 *Massachusetts Baptist Missionary Magazine* 4, no. 6 (June 1815) : 181.
73 For example, *American Baptist Magazine* 1, no. 4 (July 1817) : 138; 1, no. 11 (Sept. 1818) : 413; 1, no. 12 (Nov. 1818) : 445. There were innumerable sermons like Thomas Baldwin's *Missionary Exertions Encouraged* and Samuel Nott's *Sermon on the Idolatry of the Hindoos.*
74 *American Baptist Magazine* 1, no. 1 (Jan. 1817) : 32–33.
75 *American Baptist Magazine* 1, no. 12 (Nov. 1818) : 458.
76 *Connecticut Evangelical Magazine* 5, no. 11 (Nov. 1812) : 429.
77 *Church Record* 1, no. 19 (Nov. 2, 1822) : 157.
78 *American Baptist Magazine* 1, no. 7 (Jan. 1818) : 279.
79 *American Baptist Magazine* 1, no. 8 (Mar. 1818) : 312.
80 *American Baptist Magazine* 2, no. 2 (Jan. 1819) : 40.
81 Joseph Tracy et al., *History of American Missions to the Heathen,* pp. 30, 355.
82 *American Baptist Magazine* 1, no. 12 (Nov. 1818) : 446.
83 *American Baptist Magazine* 1, no. 5 (Sept. 1817) : 200.
84 *American Baptist Magazine* 1, no. 6 (Nov. 1817) : 240.
85 *Christian Journal and Literary Register* 1, no. 14 (July 1817) : 219.
86 *Evangelical Guardian and Review* 1, no. 5 (Sept. 1817) : 235–39.
87 *Christian Messenger,* Sept. 13, 1817; Sept. 27, 1817.
88 *American Baptist Magazine* 1, no. 5 (Sept. 1817) : 178.
89 *Christian Monitor* (Virginia), Mar. 9, 1816. This was an extremely popular idea and dated back to the fast sermons of 1812 and beyond.
90 *American Baptist Magazine* 1, no. 9 (May 1818) : 330.
91 Ruhl Bartlett, ed., *The Record of American Diplomacy,* p. 258.
92 *American Baptist Magazine* 1, no. 5 (Sept. 1817) : 178.
93 *Christian Secretary,* Aug. 10, 1822.
94 *Christian Monitor* (Richmond), Mar. 9, 1816.
95 *Panoplist* 11, no. 1 (Jan. 1815) : 1.
96 *Panoplist* 15, no. 10 (Oct. 1819) : 443.
97 *Christian Chronicle,* Mar. 14, 1818.
98 *Christian Chronicle,* Oct. 17, 1818.

BIBLIOGRAPHY

NEWSPAPERS

District of Columbia: *Federal Republican; National Intelligencer.*
Georgia: *Republican and Savannah Evening Ledger.*
Kentucky: *Lexington Reporter.*
Maryland: *Baltimore Patriot; Baltimore Whig; Niles' Weekly Register.*
Massachusetts: *American Advocate; Boston Yankee; Eastern Argus.*
New Hampshire: *New Hampshire Patriot.*
New Jersey: *Centinel of Freedom; Guardian or New Brunswick Advertiser; Trenton Federalist; Trenton True American.*
New York: *Albany Argus; Lansingburg Gazette; Long Island Star; Military Monitor and American Register; New York Columbian; Shamrock.*
North Carolina: *Carolina Federal Republican; Hornet's Nest.*
Ohio: *Fredonian; Liberty Hall; Ohio Federalist and Belmont Repository; Supporter.*
Pennsylvania: *Aurora; Cumberland Register; Downington American Republican; Franklin Repository; Pittsburg Gazette; Somerset Whig.*
Rhode Island: *Columbian Phenix; Rhode Island Republican.*
South Carolina: *Charleston Courier.*
Vermont: *Rutland Herald; Vermont Republican; Washingtonian.*
Virginia: *Farmer's Repository; Martinsburg Gazette.*

RELIGIOUS JOURNALS AND NEWSPAPERS

Almoner.
American Baptist Magazine and Missionary Intelligencer.
Analect Magazine.
Christian Chronicle.

Christian Disciple and Theological Review.
Christian Journal and Literary Register.
Christian Messenger.
Christian Mirror.
Christian Monitor (Maine).
Christian Monitor (Virginia).
Christian Monitor and Religious Intelligencer.
Christian Secretary.
Christian Visitant.
Christian's Magazine.
Church Record.
Churchman's Magazine.
Connecticut Evangelical Magazine.
Evangelical Guardian and Review.
Evangelical Record and Western Review.
Evangelical Witness.
General Repository and Review.
Gospel Visitant.
Halcyon Luminary and Theological Repository.
Herald of Gospel Liberty.
Massachusetts Baptist Missionary Magazine.
New England Missionary Magazine.
Panoplist.
Religious Enquirer.
Religious Magazine.
Utica Christian Magazine.
Vehicle, or Madison and Cayuga Christian Magazine.
Vermont Baptist Missionary Magazine.
Vermont Evangelical Magazine.
Weekly Recorder.

POLITICAL LITERATURE OF THE WAR

An Address of Members of the House of Representatives of the Congress of the United States to their Constituents, on the subject of the War with Great Britain. Haverhill: W. B. & H. G. Allen, 1812.

Address of the Convention to the free electors of New-Jersey. N.p., n.d.

Address of the Republican Committee of the City of New York. New York, 1812.

Aiken, Solomon. *Address to Federal Clergymen on the Subject of the War.* Boston, 1813.

Bailey, Henry. *A Federal Call to the People of the United States to come forward at the ensuing elections and save their country.* Philadelphia, 1812.

Bliss, Henry. *An Oration, delivered at the Baptist Meeting-House in Colebrook, (Con.) on the National Thanksgiving.* N.p., 1815.

Carey, Mathew. *The Olive Branch: or, faults on both sides, federal and democratic.* 2d ed. Philadelphia: Mathew Carey, 1815.

———. *The Olive Branch: or, faults on both sides, federal and democratic.* 7th ed., Middlebury, Vt.: William Slade, 1816.

Declaration of the County of Essex, in the Commonwealth of Massachusetts by its Delegates, assembled in convention at Ipswich. Salem: Thomas Cushing, 1812.

Evarts, Jeremiah. *An oration delivered in Charlestown, (Mass.) on the fourth of July, 1812, in commemoration of American Independence.* Charlestown: Samuel Etheridge, 1812.

Hector Benevolus. *The Hartford Convention in an Uproar! and the Wise Men of the East Confounded!* . . . Windsor, Vt., 1815.

Hilliard, Isaac. *A Wonderful and Horrible Thing is Committed in the Land.* Poughkeepsie: at the Herald Office for the author, 1814.

A Layman [William Plumer]. *An Address to the Clergy of New-England, on their opposition to the Rulers of the United States.* Concord: I. & W. R. Hill, 1814.

[McFarland, Asa]. *A Defence of the Clergy of New-England, against the charges of interfering in our political affairs, and condemning the policy of the present war.* Concord: George Hough, 1814.

Merrill, Orsamus. *An Oration, delivered at the Meeting House in Bennington, Vermont, on the sixteenth of August, anno domini 1815.* Bennington: Darius Clark, 1815.

Milo. *Letters addressed to a friend at Pittsburg, on the character and conduct of DeWitt Clinton, Esq.* New York, 1812.

Proceedings of a Convention of Delegates from forty one towns, in the County of Worcester. Worcester: Isaac Sturtevant, 1812.

The Republican Crisis: or, an exposition of the political Jesuitism of James Madison, president of the United States of America. By an observant citizen of the District of Columbia. Alexandria, 1812.

Speech of the Hon. George Sullivan, at the late Rockingham Convention, with the Memorial and Resolutions, and Report of the Committee of election. 2d ed. Exeter: Constitutionalist Press, 1812.

Stockton, Lucius. *An Address before the Convention of the Friends of Peace of the State of New-Jersey, July 4, 1814.* N.p., 1814.

Touchstone to the People of the United States, on the Choice of a President. New York: Pelsue & Gould, 1812.

True Republican. *Jefferson against Madison's War.*

Tufts, Joseph. *Oration, pronounced before the Federal Republicans of Charlestown, Massachusetts, July 4, 1814.* Charlestown: Samuel Etheridge, 1814.

Voice of the Yeomanry! Proceedings of the York Convention, holden at Alfred, Sept. 10, 1812. Boston: Munroe & French, 1812.

Washington: to the people of the United States, on the choice of a President. Boston, 1812.

DENOMINATIONAL AND CONTROVERSIAL LITERATURE

The Acts and Proceedings of the General Synod of the Reformed Protestant Dutch Church in North America. New York: Board of Publication of the Reformed Protestant Dutch Church, 1859.

Andrews, Elisha. *A Brief Reply to Bickerstaff's short epistle to the Baptists.* Sutton: Sewall Goodridge, 1810.

Ballou, Hosea. *Divine Benevolence: being a reply to a Pamphlet, entitled Serious and Important reasons against becoming a Universalist.* Boston: Rowe & Hooper, 1815.

Benedict, David. *A General History of the Baptist Denomination in America, and other parts of the world.* Boston: Manning & Loring, 1813.

Brown, Francis. *Reply to Rev. Martin Ruter's Letter, relating to Calvin and Calvinism.* Portland: A. & J. Shirley, 1815.

Christian Advices: published by the Yearly Meeting of Friends, held in Philadelphia. Philadelphia: Kimber & Conrad, 1808.

Clarke, Henry. *A History of the Sabbatarians or Seventh Day Baptists in America.* Utica: Seward & Williams, 1811.

Constitution of the Presbyterian Church in the United States of America. Philadelphia: Anthony Finley, 1821.

The Constitution of the Reformed Dutch Church in the United States of America. New York: George Forman, 1815.

Dalcho, Frederick. *An Historical Account of the Protestant Episcopal Church in South Carolina.* Charleston: E. Thayer, 1820. Contains the Journals of the Diocese of South Carolina.

Dashiell, Thomas. *A Digest of the Proceedings of the Conventions and Councils in the Diocese of Virginia.* Richmond: William Jones, 1883.

A Declaration of the Society of People (commonly called Shakers) shewing their reasons for refusing to aid or abet the cause of war and bloodshed by bearing arms, paying fines, hiring substitutes, or rendering any equivalent for military services. Hartford: Hudson & Goodwin, 1815.

The Documentary History of the Protestant Episcopal Church in the Diocese of Vermont, including the Journals of the Conventions from the years 1790 to 1832 inclusive. New York: Pott & Amery, 1870.

DuBourg, William. *The Sons of St. Dominick: A Dialogue Between a Protestant and a Catholic, on the Occasion of the Late Defence of the Pastoral Letter, of the Presbytery of Baltimore, against the Vindication of St. Mary's Seminary, and Catholics at large.* Baltimore: Bernard Dornin, 1812.

Extracts from the Minutes of the General Association of the Presbyterian Church in the United States of America, A.D. 1812. Philadelphia: Jane Aitken, 1812.

Extracts from the Minutes of the General Association of the Presbyterian Church in the United States of America, A.D. 1814. Philadelphia: Jane Aitken, 1814.

Extracts from the Minutes of the Proceedings of the Ninth General Synod of the Associate Reformed Church in North America. Philadelphia: Jane Aitken, 1812.

Fristoe, William. *A Concise History of the Ketocton Baptist Association.* Staunton: William Lyford, 1808.

Hibbard, Billy. *An Address to the Quakers: including the pamphlet entitled, Errors of the Quakers &c.* New York: for the author, 1811.

Hobart, John. *The Origin, the General Character, and the Present Situation of the Protestant Episcopal Church in the United States of America.* Philadelphia: Bradford & Inskeep, 1814.

Hymns composed by different authors, at the request of the General Convention of Universalists of the New England states and others. 2d ed. Charlestown: Samuel T. Armstrong, 1810.

Jones, David. *Peter Edward's Candid Reasons examined and answered.* Philadelphia: Dennis Heartt, 1811.

Journal of a Convention of the Protestant Episcopal Church, held in St. Paul's, Baltimore, June 9, 1813. Baltimore: J. Robinson, 1813.

Journal of a Convention of the Protestant Episcopal Church of Maryland, held in Christ Church, Easton, May 17th, 18th, & 19th, 1815. Baltimore: J. Robinson, 1815.

Journal of the Convention of the Protestant Episcopal Church of the State of New Jersey, 1785–1816. New York: John Polhemus, 1890.

Journal of the 29th Convention of the Protestant Episcopal Church in the State of Pennsylvania. Philadelphia: William Fry, 1813.

Journal of the 30th Convention of the Protestant Episcopal Church in the State of Pennsylvania. Philadelphia: James Maxwell, 1815.

Journals of the Conventions of the Protestant Episcopal Church in the Diocese of Massachusetts, from the year 1784 to the year 1828. Boston: James Dow, 1849.

Journals of the Conventions of the Protestant Episcopal Church in the Diocese of New York. New York: Henry M. Onderdonk, 1844.

Journals of the Conventions of the Protestant Episcopal Church in the Diocese of Rhode Island. Providence, 1859.

Journals of the General Conference of the Methodist Episcopal Church. Vol. 1 : 1796–1836. New York: Carlton & Phillips, 1855.

Journals of the General Conventions of the Protestant Episcopal Church in the United States, 1785–1835. Claremont, N. H.: Claremont Manufacturing Co., 1874.

Kelly, John. *Solemn and Important Reasons against becoming a Universalist.* Haverhill: Burrill & Tileston, 1815.

Kersey, Jesse. *A Treatise on the fundamental doctrines of the Christian Religion: in which are illustrated the profession, ministry, worship and faith of the Society of Friends.* Philadelphia: Solomon Conrad, 1815.

M'Henry, Barnabas. *Remarks on some passages in a periodical work, printed in Lexington, K., entitled "The Evangelical Record and Western Review."* Lexington: Smith, 1813.

Minutes of the Annual Conferences of the Methodist Episcopal Church, for the years 1775–1828. New York: T. Mason & G. Lane, 1840.

Minutes of the Boston Baptist Association, held at the Meeting-House of the Third Baptist Church in Boston, September 20 & 21, 1815. Boston: Lincoln & Edmands, 1815.

Minutes of the Dover Association held at Hopeful Meeting-House . . . October ninth, tenth, & eleventh, 1813. Richmond: Ritchie & Truehart, 1813.

Minutes of the Philadelphia Baptist Association, Held, by appointment, in Philadelphia. October 5th, 6th, and 7th, 1813. N.p., n.d.

Minutes of the Philadelphia Baptist Association, held in the Meeting House of the First Baptist Church in Philadelphia. October 3d, 4th, and 5th, 1815. N.p., n.d.

Pastoral Letters, from the House of Bishops to the Clergy and Members of the Protestant Episcopal Church in the United States. Philadelphia: Edward Biddle, 1845.

Rice, John. *An illustration of the character and conduct of the Pres-*

byterian Church in Virginia. Richmond: Du Val & Burke, 1816.

Ruter, Martin. *A Letter, addressed to Rev. Francis Brown . . . containing an answer to his defence of Calvin and Calvinism*. Portland: F. Douglas, 1815.

Sweet, William, ed. *Circuit-Rider Days Along the Ohio*. New York: Methodist Book Concern, 1923. Contains the Journals of the Ohio Conference from 1812.

———. *The Rise of Methodism in the West, being the Journal of the Western Conference 1800–1811*. New York: Methodist Book Concern, 1920.

Themistus. *Madison and Religion: or a Warning to the People of the United States of America*. Philadelphia: at the Herald Office, 1811.

Willis, Thomas. *The Doctrine and Principles of the people called Quakers, explained and vindicated*. New York: Samuel Wood, 1812.

Sermons on the War

Abercrombie, James. *Two Sermons; the first, preached on Thursday, July 30; the second, preached on Thursday, August 20, 1812: being days of fasting, humiliation, and prayer, appointed by Public Authority*. Philadelphia: Moses Thomas, 1812.

Andros, Thomas. *The place of the church in the grand chart of scripture prophecy, or the great battle of Armageddon*. Boston: Samuel Armstrong, 1814.

Appleton, Jesse. *A Sermon delivered at Brunswick, April 13, 1815, appointed as a day of National Thanksgiving*. Hallowell: Ezekiel Goodale, 1815.

Austin, Samuel. *The Apology of Patriots, or the heresy of the Friends of the Washington and peace policy defended*. Worcester: Isaac Sturtevant, 1812.

———. *Sermon preached in Worcester, Massachusetts, on the occasion of the special fast, July 23, 1812*. Worcester: Isaac Sturtevant, 1812.

Ballou, Hosea. *A Sermon delivered at Portsmouth, N. H., appropriate to the occasion of a day of Humiliation and Prayer*. Portsmouth: W. Weeks, 1812.

Beecher, Lyman. "A reform of morals practicable and indispensable." In *Sermons, delivered on various occasions*, 2 : 75–113. Boston: John P. Jewett & Co., 1852.

Bell, Benjamin. *A Sermon preached at Steuben, April, 1813, in which are shewn the evil effects of war and when it may be lawful to go to war.* Sangerfield: J. Tenny, 1814.

Beman, Nathan. *A Sermon delivered at the meeting house of the Second Parish in Portland, August 20, 1812, on the occasion of the National Fast.* Portland: Hyde, Lord & Co., 1812.

Blatchford, Samuel. *A Sermon, delivered to the United Presbyterian Congregations of Lansingburg and Waterford, April 13, 1815.* Albany: Websters & Skinners, 1815.

Bradford, John. *The Fear of the Lord, the Hope of Freedom. A Sermon, on the present struggle of the Dutch for emancipation.* Albany: E. & E. Hosford, 1814.

———. *The Schools of the Prophets: A Sermon, delivered at New-Brunswick, New-Jersey, before the Board of Superintendants, of the Theological School of the Reformed Dutch Church, on Wednesday, 28th April, 1813.* Albany: Green & Co., 1813.

Brown, Francis. *A Sermon delivered July 23, 1812, on occasion of the state fast, appointed in consequence of the Declaration of War against Great Britain.* Portland: Gazette Press, 1812.

Cary, Samuel. *A Sermon preached before the ancient and honourable artillery Company, in Boston, June 6, 1814.* Boston: Wells, 1814.

Channing, William. *A discourse delivered in Boston, at the solemn festival in commemoration of the goodness of God in delivering the Christian world from military despotism, June 15, 1814.* Boston: Henry Channing, 1814.

———. *A Sermon, preached in Boston, August 20, 1812.* Boston: C. Stebbins, 1812.

———. *A sermon preached in Boston, July 23, 1812.* Boston: Greenough & Stebbins, 1812.

Church, John Hubbard. *Advantages of Moderation, A Sermon delivered at Pelham, N. H. August 20, 1812.* Haverhill: W. B. & H. G. Allen, 1812.

Clark, Daniel Atkinson. *Independence Sermon delivered July 4, 1814 at Hanover, New Jersey.* Newark: John Tuttle & Co., 1814.

Curtis, Jonathan. *Two Sermons, delivered at Epsom, New Hampshire . . . April 13, 1815.* Concord: George Hough, 1815.

Cushman, Elisha. *Christian Fortitude, A Discourse, delivered at the Baptist Meeting-House, in Hartford, May 30th, 1813.* Hartford: John Russell, 1813.

Dow, Moses. *A Sermon preached in Beverly, August 20, 1812 . . . and again at the Tabernacle in Salem, April 8, 1813.* Salem: Joshua Cushing, 1813.

Dunlap, John. *The Power, Justice and Mercy of Jehovah, exercised upon his Enemies and his People. A Sermon, delivered on Board the Fleet, at Whitehall, December 18, 1814.* Albany: Websters & Skinners, 1815.

Dwight, Timothy. *Discourse, in Two parts, delivered August 20, 1812, on the National Fast, in the chapel of Yale College.* 2d ed. Boston: Cummings & Hilliard, 1813.

———. *A Discourse, in two parts, delivered July 23, 1812, on the Public Fast in the Chapel of Yale College.* 2d ed. Boston: Cummings & Hilliard, 1813.

Emerson, Brown. *The Causes and Effects of War. A Sermon, delivered in Salem, August 20, 1812, the day of National humiliation and Prayer.* Salem: Joshua Cushing, 1812.

———. *The Equity of God's dealings with Nations, A Sermon, preached in Salem, July 23, 1812.* Salem: Joshua Cushing, 1812.

Fiske, John. *A Sermon delivered at New-Braintree, August 20, 1812.* Brookfield, Mass.: E. Merriam & Co., 1812.

French, Jonathan. *Sermons, delivered on the 20th of August, 1812 . . . to which are added Observations on the Propriety of preaching occasionally on Political Subjects.* Exeter: E. G. Beals, 1812.

Gardiner, John. *A discourse, delivered at Trinity Church, Boston, April 9, 1812 on the day of the Publick Fast.* Boston: Munroe & Francis, 1812.

———. *A Discourse delivered at Trinity Church, Boston, July 23, 1812 on the day of Publick fast in Massachusetts.* Boston: Munroe & Francis, 1812.

Giles, John. *Discourses delivered to the second Presbyterian society in Newburyport, August 20, 1812 . . . with a copious appendix.* Haverhill: W. B. & H. G. Allen, 1812.

———. *Two discourses delivered to the second Presbyterian society in Newburyport, August 20, 1812.* 3d ed. Newburyport: W. & J. Gilman, 1812.

Hart, Joshua. *A Sermon delivered at Huntington, July 4, 1813; being the anniversary of American Independence.* Brooklyn: Alden Spooner, 1813.

———. *A Sermon, prepared for the General Fast, shewing the lawfulness of defending ourselves and our leaders by the sword, at the risk of our lives, when attacked. Delivered at Huntington, Long-Island, Jan. 12, 1815.* Brooklyn: Alden Spooner, 1815.

Hobart, John. *The Security of a Nation. A Sermon, Preached in Trinity Church . . . April 13, 1815.* New York: T. & J. Swords, 1815.

Holcomb, Reuben. *A Discourse in Two parts, delivered at Sterling,*

Massachusetts, Thursday, July 23, 1812, at the State Fast. Worcester: Isaac Sturtevant, 1812.

Jarvis, Samuel. *The duty of offering unto God thanksgiving. A Sermon, preached in St. Michael's Church, Bloomingdale, on the Second Thursday in April, A.D. 1815.* New York: Eastburn, Kirk, & Co., 1815.

Knox, Samuel. *A Discourse, delivered in the Second Presbyterian Church, in the City of Baltimore, on Thursday, the 20th of August, 1812.* Baltimore: William Warner, 1812.

Lathrop, John. *A Discourse, delivered in Boston, April 13, 1815, the day of Thanksgiving appointed by the President of the United States in consequence of the Peace.* Boston: J. W. Burditt, 1815.

———. *A Discourse on the law of retaliation, delivered in the New Brick Church, February 6, 1814.* Boston: J. W. Burditt, 1814.

———. *The present war unexpected, unnecessary, and ruinous.* Boston: J. W. Burditt, 1812.

Latta, John. *A Sermon Preached at New-Castle, (Del.) on the Thirteenth Day of April, 1815.* Wilmington: Robert Porter, 1815.

———. *A Sermon Preached on the 20th of August, 1812.* Wilmington: Robert Porter, 1812.

Long, David. *A Discourse, delivered in Milford, (Mass.) on Lord's Day, October 30, 1814: occasioned by the return of a company of artillery, under Captain Rufus Thayer, from Camp, at South-Boston.* Boston: S. T. Armstrong, 1814.

Mathews, Philip. *An Oration, delivered on the 5th of July, 1813.* Charleston: John MacKey & Co., 1813.

McLeod, Alexander. *A Scriptural View of the Character, causes, and ends of the present war.* New York: Eastburn, Kirk, & Co., 1815.

Merrill, Daniel. *Balaam Disappointed. A Thanksgiving sermon, delivered at Nottingham-West, April 13, 1815.* Danville, Vt.: Ebenezer Eaton, 1816.

Miltimore, William. *A Discourse, delivered at Falmouth, March 1, 1815, on the ratification of peace, between America and Great Britain.* Portland: F. Douglas, 1815.

Moore, Humphrey. *An Oration, delivered at Milford, N. H. March 9, 1815, occasioned by the Treaty of Peace, made and ratified, between Great-Britain and the United States.* Amherst: R. Boylston, 1815.

Morse, Jedidiah. *A Sermon delivered at Charlestown, July 23, 1812.* Charlestown: Samuel Etheridge, 1812.

Osgood, David. *A Solemn Protest against the late declaration of war, in a Discourse, delivered on the next Lord's Day after the tidings of it were received.* 2d ed. Exeter: C. Norris & Co., 1812.

Parish, Elijah. *A Protest against the War, a Discourse delivered at Byfield, Fast Day, July 23, 1812.* Newburyport: E. W. Allen, 1812.

Parker, Freeman. *A Sermon delivered at Dresden, July 23, 1812; the day appointed by the governor and Council for a State Fast: and at Wiscasset, on the 20th of August following: the day recommended by the President of the United States for a National Fast.* Portland: Arthur Shirley, 1812.

Parkinson, William. *A Sermon preached in the meeting house of the first Baptist Church in the city of New York, August 20, 1812.* New York: John Tiebout, 1812.

Payson, Seth. *An Abridgment of Two Discourses, preached at Rindge, N. H. at the Annual Fast, April 13, 1815.* New-Ipswich: Simeon Ide, 1815.

Popkin, John. *A Discourse delivered on the day of National Thanksgiving for Peace, April 13, 1815.* Newburyport: W. B. Allen, 1815.

Richardson, Joseph. *The Christian Patriot Encouraged. A Discourse, delivered before the first Parish in Hingham, on Fast Day, April 8, 1813.* Boston: Joshua Belcher, 1813.

Romeyn, John B. "The Duty of America in the Present Crisis." In *Sermons in two volumes,* 2 : 308–74. New York: Eastburn, Kirk, & Co., 1816.

Rowan, Stephen. *The Sin and Danger of Insensibility under the calls of God to Repentance. Two Sermons, delivered in the Reformed Dutch Church at Greenwich, in the city of New York, on Thursday, July 30, 1812.* New York: Whiting & Watson, 1812.

Speece, Conrad. *A Sermon, delivered at Peterville Church, on Thursday, August 20, 1812.* Richmond: Blagrove & Truehart, 1812.

Stansbury, Arthur. *God Pleading with America, a Sermon delivered on the late fast day.* Goshen, N. Y.: T. B. Crowell, 1813.

Stevens, John. *A Discourse, delivered in Stoneham, (Mass.) April 8, 1813 being the day of the State Fast.* Bennington: Darius Clark & Co., 1813. This sermon was published in New York, Boston, and other cities under the title, *The Duty of Union in a Just War.*

Stone, Micah. *Danger and Duty pointed out, in a Discourse, delivered at Brookfield, South Parish, July 23, 1812.* Brookfield, Mass.: E. Merriam & Co., 1812.

Strong, Nathan. *A fast sermon, delivered in the North Presbyterian*

Meeting House in Hartford, July 23, 1812. Hartford: Peter Gleason and Co., 1812.

Thayer, Nathaniel. *A Sermon delivered August 20, 1812.* Worcester: Isaac Sturtevant, 1812.

Truair, John. *The Alarm Trumpet. A Discourse, delivered at Berkshire, September 9, 1813.* Montpelier: Walton & Goss, 1812.

Turner, Edward. *The Substance of a Discourse, delivered at the Universalist Meeting-House in Charlestown, Mass. April 13, 1815.* Charlestown: J. Howe, 1815.

Vanpelt, Peter. *A Discourse, delivered on the Fourth of July, in the North Brick Church.* New York, 1812.

Walker, Samuel. *Two Discourses delivered July 23, 1812, being the day appointed by the Governor of Massachusetts for fasting and prayer, on account of the war with Great-Britain.* Salem: Joshua Cushing, 1812.

Whelpley, Samuel. *The fall of Wicked Nations. A Sermon, delivered in the First Presbyterian Church, Newark, September 9, 1813, A Day of Fasting and humiliation.* New York: Pelsue & Gould, 1813.

Whitaker, Nathaniel. *The Reward of Toryism, a discourse on Judges V. 23, delivered at the Tabernacle in Salem, May 1783.* Boston: reprinted at the Yankee Office, 1813.

Williams, Thomas. *A Discourse, occasioned by the Proclamation of Peace between Great Britain and the United States of America.* Providence: H. Mann & Co., 1815.

Wilson, Joshua. *A Sermon, delivered in the Presbyterian Meeting House in Cincinnati, Ohio, to the Cincinnati Light Companies. May 14, 1812.* Concord: I. & W. R. Hill, 1812.

Worcester, Noah. *Abraham and Lot, A Sermon on the Way of Peace, and the Evils of War, delivered at Salisbury, in New-Hampshire, on the day of the National Fast.* Concord: George Hough, 1812.

———. *The Substance of Two sermons, occasioned by the late declaration of war, preached at Salisbury, New-Hampshire on Lord's Days, June 28th and July 5th, 1812.* Concord: George Hough, 1812.

Worcester, Samuel. *Calamity, Danger, and Hope, A Sermon preached at the Tabernacle in Salem, July 23, 1812, the day of the publick fast in Massachusetts, on account of the War with Great-Britain.* Salem: Joshua Cushing, 1812.

———. *Courage and Success to the Good, A Discourse delivered at the Tabernacle in Salem, August 20, 1812 . . . and the Substance of a Discourse, delivered Sabbath Day, August 9, 1812.* Salem: Joshua Cushing, 1812.

Miscellaneous Sources

An American Layman [Elias Boudinot]. *The Second Advent, or coming of the Messiah in Glory.* Trenton: D. Fenton & S. Hutchinson, 1815.

Buchanan, Claudius. *Christian Researches in Asia: with notices of the translation of the Scriptures into the Oriental languages.* 2d ed. Boston: Samuel Armstrong, 1811.

Dwight, Timothy. *Greenfield Hill.* New York: Childs & Swain, 1794.

Kinne, Aaron. *A Display of Scriptural Prophecies.* Boston: Samuel Armstrong, 1813.

Morse, Jedidiah, and Parish, Elijah. *A Compendious History of New England.* 2d ed. Newburyport: Thomas & Whipple, 1809.

————. *A Compendious History of New England.* 3d ed. Charlestown: Samuel Etheridge, 1820.

Second Report of the New-Hampshire Bible Society. Concord: George Hough, 1813.

Other Literature Cited

Adams, Henry. *History of the United States during the Administration of Jefferson and Madison.* 9 vols. New York: Charles Scribner's Sons, 1889–91.

Armitage, Thomas. *The Funeral Sermon on the Death of Rev. Spencer Houghton Cone.* New York: Holman & Gray, 1855.

Ballou, Maturin. *Biography of Rev. Hosea Ballou.* Boston: Abel Tompkins, 1852.

Bangs, Nathan. *A History of the Methodist Episcopal Church.* 2 vols. New York: T. Mason & G. Lane, 1839.

Banner, James. *To the Hartford Convention: The Federalists and the Origins of Party Politics in Massachusetts, 1789–1815.* New York: Alfred A. Knopf, 1970.

Bartlett, Ruhl, ed. *The Record of American Diplomacy.* New York: Alfred A. Knopf, 1959.

Beardsley, E. Edwards. *The History of the Episcopal Church in Connecticut.* New York: Hurd & Houghton, 1868.

Bentley, William. *The Diary of William Bentley, D.D.* 4 vols. Gloucester: Peter Smith, 1962.

Bernheim, G. D. *History of the German Settlements of the Lutheran Church in North and South Carolina.* Philadelphia: Lutheran Book Store, 1872.

Blied, Benjamin. *Catholic Aspects of the War for Independence, the War of 1812, the War with Mexico, the War with Spain: Four Essays.* Milwaukee, 1949.

Boehm, Henry. *Reminiscences, historical and biographical, of sixty-four years in the ministry.* New York: Carlton & Porter, 1866.

Brant, Irving. *James Madison, Commander in Chief 1812–1836.* Indianapolis: Bobbs-Merrill Co., 1961.

Brock, Peter. *Pacifism in the United States from the Colonial Era to the First World War.* Princeton: Princeton University Press, 1968.

Brown, Mrs. Douglas S. *A History of Lynchburg's Pioneer Quakers and Their Meeting House 1754–1936.* Lynchburg: Douglas Brown, 1936.

Campbell, Jesse. *Georgia Baptists, Historical and Biographical.* Richmond: H. K. Ellyson, 1847.

Carter, Cullen. *History of the Tennessee Conference.* Nashville: C. T. Carter, 1948.

Cassara, Ernest. *Hosea Ballou, the Challenge to Orthodoxy.* Boston: Beacon Press, 1961.

Clark, D. W. *Life and Times of Rev. Elijah Hedding, Late senior bishop of the Methodist Church.* New York: Carlton & Phillips, 1855.

Clark, Elmer, et al., eds. *The Journal and Letters of Francis Asbury.* 3 vols. Nashville: Abingdon Press, 1958.

Cone, Edward. *Some Account of the Life of Spencer Houghton Cone.* New York: Livermore & Rudd, 1856.

Cummings, Asa. *Memoir and Select Thoughts of the late Rev. Edward Payson.* New York: William Hyde, 1849.

Davis, Isaac. *An Historical Discourse on the Fiftieth Anniversary of the First Baptist Church in Worcester, Mass.* Worcester: Henry Howland, 1863.

Donald, David. *Lincoln Reconsidered.* New York: Alfred A. Knopf, 1956.

Doubourg, J. Huen [André Hamon]. *Life of the Cardinal de Cheverus.* Philadelphia: Hooker & Caxton, 1839.

Drury, Clifford. *The History of the Chaplain Corps, United States Navy.* Washington, D. C.: U. S. Government Printing Office, 1948.

DuBose, Horace. *Life of Joshua Soule.* Nashville: Publishing House of the Methodist Episcopal Church South, 1911.

Engelman, Fred. *The Peace of Christmas Eve.* New York: Harcourt, Brace and World, 1962.

Evans, Charles. *Journal of the Life and Religious Services of William Evans.* Philadelphia: Caxton Press, 1870.

Fischer, David. *The Revolution of American Conservatism.* New York: Harper & Row, 1965.

Fiske, John. *Recollections and Anticipations. A half-century and dedicatory discourse, delivered in New-Braintree, Massachusetts, October 26, 1846.* Greenfield: Merriam & Mirick, 1846.

Foster, Charles. *An Errand of Mercy: The Evangelical United Front, 1790–1837.* Chapel Hill: University of North Carolina Press, 1960.

Freese, J. R. *A History and Advocacy of the Christian Church.* 3d ed. Philadelphia: Christian General Book Concern, 1852.

Gabriel, Ralph Henry. *The Course of American Democratic Thought.* 2d ed. New York: Ronald Press, 1956.

Gadsden, Christopher. *A Discourse . . . on the occasion of the Death of Bishop Dehon.* Charleston: A. E. Miller, 1817.

——. *An Essay on the Life of the Right Reverend Theodore Dehon, D.D.* Charleston: A. E. Miller, 1833.

Geffen, Elizabeth. *Philadelphia Unitarianism 1796–1861.* Philadelphia: University of Pennsylvania Press, 1961.

Goodykoontz, Colin. *Home Missions on the American Frontier.* Caldwell, Idaho: Caxton Press, 1939.

Greene, L. K., ed. *The Writings of the Late Elder John Leland.* New York: G. W. Wood, 1845.

Guilday, Peter. *The Life and Times of John Carroll, Archbishop of Baltimore.* 2 vols. New York: The Encyclopedia Press, 1922.

Gummere, Amelia. *Friends in Burlington.* Philadelphia: Collins, 1884.

Hawkins, William. *Life of John H. W. Hawkins.* Boston: John P. Jewett & Co., 1859.

Hay, Charles. *Memoirs of Rev. Jacob Goering; Rev. George Lochman, D.D.; and Rev. Benjamin Kurtz, D.D., LL.D.* Philadelphia: Lutheran Publication Society, 1887.

Henshaw, John. *Memoir of the Life of the Rt. Rev. Richard Channing Moore, D.D.* Philadelphia: William Stanely & Co., 1843.

Hibbard, Billy. *Memoirs of the Life and Travels of Billy Hibbard.* 2d ed. New York: published by the author, 1843.

Hicks, Elias. *Journal of the Life and Labours of Elias Hicks.* New York: Isaac Hopper, 1832.

Hoag, Joseph. *Journal of the Life of Joseph Hoag, an eminent minister of the Gospel, in the Society of Friends.* Auburn: Knapp & Peck, 1861.

Horsman, Reginald. *The Causes of the War of 1812.* Philadelphia: University of Pennsylvania Press, 1962.

James, Marquis. *Andrew Jackson, the Border Captain.* New York: Grosset and Dunlap, 1964.

Jones, Abner D. *Memoir of Elder Abner Jones*. Boston: William Crosby & Co., 1842.

Journal of Joseph Valpy, Jr. of Salem, Nov., 1813–April, 1815. Detroit: Michigan Society of Colonial Wars, 1922.

Kendrick, Ariel. *Sketches of the Life and Times of Elder Ariel Kendrick*. Ludlow, Vt.: Barton & Tower, 1847.

Kerber, Linda. *Federalists in Dissent: Imagery and Ideology in Jeffersonian America*. Ithaca: Cornell University Press, 1970.

Kersey, Jesse. *A Narrative of the early life, travels, and gospel labors of Jesse Kersey, late of Chester County, Pennsylvania*. Philadelphia: T. Elwood Chapman, 1851.

Kidder, Daniel. *Recollections of William Theophius, a Pilgrim of Fourscore*. New York: Lany & Scott, 1852.

Kirkpatrick, John. *Timothy Flint, Missionary, Author, Editor, 1780–1840*. Cleveland: Arthur Clark Co., 1911.

Kite, William. *Memoirs and Letters of Thomas Kite*. Philadelphia: Friends' Book Concern, 1883.

Koch, Gustaf. *Republican Religion: The American Revolution and the Cult of Reason*. New York: Henry Holt & Co., 1933.

Lewis, David. *Recollections of a Superannuate: or, sketches of life, labor, and experience in the Methodist itineracy*. Cincinnati: Methodist Book Concern, 1857.

Marshall, B. D. *Historical Sketches of the First Baptist Church of Worcester*. Worcester: Henry Howland, 1877.

Martin, Isaac. *A Journal of the life, travels, labours, and religious exercises of Isaac Martin*. Philadelphia: William Gibbons, 1834.

Melville, Annabelle. *Jean Lefebvre de Cheverus*. Milwaukee: Bruce, 1958.

Merrill, Daniel, et al. *Centennial of the First Baptist Church of Sedgwick, Maine, June 11–18, 1905*. N.p., 1905.

Milnor, James. *Sermon occasioned by the death of his Excellency DeWitt Clinton*. New York: Gray & Bruce, 1828.

Nichols, Roy F. *The Disruption of American Democracy*. 2d ed. New York: Macmillan, 1948.

Osborn, Charles. *Journal of that faithful Servant of Christ, Charles Osborn*. Cincinnati: Achilles Pugh, 1854.

Pearson, Hugh. *Memoirs of the Life and Writings of Rev. Claudius Buchanan*. Oxford: At the University Press, 1817.

Peck, George. *Early Methodism within the bounds of the old Genesee Conference from 1788 to 1828*. New York: Carlton & Porter, 1860.

Perkins, Bradford. *Prologue to War.* Berkeley: University of California Press, 1961.

Proudfit, Alexander. *The Agency of God in the Elevation of Man.* Salem: Dodd & Stevenson, 1828.

Renwick, James. *Life of DeWitt Clinton.* New York: Harper & Bros., 1840.

Richardson, James, ed. *A Compilation of the Messages and Papers of the Presidents 1789–1902.* Washington, D.C.: Bureau of National Literature and Art, 1905.

Rudolph, L. C. *Francis Asbury.* Nashville: Abingdon Press, 1966.

Shea, John G. *Life and Times of the Most Reverend John Carroll.* 2 vols. New York: John G. Shea, 1888.

Smith, Stephen. *Historical Sketches and Incidents, illustrative of the establishment and progress of Universalism in the state of New York.* Buffalo: Steele's Press, 1843.

Spalding, Martin. *Sketches of the life, times, and Character of the Rt. Rev. Benedict Joseph Flaget, First Bishop of Louisville.* Louisville: Webb & Levering, 1852.

Sprague, William. *Annals of the American Pulpit.* 9 vols. New York: Robert Carter & Bros., 1857–69.

Staats, Cuyler. *Tribute to the Memory of DeWitt Clinton.* Albany: Webster & Wood, 1828.

Stabler, William. *A Memoir of the Life of Edward Stabler.* Philadelphia: John Richards, 1846.

Stauffer, Vernon. *New England and the Bavarian Illuminati.* New York: Columbia University Press, 1918.

Stewart, I. D. *The History of the Freewill Baptists, for half a century.* Dover: Freewill Baptist Printing Establishment, 1862.

Stone, Jesse. *Memoir of the Life of the Rt. Rev. Alexander Viets Griswold, D.D.* Philadelphia: Stanely & McCalla, 1844.

Strickland, William, ed. *Autobiography of Dan Young, a New England preacher of the Olden Time.* New York: Carlton & Porter, 1866.

———. *Life of Jacob Gruber.* New York: Carlton & Porter, 1860.

Tallcot, Joseph. *Memoir of Joseph Tallcot.* Auburn: Miller, Orton, & Mulligan, 1855.

Tracy, Joseph, et al. *History of American Missions to the Heathen.* Worcester: Spooner & Howland, 1840.

Train, Charles. *An Oration, delivered in Hopkington, (Mass.) on the forty-seventh anniversary of our National Independence, July 4, 1823.* Worcester: William Manning, 1823.

Turner, Lynn. *William Plumer of New Hampshire 1759–1850.* Chapel Hill: University of North Carolina Press, 1962.

Wallace, Adam. *The Parson of the Islands; a biography of the Rev. Joshua Thomas.* Philadelphia: published by the author, 1861.

Ware, Henry. *Memoirs of the Rev. Noah Worcester.* Boston: James Munroe & Co., 1844.

Wentz, Abdel. *History of the Lutheran Church of Frederick, Maryland, 1738–1938.* Harrisburg: Evangelical Press, 1938.

White, William. *Memoirs of the Protestant Episcopal Church in the United States of America.* Philadelphia: S. Potter & Co., 1820.

Whitehill, Walter, ed. *New England Blockaded in 1814: The Journal of Henry Edward Napier, Lieutenant in H. M. S. Nymphe.* Salem: Peabody Museum, 1939.

Whittemore, Thomas. *Life of Rev. Hosea Ballou.* Boston: James Usher, 1854.

Wilson, Bird. *Memoir of the Life of the Rt. Rev. William White, D.D.* Philadelphia: James Kay, 1839.

Worcester, S. M. *Life and Labors of Rev. Samuel Worcester.* Boston: Crocker & Brewster, 1852.

Young, Jacob. *Autobiography of a Pioneer.* Cincinnati: L. Swormstedt & A. Poe, 1859.

Articles Cited

"Diary of Archelaus Putnam of New Mills." *Danvers Historical Collections* 6 (1918) : 11–29.

Fairbank, John K. "Assignment for the '70's." *American Historical Review* 74, no. 3 (Feb. 1969) : 861–79.

Goodman, Warren. "The Origins of the War of 1812: A Survey of Changing Interpretations." *Mississippi Valley Historical Review* 28 (1941–42) : 171–86.

Gribbin, William. "American Episcopacy and the War of 1812." *Historical Magazine of the Protestant Episcopal Church* 38, no. 1 (Mar. 1969): 25–36.

———. "The Covenant Transformed: The Jeremiad Tradition and the War of 1812." *Church History* 40, no. 3 (Sept. 1971) : 297–305.

———. "The War of 1812 and American Presbyterianism: Religion and Politics during the Second War with Great Britain." *Journal of Presbyterian History* 47, no. 4 (Dec. 1969) : 320–39.

Jacobsen, Edna, ed. "Aaron Hampton's Diary." *New York History* 21 (1940) : 324–34, 431–42.

"Journal of Nathaniel Pierce of Newburyport, Kept at Dartmoor

Prison, 1814–1815." *Essex Institute Historical Collections* 73 (1937) : 24–59.

"Letters of Samuel Taggart, Representative in Congress, 1803–1814." *Proceedings of the American Antiquarian Society* 33 (1923–24) : 297–438.

Morison, Samuel Eliot. "Our Most Unpopular War." *Proceedings of the Massachusetts Historical Society* 80 (1968) : 38–54.

"Notes from Memorandum Book of John Stone, Deacon of the First Church, Salem." *Essex Institute Historical Collections* 61 (1925) : 97–112, 259–64.

Richards, Leonard. "John Adams and the Moderate Federalists: The Cape Fear Valley as a Test Case." *North Carolina Historical Review* 43 (1966) : 14–30.

Robinson, William A. "The Washington Benevolent Society in New England: A Phase of Politics during the War of 1812." *Proceedings of the Massachusetts Historical Society* 49 (1915–16) : 274–86.

OTHER LITERATURE OF SPECIAL UTILITY

Adams, Henry, ed. *Documents Relating to New-England Federalism.* Boston: Little, Brown & Co., 1877.

Armstrong, James. *History of the Old Baltimore Conference.* Baltimore: published by the author, 1907.

Baker, George. *An Introduction to the History of Early New England Methodism, 1789–1839.* Durham: Duke University Press, 1941.

Bangs, Nathan. *Life of Rev. Freeborn Garrettson.* 2d ed. New York: Emory & Waugh, 1830.

Block, Marguerite. *The New Church in the New World: A Study of Swedenborgianism in America.* New York: Henry Holt & Co., 1932.

Bodo, John. *The Protestant Clergy and Public Issues, 1812–1848.* Princeton: Princeton University Press, 1954.

Boyd, Jesse. *History of Baptists in America.* New York: American Press, 1957.

Brown, Roger. *Republic in Peril: 1812.* New York: Columbia University Press, 1964.

Brunson, Alfred. *A Western Pioneer: or, incidents of the life and times of Rev. Alfred Brunson.* Cincinnati: Hitchcock & Walden, 1872.

Bucke, Emory, et al. *History of American Methodism.* 3 vols. New York: Abingdon Press, 1964.

Burr, Nelson. *A Critical Bibliography of Religion in America.* Re-

ligion in American Life, edited by J. W. Smith and A. L. Jameson, vol. 4, pts. 3, 4, and 5. Princeton: Princeton University Press, 1961.

Crocker, Henry. *Elder Aaron Leland.* Burlington: Vermont Historical Society, 1906.

Davidson, Robert. *History of the Presbyterian Church in the State of Kentucky.* New York: Robert Carter, 1847.

Easton, S. J. M. *History of the Presbytery of Erie.* New York: Hurd & Houghton, 1868.

Eddy, Richard. *Universalism in America.* 2 vols. Boston: Universalist Publishing House, 1886.

Elliott, Charles. *The Life of the Rev. Robert R. Roberts.* New York: G. Lane & C. B. Tippett, 1844.

Elsbree, Oliver. *The Rise of Missionary Spirit in America 1790–1815.* Williamsport, Pa.: Williamsport Printing and Binding Co., 1928.

Gillette, E. H. *History of the Presbyterian Church in the United States of America.* 2 vols. Philadelphia: Presbyterian Publication Committee, 1864.

Griffin, Martin. *History of Rt. Rev. Michael Egan.* Philadelphia, 1893.

Hotchkin, James. *A History of the Purchase and Settlement of Western New York, and of the Presbyterian Church in that section.* New York: M. W. Dodd, 1848.

Jacobs, Sarah. *Memoir of Rev. Bela Jacobs.* Boston: Gould, Kendall & Lincoln, 1837.

Kilgore, Charles. *The James O'Kelly Schism in the Methodist Episcopal Church.* Mexico City: Casa Unida de publicaciones, 1963.

Livermore, Shaw. *The Twilight of Federalism: The Disintegration of the Federalist Party, 1815–1830.* Princeton: Princeton University Press, 1962.

Ludlum, David. *Social Ferment in Vermont 1791–1850.* New York: Columbia University Press, 1939.

Mallary, Charles. *Memoirs of Elder Edmund Botsford.* Charleston: W. Riley, 1832.

Manross, William. *Episcopal Church in the United States, 1800–1840.* New York: Columbia University Press, 1938.

Morse, James. *Jedidiah Morse.* New York: Columbia University Press, 1939.

Mudge, James. *History of the New England Conference of the Methodist Episcopal Church, 1796–1910.* Boston: published by the conference, 1910.

Phillips, Clifton. *Protestant America and the Pagan World: The First*

Half-Century of the American Board of Commissioners for Foreign Missions, 1810–1860. Cambridge: Harvard University Press, 1969.

Posey, Walter B. *The Baptist Church in the Lower Mississippi Valley 1776–1845.* Lexington: University of Kentucky Press, 1957.

———. *The Development of Methodism in the Old Southwest 1783–1824.* Nashville: Vanderbilt University Press, 1933.

———. *Religious Strife on the Southern Frontier.* Baton Rouge: Louisiana State University Press, 1965.

Purcell, Richard. *Connecticut in Transition.* Washington, D. C.: American Historical Association, 1918.

Robinson, William. *Jeffersonian Democracy in New England.* New Haven: Yale University Press, 1916.

Sapio, Victor. *Pennsylvania in the War of 1812.* Lexington: University Press of Kentucky, 1970.

Sonne, Niehls. *Liberal Kentucky 1780–1828.* New York: Columbia University Press, 1939.

Stevens, Abel. *Life and times of Nathan Bangs.* New York: Carlton & Porter, 1863.

Stokes, Anson P. *Church and State in the United States.* 3 vols. New York: Harper & Bros., 1950.

Stone, John. *A Memoir of the Life of James Milnor, D.D.* New York: American Tract Society, 1848.

Sweet, William. *Religion in the Development of American Culture 1765–1840.* Gloucester: Peter Smith, 1963.

Terry, Ezekiel. *Memoir of the life and character of the late Rev. George Atwell.* Palmer, Mass.: Ezekiel Terry, 1815.

Tracy, Ebenezer. *Memoir of the Life of Jeremiah Evarts, Esq.* Boston: Crocker & Brewster, 1845.

Whitehill, Walter. *A Memorial to Bishop Cheverus.* Boston: Boston Athenaeum, 1951.

Wylie, Samuel. *Memoir of Alexander McLeod, D.D.* New York: Charles Scribner, 1855.

INDEX